BLACK AND WHITE
IN THE SOUTHERN STATES

P. Bennett
2023

SOUTHERN CLASSICS SERIES

John G. Sproat, General Editor

BLACK
and WHITE
in the SOUTHERN STATES

A Study of the Race Problem in the United States
from a South African Point of View

MAURICE S. EVANS

With a new introduction by
George M. Fredrickson

UNIVERSITY OF SOUTH CAROLINA PRESS
Published in cooperation with the Institute for
Southern Studies and the South Caroliniana Society
of the University of South Carolina.

UNIVERSITY OF SOUTH CAROLINA *BICENTENNIAL*

© 2001 University of South Carolina

Published in Columbia, South Carolina, by the
University of South Carolina Press

Manufactured in the United States of America

05   04   03   02   01   5   4   3   2   1

Library of Congress Cataloging-in-Publication Data
Evans, Maurice S. (Maurice Smethurst), 1854–1920.
   Black and white in the southern states : a study of the race problem in
the United States from a South African point of view / Maurice S.
Evans ; with a new introduction by George M. Frederickson.
       p.   cm. — (Southern classics series)
   "Published in cooperation with the Institute for Southern Studies and
the South Caroliniana Society of the University of South Carolina."
   Previously published: London : Longmans, Green and Co., 1915.
With new introd.
   Includes bibliographical references and index.
   ISBN 1-57003-409-5 (pbk. : alk. paper)
   1. African Americans—Civil rights—Southern States—History—
20th century. 2. African Americans—Southern States—Social
conditions—20th century. 3. Southern States—Race relations.
4. Southern States—Foreign public opinion, South African. 5. Public
opinion—South Africa. I. Title. II. Series.
E185.61 .E92   2001
305.8'00973—dc21   00-054512

CONTENTS

GENERAL EDITOR'S PREFACE

IF for no other reason than that Maurice Evans was a South African and a thoroughly committed segregationist, his inquiry into race relations in the American South in the early twentieth century, *Black and White in the Southern States*, presents readers with a unique perspective on the subject. As George M. Fredrickson reveals in his insightful introduction to this classic, however, Evans's conclusions about the "place" of African Americans in American society, then and for the future, were not quite what one might expect from a forefather of apartheid.

Southern Classics returns to general circulation books of importance dealing with the history and culture of the American South. Sponsored by the Institute for Southern Studies and the South Caroliniana Society of the University of South Carolina, the series is advised by a board of distinguished scholars who suggest titles and editors of individual volumes to the general editor and help establish priorities in publication.

Chronological age alone does not determine a title's designation as a Southern Classic. The criteria also include significance in contributing to a broad understanding of the region, timeliness in relation to events and moments of peculiar interest to the American South, usefulness in the classroom, and suitability for inclusion in personal and institutional collections on the region.

JOHN G. SPROAT
General Editor

vii

INTRODUCTION

WHY should the Southern Classics Series reprint a book about race relations by a South African segregationist who traveled through the South for a few weeks in the late spring and early summer of 1914? There are at least three good reasons. First, the book provides a fairly comprehensive report on the racial thought and attitudes of the time. Maurice Evans talked with a substantial number of southerners—of both races and all shades of opinion—to learn what they thought about "the Negro problem," as well as to observe their behavior. (His endorsement in principle of racial separation did not prevent him from being a respectful guest in black homes.) He brought to his task a broad knowledge of the literature on black-white relations in the United States and an outsider's perspective that enabled him to see the peculiarity of beliefs and practices that many Americans regarded as normal and inevitable. Although it came to conclusions very different from those of Gunnar Myrdal's *An American Dilemma*, Evans's book is arguably the most revealing assessment of racial attitudes and ideologies in the Jim Crow South prior to Myrdal's classic study of 1944. His reports and judgments reveal that racism or race consciousness can take a variety of forms with differing policy implications.

A second reason why the book is still worth reading is the insights it provides into the similarities and differences between the racial orders being established under the common rubric of "segregation" in the American South and South Africa during the early years of the twentieth century. In his brief discussion of *Black and White in the Southern States* in *The Strange Career of Jim Crow*, C. Vann Woodward quotes some passages suggesting that Evans viewed the current situation and future prospects of black-white relations in the two places as virtually identical.[1] John Cell, whose *The Highest Stage of White Supremacy* is the only full-blown comparative study of the two segregation movements, made significant use of Evans to make a case for the fundamental similarity of Crow and "native segregation."[2] But Evans can also be read to support my argument in *White Supremacy* that the differences outweigh the parallels. (I quoted Evans on the relative lack of an economic color bar in the South and extracted from his earlier book on South Africa a passage describing the lack of segregated public facilities in Cape Town.)[3] Readers will now be able to make up their own minds on what Evans contributes to this ongoing debate between the "lumpers" and the "splitters" among comparative historians of white supremacy in the two Souths.[4]

A third value of *Black and White in the Southern States* is what it actually reveals about conditions in the South in 1914. Evans's racial biases did prevent him from making some acute observations about what African Americans were up against at the height of the Jim Crow era. Differences in the spirit and programmatic content of early-twentieth-century segregationism in the two countries provided him with a vantage point from which he could expose the injustice and brutality of some of the racist practices that he found in the South. In places, his book does not read all that differently from the accounts of recent historians.[5] Even though they would disagree with Evans's explanation and proposed solutions for the abysmal state of black-white relations in the American South on the eve of World War I, these historians will have to concede that he was, on the whole, a reliable witness who got most of his facts straight.

Biographical information on Maurice Smethurst Evans (1854–1920) is surprisingly hard to come by. I could not find a memoir, biography, or even a detailed encyclopedia entry. I was able to determine, however, that he was born in Manchester, England, in 1854 and immigrated to the British East African colony of Natal in 1875. For more than twenty years, he seems to have devoted himself mainly to agriculture. In the 1890s, he helped his brother, Edward William Evans, establish a large and successful farm that produced a variety of crops in the Dronkvlei area of southern Natal. In 1897, Maurice Evans was elected to the Natal parliament, where he served for many years and was apparently a popular and influential legislator. He was reelected in 1906 as the largest vote getter among a number of candidates running for the several seats from

Durban, the center of white population in Natal. In that same year, he published a pamphlet, entitled *The Native Problem in Natal*, that was written in response to a localized Zulu rebellion that aroused great anxiety among the white settlers in the colony.[6]

Despite the uprising, Evans sounded the note of cautious optimism and benevolent paternalism that would continue to characterize his writings on black-white relations in South Africa. "I range myself," he wrote in his pamphlet, "with those who hold a reasonable optimism. I feel that we have a fine race of people given into our charge who, while rapidly changing, are not degenerate—a people who under the right guidance are capable of much, and who under firm, considerate and wise rule are easily governed."[7] (In his comments on the Zulus here and elsewhere in his writings, Evans tends to portray them as a relatively unspoiled race of noble savages.) Emerging as a leading white expert on "native affairs," Evans served on the Natal Native Commission of 1906–7 that met to evaluate relations between Europeans and Zulus in the wake of the recent rebellion.[8]

Building on the knowledge he had derived from his work with the Commission, Evans turned his hand to writing a major book on black-white relations in southern Africa, which compared the conditions he knew well in Natal with those existing in other parts of the self-governing Union of South Africa that had just been created by the joining of two British colonies—Natal and the Cape of Good Hope—with the former Afrikaner republics of the Transvaal and the Orange Free State. He also described the governance and prospects of Africans in the territories bordering on South Africa that remained under direct British rule. *Black and White in South East Africa*, completed in 1910 but not published until 1913, is notable for its prescription of territorial segregation as the solution to South Africa's "native problem."[9]

Evans's "Study in Sociology" was a major contribution to the debate that had been taking place for several years over the direction of native policy in a unified South Africa. Three distinctive ideologies had competed for support among the founding fathers of the new central government, each associated with one of the territorial components that were being welded together. One was the "liberalism" associated with the Cape Colony. Its slogan of "equal rights for

every civilized man" meant that Africans who could meet a civilization test based on property and education became equal before the
law and could be admitted to the suffrage, as had been the policy in
the Cape since 1852. An opposite orientation was that of the Transvaal and the Orange Free State. Here the prevailing philosophy had
been expressed in Afrikaans as *Baaskap*, or unrestrained white domination—a South African equivalent of Chief Justice Roger Taney's
opinion in the Dred Scott decision of 1857 that African Americans
had no constitutional rights that whites were bound to respect. Consequently, Africans had possessed virtually no legal and political status at all under the republican constitutions and were ruled, for the
most part, by naked force.

The British colony of Natal had pioneered a third alternative—
territorial segregation and a dual legal system. Before Natal was
granted responsible government under its own parliament in 1893,
a Crown-appointed head of the Native Affairs Department and a
corps of district commissioners presided over large African reserves
within which, for most purposes, chiefs exercised their traditional
authority and tribal customs prevailed. After Natal was granted self-
government, the same basic system persisted, but the representatives
of the settlers saw to it that the reserves were reduced in size whenever the land hunger of whites made it politically expedient to do so.
Africans in the reserves were also heavily taxed, not only to pay the
costs of administering these areas, but, more importantly, to force an
adequate number of them to come out of their designated territories
to work for white farmers at low wages. Mission-trained "civilized"
Africans could apply for exemptions from traditional authority as
interpreted by white magistrates and thereby exercise the same
rights as the white settlers, but so few exemptions were granted that
this whiff of liberalism had almost no practical consequences.[10]

Differences on native policy among the representatives of the
various provinces at the South African constitutional convention of
1908 had led to an apparent compromise: Each province could
decide for itself whether or under what conditions Africans could be
admitted to the franchise and full equality under the law. But since
only whites could be elected to the Union parliament, the Cape
principle of official colorblindness was decisively rejected as a policy
for the country as a whole and remained a local exception, subject to

being overruled by a two-thirds vote of both houses of parliament sitting together. (In 1936 and 1956 this constitutional device would be used to disfranchise first Cape Africans and then "Coloreds.")[11]

Maurice Evans was a firm believer in the essence of the traditional Natal policy, which can be viewed as an application of the indirect rule and limited interference with indigenous cultures that generally characterized British imperial rule in colonies where whites were vastly outnumbered by indigenous peoples. (The ratio in Natal at the turn of the century was roughly ten to one.) As a member of the Natal parliament, he tended to oppose laws passed for the direct economic benefit of the settler population if they seriously compromised the principle of paternalistic territorial separation—by, for example, routinely inducing or forcing masses of Africans to migrate into areas of European settlement to work for whites at low wages. In his book, he proposed that native affairs no longer be subject to the whims of an elected white parliament but, once some broad guidelines had been agreed upon, should be vested in a commission of benevolent experts appointed for long terms or even for life. Because he did not fully trust the elected representatives of the white settlers to treat blacks justly and fairly, he was strongly opposed to the unadulterated "*herrenvolk* democracy" that had characterized the Afrikaner republics. In the context of British imperialist thought in the early twentieth century, such views could seem liberal and humanitarian; they were compatible with the thinking of most missionaries and with the aboriginal protection movement that had fused with the antislavery society in Great Britain.

Evans was equally opposed, however, to the Cape liberal policy of educating and civilizing Africans with the aim of eventually incorporating them into a common society and polity, and he likened such color-blind assimilationism to what had been attempted with allegedly disastrous consequences for both races in the southern United States. In the preface to the second edition of his book on South Africa, written in the wake of his trip to the United States, he declared that the effort to establish legal equality there had been "tragic" for Negroes and, because of demographic differences, would be even worse for South African natives. "It seems clear to me," he wrote, "that the policy of equal rights in the eyes of the law, and which ignores racial differences, will not meet the case."[12]

In the conclusion to his book on South Africa, Evans set forth "three fundamental principles:

1. The white man must govern.
2. The parliament elected by the white man must realize that while it is their duty to decide upon the line of policy to be adopted, they must delegate a large measure of power to those especially qualified, and must refrain from undue interference.
3. The main line of policy must be the separation of the races as far as possible, our aim being to prevent race deterioration, to preserve race integrity, and to give both opportunity to build up and develop their race life."[13]

Evans's proposal for wholesale territorial segregation struck a responsive chord among white South Africans and was implemented, although perhaps in a more discriminatory fashion than he himself would have preferred, when the Union parliament passed the Natives' Land Act of 1913, which divided the entire country, except for the Cape Province, into areas in which the ownership or long-term occupancy of land was reserved for one race or the other—with the white minority of course receiving the lion's share. But even before he traveled in the American South, Evans had concluded that such a policy would not be feasible there. On the next-to-the-last page of *Black and White in South East Africa*, he had sobering words for Americans who might suppose that the territorial separation of the races that was still possible in South Africa could also solve their own "tragic" race problem. "Involved centuries of contact, the sin of miscegenation, the complete divorce of the Negro from his old ancestral African life, have made this solution practically impossible of realization," he concluded.[14]

The preconceptions behind *Black and White in the Southern States*—indeed the very purpose of the trip and resulting book—are thus made clearer. The American South was to serve as an object lesson for South Africa, a description of what would happen if maximal segregation was not carried out. Jim Crow, whatever its merits as a means of reducing race friction, fell far short of what was needed, but history had denied to the South the opportunity that South

Africa still possessed to ensure the "race integrity" of both black and white through territorial separation. The book is not exclusively an expression of gloom and doom. Evans identifies some trends and ideas that might make a bad situation a little better. But they do not include proposals for carving up the South into areas officially designated for the occupancy of one race or the other. Clarence Poe, the North Carolina farm editor who was inspired by Evans and the Natives' Land Act to propose land segregation in the rural South, had apparently not read Evans very carefully.[15]

As he indicates in the introduction, Evans did a great deal of reading on race relations in the United States before he left South Africa, and the critical bibliography at the end of this book makes it possible to place his views within the American debate of the early twentieth century on the situation and prospects of African Americans. One is struck by his dismissive comments on the works of extreme racists (the "Negro-as-beast" school) and his appreciative responses to the writings of W. E. B. Du Bois. He also pays Du Bois the tribute of plagiarizing from him in his introduction: he ends his first paragraph affirming without attribution that "The problem of the Twentieth Century is the problem of the colour line." But he reserves his greatest praise for the works of Edgar Gardner Murphy, whose books simply "must be read." He also indicates in the introduction that he consulted Murphy in New York before he left for the South and received from him "advice which struck the right note" (p. xxvi). It is clear that Murphy was the American authority on race who Evans felt closest to and whose views most nearly paralleled his own.

Edgar Gardner Murphy (1869–1913) was an Episcopal clergyman born in Arkansas, who became interested in race issues while ministering to a church in Montgomery, Alabama, around the turn of the century. After organizing a major conference, "Race Problems of the South," in 1900, he left the ministry to become a full-time writer on social issues and a spokesman for the humanitarian wing of southern Progressivism. His views on black-white relations have been variously characterized by historians as neopaternalism, "accommodationist racism," or "Volksgeistian conservatism."[16] As a "liberal" or moderate proponent of segregation, he tried to make the case that separation, if implemented with fairness, would enable each race to develop its distinctive gifts and capacities. Murphy's belief in the cosmic value of race consciousness and race solidarity has led Joel Williamson to argue that he developed what amounted to a concept of "white soul" that stemmed from the same Germanic idealism and romantic nationalism that originally inspired W. E. B. Du Bois's conception of "black soul."

This form of race thinking derived ultimately from the writings of the German philosopher Johann Gottfried von Herder, whose late-eighteenth-century critique of Enlightenment universalism and cosmopolitanism anticipated the romantic nationalism of the nineteenth century.[17] According to Herder and subsequent advocates of romantic cultural pluralism, each historic or emerging nation or people had its own unique "genius" that manifested itself in language, art, and special forms of spirituality. The achievement of human potential was not, as the Enlightenment had affirmed, the result of individuals developing the rational faculties and moral sentiments that they shared with the rest of humanity, but could only come to full expression if each ethnic group or nation was relatively isolated from external or cosmopolitan influences.

When correlated, as it often was, with physical differences—or "race" in the biological sense—this romantic celebration of ethnic or cultural diversity (*among*, but not *within*, nation-states) could turn into a form of racialism that is distinguishable from the rationalistic racial Darwinism that most historians believe predominated in the thinking of white colonialists and segregationists in the late nineteenth and early twentieth centuries. The emphasis here was on difference rather than natural or permanent hierarchy and on coexistence rather than a "struggle for existence." A special problem existed, however, when two peoples or races with differing *volksgeists* found themselves in close proximity and under the same political authority. The best that could happen under these circumstances, according to these romantic racialists, was a form of segregation that would permit each people or race to develop along its own lines. They also adhered to a standard concept of sociocultural evolution—each *volk* moved in its own way and at its own pace from savagery (hunting and gathering) to barbarism (agriculture) to its own special variety of civilization (urbanization and industrialism). Consequently, their relativism did not extend to the notion that the less developed or "civilized" group in a contact situation could make progress, even its own peculiar way, without some guidance and protection from the more advanced and therefore dominant group. The worst that could happen, however, would be to attempt to assimilate barbarous people into a civilization that was not of their own making. Such a policy would block their spiritual development as a distinctive people and lead only to degeneracy as they vainly attempted to imitate those with different temperaments and capacities. Separation under the hegemony of the relatively more civilized group should allow the less-civilized enough autonomy so that its own special genius could flower.[8]

Evans clearly belonged to this romantic and pseudo-relativistic school of racial thought, rather than to the one that was straightforward in its belief in the biological inferiority of "the lower races" and the likelihood that they would simply disappear as a result of unequal competition with the superior races. Racial Darwinists tended to advocate segregation as a means of quarantining degenerating and vanishing races; romantic racialists of the early-twentieth-century type, like Murphy and Evans, prescribed it as a means of ensuring the integrity and further development of all races. In the preliminary chapter entitled "Some Thoughts on Race," Evans made his position clear. "Race is deeper than culture," he affirmed. "And so I would wish it. To mold all the peoples of this wonderful varied world into one type does not seem to me to be desirable. We have our different gifts, and I would allow all such free play." He then went on to quote extensively from Edward Blyden, the pioneer theorist of black nationalism who was active in West Africa, in support of this benign conception of racial pluralism (15–16). He could easily have quoted the early W. E. B. Du Bois as well.[19]

From a contemporary perspective, there might seem to be little practical difference between Evans's romantic or Volksgeistian racism and the viewpoint of America's radical racists—those professional Negrophobes whose biological determinism or bizarre interpretations of certain passages in the book of Genesis led them to believe that blacks were not simply inherently inferior but also, except perhaps when enslaved to whites, incapable of progress and doomed to degeneration or extermination. In fact it was the kind of thinking that Evans represented that would later provide much of the ideological rationale for apartheid in South Africa. Allowing each race "to develop along its own lines" would serve as a convenient cover for the most blatant forms of brutality and exploitation. But understanding his racial philosophy makes comprehensible Evans's surprisingly critical and at times outraged reactions to the way southern whites treated blacks at the height of Jim Crow. Paternalistic southern "liberals" like Murphy, Willis D. Weatherford, and Benjamin F. Riley might feel much the same way, but they could not afford to be as outspoken as a visitor from South Africa. Booker T. Washington, whom Evans greatly admired, was under even more obvious constraints and would probably have lost all his influence on the white southern elite if he had made some of the statements that can be found in this book.

After providing a mass of evidence showing the intense and unjustified prejudice of most southern whites toward African Americans and the shocking atrocities that resulted, Evans let fly: "It is painful to have to record that a people of our own race should be so saturated with hostility toward a weaker one, which is unable to defend itself, either at law or by force of arms. . . . What is happening [in the South] is a subversion of right and justice with its maleficent reflex action on character" (80). As a segregationist who wished to minimize contact between the races, Evans had no good reason to criticize the Jim Crow laws themselves, provided that they offered blacks adequate facilities. He traveled by train throughout the South and professed to find no significant differences between the separate accommodations reserved for each race. What he found intolerable was the unrestrained and unpunished violence against blacks, most obviously by lynch mobs, and their failure to receive justice in the courts or at the hands of the police. Racial separation was one thing—he could understand that; but the kind of racial hostility that led to murder, brutality, and the denial to blacks of any protection or defense against such barbarism was something else. "Whatever may be the opinion of the Jim Crow car, the denial to places of entertainment, and separation of the races in school and church," he wrote, "it is essential that if the South is to escape the condemnation of the civilized world, it must see to it that the Negro receives equal justice in the courts, that lynching be made impossible, and that the standards of honour be so raised that the chastity of the Negro woman is safeguarded as that of her white sister" (191). (His last point was less an aspersion on the sexual morality of black women than a criticism of the white men who took advantage of them. As a fierce opponent of miscegenation in any form, Evans was appalled at the high incidence of illicit interracial sex that he found in the South.)

Evans believed that South African whites treated black people much more humanely than white southerners, and—at the time he wrote at least—he was probably right, which is not to say that black Africans were treated well. But South African white supremacy relied mainly on discriminatory law rather than on extra-legal violence, which at least made life a little more predictable for Africans, who may have been greatly disadvantaged but did not, for the most part, have to live in constant fear of white vigilantes and freelance racial terrorists.

If his condemnation of lynching, sexual exploitation, and injustice under the law strikes a positive note for contemporary readers who repudiate the racism of the past, his explanation for how the southern race relations arrived at such a state in 1914 does not. It was because of the ill-advised effort to make blacks equal citizens under Reconstruction and the constitutional changes that this entailed that whites had originally been driven to defend their superior status by such violent and irregular means. This great historical blunder did not excuse their current behavior because disfranchisement had removed any possibility of black domination or substantial political influence, but it did serve as an object lesson to South Africa to avoid the path of common citizenship and assimilation. The implication that blacks in neither country should have the right to vote made white benevolence or altruism their only protection, and this, of course, was no protection at all, as Evans should have realized on the basis of what he reported.

Although Evans found race relations in the South about as bad as they could get, he saw some signs of hope and pointed out some avenues that might lead to greater integrity for each race and a modicum of harmony between them. Where he believed that blacks had made the most progress and had the greatest opportunities was on the land. He noted that the number of black farmers who owned their own land was increasing and that some had become quite successful. The visit he made to a particularly prosperous black farmer provided him with a model for the future, although he was disconcerted by the farmer's own pessimism about the prospects for blacks in general. Cities, Evans believed, were not good habitats for blacks in either the United States or South Africa because of the corrupting and demoralizing influences to which urban life exposed them. For most African Americans the cities were "a veritable sewer and death trap." He did encounter some successful Negro urbanites but concluded that "the majority . . . were of mixed race" and thus had inherited some of the white man's aptitude for metropolitan living (235). For those of relatively pure African descent, as for the Bantu of South Africa, the countryside was the only place where they could lead a "wholesome" life. But this could only happen if adequate land was made available.

Evans's solution for South Africa, as we have seen, was to segregate Africans, as much as possible, on reserve areas that had to be large enough to sustain an agrarian way of life and autonomous enough to remain traditionally African in culture and local governance. But, in a passage that his American disciple Clarence Poe apparently failed to notice, he stated flatly: "I am not, however, in favour of such a legal territorial separation in the South land." Noting the differences "in land and people, history and customs" between the southern states and South Africa, he concluded that if a legislature passed something like the Natives' Land Act it would "be bitterly resented by the Negro people, who would regard it as an attempt to deprive them of their last hope. It would be exceedingly difficult to put into operation, would cause much hardship, and rouse the strongest race animosities." What, then, could be done in the American case? "The wisest course is to place no obstacles in the way of Negroes acquiring land, indeed help them to do so, particularly when, as the wisest of the race desire, they shall acquire it in communities, thus practically segregating themselves" (258). Evans went so far as to predict that if communities of landholding black farmers were scattered throughout the South they would receive assistance from "philanthropic whites" and eventually "State aid," because it would be acknowledged that a way had at last been found for the races to coexist in harmony and with the hope of mutual progress (259).

Evans's plan to save the South and the Negro by creating an economically independent black peasantry failed to enlist American disciples from either side of the color line. The year 1915 was an exceptionally unpropitious time to promote such a cause. Blacks in massive numbers were being drawn irresistibly to northern cities by the opportunities for decent jobs that opened up when war broke out in Europe; and rural southern whites, fearing a loss of cheap labor or competition between the races for land that poor whites might hope to acquire, would have resisted, violently if necessary, any substantial improvement in the economic status of the blacks who remained in the rural South as sharecroppers, farm laborers, or owners of tiny acreages insufficient to keep them out of debt to supply merchants or out of the labor market.

Something like what Evans proposed might have been possible during the Reconstruction era, when many of the freedpeople and a few Radical Republicans understood that access to the land as independent farmers was the most promising way for blacks to make a meaningful transition from slavery to freedom. Whether the establishment throughout the former slaveholding states of self-sufficient African American rural communities or districts in areas formerly dominated by large slave plantations—a process that actually began during Reconstruction in coastal South Carolina and the lower Mississippi valley—would have led ultimately to a de facto and equitable form of geographical separation is an intriguing, if unanswerable, question. But as Evans clearly acknowledged in the descriptive parts of this book, the lives of Southern whites and blacks had become too entangled ever to be separated, except to a limited extent by the non-consensual and constitutionally vulnerable patchwork of laws and customs that Americans called Jim Crow and that South Africans would later call "petty apartheid." "Grand apartheid," or what Evans called "absolute segregation"—the dream of an almost total geographical separation of the races that has been shared at times by black nationalists and extreme white supremacists in the United States—was never in the cards for the American South. Even in South Africa, where the idea originated with English-speaking liberal paternalists like Evans but was implemented most fully by

Afrikaner Nationalists after 1948, it turned into a nightmare from which South Africa had to be awakened by massive black resistance and international pressure.

There was simply no way that a fair division of the country with adequate provision for African autonomy and subsistence could be implemented so long as whites monopolized political power. As Evans's book itself reveals, when it is being realistic rather than utopian in its analysis of the somewhat different form of white supremacy that existed in the American South in 1914, there was no way that the powerful could be induced to be fair to the powerless. White interests and prejudices would always prevail over the concerns and aspirations of blacks, sometimes violently and extra-legally, and sometimes through the matter-of-fact workings of a bureaucracy enforcing unjust laws. The political and economic empowerment of blacks is, in both countries, the sine qua non of racial justice.

GEORGE M. FREDRICKSON

NOTES

1. C. Vann Woodward, *The Strange Career of Jim Crow*, 3rd rev. ed. (New York: Oxford University Press, 1974), 111–12.

2. John W. Cell, *The Highest Stage of White Supremacy: The Origins of Segregation in South Africa and the American South* (Cambridge, U.K.: Cambridge University Press, 1982), 27–33.

3. See George M. Fredrickson, *White Supremacy: A Comparative Study in American and South African History* (New York: Oxford University Press, 1981), 236, 266–67. The latter quote is drawn from *Black and White in South East Africa*, cited fully below. The general argument for sharply differentiating the two forms of segregation is made on pp. 239–57.

4. For a historiographic analysis of this debate, see my "The South and South Africa" in *The Arrogance of Race: Historical Perspectives on Slavery, Racism, and Social Inequality* (Middletown, Conn.: Wesleyan University Press, 1988), 254–69.

5. A prime example is Leon Litwack's magisterial *Trouble in Mind: Black Southerners in the Age of Jim Crow* (New York: Knopf, 1998), which uses Evans as a source.

6. Maurice S. Evans, *The Native Problem in Natal* (Durban: P. Davis, 1906). Biographical information is from *The Natal Who's Who* (Durban:

Natal Who's Who Publishing Co., 1906), 65, and from the entry on his brother, Edward William Evans, in *Dictionary of South African Biography*, vol. 4 (Durban: Nasionale Boekhandel, 1981), 148.

7. Evans, *Native Problem*, 8.

8. On the rebellion and the work of the commission, see Shula Marks, *Reluctant Rebellion: The 1906–1908 Disturbances in Natal* (Oxford: Oxford University Press, 1970).

9. Maurice S. Evans, *Black and White in South East Africa: A Study in Sociology* (London: Longmans, Green, 1916, 2nd ed.; orig. pub. 1913). The second edition has the same text as the first and merely adds a new introduction commenting on how his study of the American South had reinforced his views on South Africa.

10. The authoritative study of the Natal policy is David Welsh, *The Roots of Segregation: Native Policy in Natal, 1845–1910* (Cape Town: Oxford University Press, 1971).

11. See Leonard Thompson, *The Unification of South Africa, 1902-1910* (Oxford: Oxford University Press, 1960).

12. Evans, *South East Africa*, vii, viii.

13. *Ibid.*, 310.

14. *Ibid.*, 326.

15. On Poe's proposals and activities, see Jeffrey J. Crow, "An Apartheid for the South: Clarence Poe's Crusade for Rural Segregation," in *Race, Class, and Politics in Southern History: Essays in Honor of Robert F. Durden*, Crow et al., eds. (Baton Rouge: Louisiana State University Press, 1989), 216–59.

16. See especially George M. Fredrickson, *The Black Image in the White Mind: The Debate on Afro-American Character and Destiny, 1817–1914* (Middletown, Conn.: Wesleyan University Press, 1987, orig. pub. 1971), 283–319; and Joel Williamson, *The Crucible of Race: Black-White Relations in the American South Since Emancipation* (New York: Oxford University Press, 1984), 415–21 and *passim*. Murphy was the author of two influential books on southern race relations: *Problems of the Present South* (New York: Macmillan, 1904) and *The Basis of Ascendency* (New York: Longmans, Green, 1909).

17. Johann Gottfried von Herder, *Reflections on the Philosophy of the History of Mankind*, ed. Frank E. Manuel (Chicago: University of Chicago Press, 1968). I describe the effect of this kind of thinking about human diversity on antebellum American conceptions of black character and destiny in *The Black Image*, 97–129.

18. For the most part, intellectual historians have ignored or downplayed this variety of race thinking. The extent to which Murphy and Evans reflected an important strand of Western imperialist and/or segregationist thinking around the turn of the century requires further study. A compari-

son with the at least superficially similar Pan-Africanist ideologies of the same period might also prove illuminating.

19. See W. E. B. Du Bois, "The Conservation of Races" (1897), in *W. E. B. Du Bois Speaks: Speeches and Addresses, 1890–1919*, ed. Philip S. Foner (New York: Pathfinder Press, 1970), 73–85.

INTRODUCTION TO THE FIRST EDITION

I MAKE no apology for adding another to the mass of books already written on this subject. Before it loses its intense burning interest for students of mankind, long before the black man and the white man live together in harmony on a basis mutually acceptable, many more books will be written. The keen intellect and tender conscience of the Twentieth Century both imperatively demand that the illogical and unethical attitude in which the races face each other in the Southern States and in South Africa shall be changed for one that we can justify, and with which the black man shall be satisfied. Our question is one phase of the greater problem of race and colour which touches all the European nations, and nearly every backward race and tribe throughout the wide world. The problem of the Twentieth Century is the problem of the colour line.

So far as I know only two men intimately acquainted by personal experience and residence in other countries in which black and white come together, have visited the Southern States and written their experiences thereon. One of these is Sir H. H. Johnston, who knows many parts of Africa with a knowledge that is in some respects unique. The other is Mr. W. P. Livingstone, author of "Black Jamaica," who writes on the North American Negro in "The Race Conflict," and who has a practical acquaintance with the race in Jamaica.

The Union of South Africa is the country in which the problem is most nearly like what it is in the Southern States. As far as my knowledge goes no South African has gone through the South with a view to study the question, certainly no South African has written upon it.

These facts should warrant me, even in view of the many scores of volumes already in print.

They will, however, only justify me if the question is approached in a right spirit, and with a full sense of the responsibility which attaches to all who attempt to guide public opinion on a question so closely touching the lives and happiness of millions. The partisan spirit, partial to one race or the other, permeates most of the writings on the subject. Probably much bitterness, as well as false views, have been due to this: With any power of mind and will I possess I will strive to avoid this pitfall. The issues are too great, the, results for good or evil may be so immense, that no preconceived ideas or partiality should be allowed to cloud clarity of view, or warp the judgment.

The method must be scientific, facts observed and noted with scrupulous care, and no conclusion drawn until the body of data fully warrants it. Willingness to cast aside, as well as to gather up, must be a ruling principle of such an inquiry. Yet with the clear eye and balanced mind must be an impressionable openness, a waiting spirit, through which shall freely, flow the genius of the people and the land. In this spirit I endeavour to unravel some of the knots in this tangled skein of human endeavour and error.

I have not written an itinerary of my journeyings. It will be sufficient to say that I went by ordinary trains from New York to New Orleans by one route and returned by another, making many side journeys from the railway to the more remote country districts. I never once travelled by night, daylight was too valuable. I talked with the men I met on the trains, the roads, the farms, and at the hotels, and I stayed at the homes of both black and white. I visited quays, markets, courts, factories, churches, schools, institutions of all kinds, wherever men did most congregate, and wherever their activities were being carried on.

Before leaving New York, among other friends, I met Mr. Edgar Gardner Murphy, author of "The Basis of Ascendancy," "The Present South," and other works, and an authority on the racial situation in America.

From him I received advice which struck the right note. Often I had seen well-intentioned visitors to South Africa, who, anxious to receive true impressions, got but a blurred, one-sided, distorted picture of men and things in our country. Mr. Murphy in effect said: Remember there is a white South as well as a black one; too many in their desire for startling effect and the unusual, only see the unaccustomed black man, and are blind to the white man; who is as much a factor in the problem as the other. Also beware of being personally conducted by those holding one-sided views, for, he said, I have seen students come to this country and leave it having only seen one side of the shield, and not knowing there was another. You will hear the most contradictory statements, each purporting to be statements of facts and the most diverse opinions based upon them; listen to all, check all by your own observations, try to hold the balance level, and draw your own conclusions. I found my South African experience of value here in keeping me clear of pitfalls into which I had seen others fall.

I find myself now in the position of those who have so often excited the ire and contempt of my fellow-colonists in South Africa, those who, after a few short months of travel, presume to write a book and give opinions and advice on subjects on which, they, the long experienced, feel diffident to express an opinion: Always recognizing that these impressionist writings vary much in value, and that many are inaccurate and hasty, I never endorsed the opinion that nothing of value could come from those who visited our land. Rather I was always keenly desirous to learn the impressions of those who came with open eye and fresh mind to view us, and I have often found much of value in what they said and wrote.

I know how often the first fresh and bright impressions become dim and cloudy from familiarity. I know how the angle becomes fixed, and how we see only what we saw; how often the old resident cannot see the wood for trees.

Admitting that the studies of the man who knows every detail, and yet can keep his detachment and hold the balance level, are the most valuable, I do not lightly estimate the contributions of he qualified visitor who can take the big view. I feel that the man with the open mind, concentrating on the subject, who is qualified by previous study, and knowledge of conditions in other lands, may often grasp the broad outlines of a situation hidden from the local man by a mass of detail. Such a one can also supply the enlightenment that comes from comparison.

I cannot in this effort pretend to be more. than an impressionist, and if error has crept into my pages will be only too glad to have it pointed out, and retract as far as possible.

Before leaving for America I spent some months in reading the literature of the subject, and I think I may say, saturated myself with it. I found much that was of value, much that was inaccurate and prejudiced. I trust that, though I read with avidity, I exercised some discretion. Owing in part to our remoteness, and to the fact that we are not yet a literary people, most of this intensely interesting literature is quite unknown to South Africans. In what I write I shall freely draw upon this source of information, giving as far as possible the authority when doing so.

I also append a Bibliography of the subject. I do not pretend that this is complete, but it includes those books which for different reasons I found of most value, and I give briefly my impressions on each, in the hope that what I found of such intense interest may also be read by my fellow-colonists. For if we are ever to justify our presence here in South Africa, the present indifference on the one hand, and hasty conclusions on the other, must give place to close study, accurate thinking, and just and statesmanlike action.

It may be that some Southerners will do me the honour of reading this book. Knowing their own people and locality intimately, they will probably find that what I say does not altogether apply to their conditions, and that they can point to many exceptions. I am fully aware that I am dealing with a big country, singularly alike in its general social conditions, yet necessarily with many local variations. Richmond Virginia, and Charleston South Carolina, are like and unlike, and both are unlike New Orleans. The position in Georgia is not the same as in Louisiana, and Tennessee is unlike both. Local investigators have made detailed study of particular cities and sections, and as far as possible I have availed myself of these to check my general statements and conclusions. I am giving a general impression, true of the whole, but perhaps not wholly true of any one part.

Without much kind help I could not have seen, heard, and experienced all I did. For this help, and for candid expressions of opinion freely given, I owe many Americans, both white and black, a deep debt of gratitude. It is impossible for me to thank all by name. Should any Southerner, feeling the similarity of the problems which demand an answer in both lands, visit South Africa on a similar quest to mine, I hope to be able to reciprocate the kindly advice, help and hospitality so freely given to me.

The first result of all these facilities of reading and observation was to overpower, almost smother me with a mass of detail, often apparently contradictory, which it seemed impossible to classify. By degrees the chaotic mass resolved itself, and the facts arranged themselves in something like order. Before I left America I formed certain definite opinions. I feel that it is in large part due to my long South African experience, and much pondering on that experience, that I was at all able to do so.

The application of certain principles outlined in the earlier chapters of the book guided me to the results I give in the later chapters. Upon these conclusions I would very much appreciate the criticism of my American friends, whether such be favourable or adverse. I approach and handle it from a somewhat different point of view to theirs; open free discussion from all standpoints is desirable if South Africans and Americans are to understand, and make that understanding the basis of action, which will result in the establishment of better race relations in both lands.

In this spirit I publish my contribution.

MAURICE S. EVANS.

HILLCREST, BEREA RIDGE,
    DURBAN, NATAL.

BLACK AND WHITE
IN THE SOUTHERN STATES

To My Wife,
ELIZABETH F. EVANS

CHAPTER I.

THE QUESTION OF THE CENTURY.

MANY signs and portents are in the air showing that among the many questions calling for solution, which are brought to the front by the rapidly changing condition of the world, that of the relations of the races hitherto regarded as civilized with those we have been accustomed to consider backward, will be the world-wide and important one.

Rapid intercommunication, the increase of travel and expansion of commerce, with the tremendous material interests involved, make it impossible for the civilized, industrial, and manufacturing nations to regard it lightly. The responsibilities they have assumed in distant parts of the world will yearly more and more force upon their attention the problem of what their attitude should be towards those for whom they have taken the responsibility of government, or to whom they are bound by political and economic ties.

Those who have assumed overlordship might be tempted to temporize, and will in fact probably do so, and only consider the question under pressure, but that pressure is not likely to be withheld for long.

For all the world over the coloured races are beginning to realize themselves and to press for answers to questions that have hitherto been evaded. The Japanese are knocking at the Western gates of the New World, and the leaders of the millions of India are asking for admittance to lands which have been so far closed to them. The development of the West African peoples goes on apace, and their increasing agricultural production is giving

I

them a status in the modern world higher than that hitherto reached by any purely African people. And in South Africa there are uneasy movements betokening awakening consciousness. All these are but the beginnings of the stirrings of the peoples.

Of the many striking changes that impress an oversea visitor to the centres of Europe, not the least is the ever-increasing number of members of alien and coloured races he sees, and this especially holds good of London. I have lately had the privilege of living there for over a year, with ample leisure to wander and study social conditions. My experience must be that of many visitors from the Colonies. In my early years, before leaving for South Africa, a black face in the streets was an object of interest and curiosity. Now no one is surprised to meet dozens during one afternoon. The majority are well dressed, and appear very much at home in their new environment, and are often accompanied by, and evidently very familiar with, men and women of English race. Inquiries need not be profound to discover that the family type of boarding-house, where they enter into the social life of the occupants, is much frequented by them. If any distinction is drawn it is not to their disadvantage.

The average Colonist shudders at this social inter-mixture, and often plainly shows disapproval, and it may be that this, combined with more intimate personal knowledge, will modify the present position and attitude in Britain. Meantime Hindoos, Chinese, Japanese and other Eastern peoples, as well as a large number of Africans, are rapidly learning the intimacies of English social life, and apparently enjoying its amenities. I found that a large number of these visitors are students at the higher seats of learning.

What may be seen in London is the outward and visible sign of race movement and race aspiration in those who have long been stationary and silent. The awakening of India, the enlightenment and uprising of Japan, the revolution in China, and the coming to consciousness of the Africans of West and South, are phenomena which will more and more demand attention from Western civilization.

The issues thus raised may be divided into three classes.

1. The relations between Europeans and (principally) Asiatics as independent States.

2. The government of tropical dependencies in which the white man cannot make a permanent home, such as the West Indies and the greater part of Africa.

3. Countries with a climate and surroundings suitable to European family life, but with a large population of a backward race, as South Africa, the Highlands of East Africa, and portions of Northern Rhodesia.

I have not a personal knowledge of conditions in the first and second classes, and there the problem differs greatly from what it is in the third class, with which I have an intimate acquaintance.

The most important countries which fall into the third class are the southern portions of the United States of America, the Union of South Africa, and probably the high plateau of British East Africa. In the two former the problem is insistent, in the last named it is gradually surging to the front.

In the Union of South Africa, and in the Southern States, it has been proved by the experience of nearly three centuries that the climate and conditions are favourable to European family life. The original settlers have increased in numbers by natural reproduction, and their descendants are a vigorous race, mentally and physically. They have the temperamental leaning of the race towards a democratic form of government, and nowhere does the democratic theory of government find stronger supporters. In both cases the theory stops at members of the dominant race.

By Federal law in the United States all men are declared free and equal, with equal rights to life, liberty, and the pursuit of happiness, and to all conveniences of civilized life.   The Constitution explicitly states that the franchise shall be the privilege of all, notwithstanding race, colour or previous condition of servitude.   In practice and by State law, one-third of the population in the South is denied social and political equality.

In the Union of South Africa one province of the four, the Cape Colony, recognizes political equality by law ; two, the Transvaal and Orange Free State, explicitly by law deny it ; and in one, Natal, there is a separate code of law for black and white.

Both South Africa and the United States are in reality not democracies, but oligarchies, and the practical discrepancy between theory and practice is one of the intricacies of the problem.   Notwithstanding the markedly different experiences through which each country has gone since European settlement first began, the visitor from South Africa to the Southern States sees much that is familiar.   Every now and then some experience brings vividly to his mind the country he has left.   He finds that the human elements being the same, the results are often strikingly similar.   It was one of the pleasures of my visit to find, so far away, how often the very conditions I had left were reproduced before my eyes, the thousands of miles melted away, and Africa was before me.   Almost as great a pleasure was noting and trying to explain the differences I saw.   These were, however, less than the resemblances.   In essence the problem is the same for both of us.   The question the Fates have set both countries is this—How to ensure that two races so different, yet living in the same land, shall each have opportunity for its full development, without clashing and without fusion.

The international relations of East and West will possibly be arranged on a mutually satisfactory basis.

The genius of the European peoples concerned will probably enable them to govern their tropical dependencies with justice and consideration, and adjust their methods to suit the development and changing needs of the governed.

Where white and black have each their permanent homes and live intermixed, as in South Africa and the United States, the problem is much more complex and difficult.   The events of the nineteenth century have accentuated and increased these difficulties.   It is the problem of the twentieth century to discover a basis of adjustment.

CHAPTER II.

FREE DISCUSSION.

To those who do not know South Africa, this short chapter will seem quite unnecessary, as in it I wish to consider the statement previously made that open frank discussion is essential if we are to arrive at the truth on this question, and get guidance for the future. To those who live elsewhere, where every subject under heaven is made matter of inquiry and debate, such a proposition is self-evident.

And it would be accepted in theory by the majority of South Africans. There is, at the same time, a feeling, often implied rather than expressed, that questions affecting the native population should be treated differently. The idea has, since Union, been expressed by one highly placed, that talking and writing on the native question only did harm. This attitude is, I think, due to the position adopted by the ruling race, a position hitherto assented to without demur by the native people, that their status and circumstances should be decided for them, and not by them.

While recognizing that justice must be the ruling principle, it is felt by many in South Africa that justice must be dispensed in the spirit of the benevolent despot. It is essential to this view that those thus governed should not be encouraged to think over and debate the position assigned to them.

Those holding this view have been familiar with the native as a tribesman, subject to the autocratic rule of a chief. Under this rule they saw the native contented and law-abiding. The white man and his government

6

taking the place of the chief, they demand the same acquiescence to the acts of government as was given to the dictates of the tribal head.

They do not fully realize that the tribal system was one evolved by, and understood and loved by, the native people. Nor do they see that while submissive to the commands, even the whims, of the chief, they felt in the marrow of their being, that the chief was of themselves, and stood, not apart, but as one representing and identical with themselves.

Judged by the ideas of freedom held by the white man, the native was often sorely oppressed by the head of his tribe. The native, conversely, felt that these acts were the prerogative of his tribal superior, and were not to be resented. Often also the white man loses sight of the fact that autocratic power was limited by the influence and advice of those councillors who knew and represented the desires of the people. At the back of the submission to tribal authority was the feeling that the ruling power is of them and by them, and their interests are identical. This feeling was at first transferred to the white ruler, and for a time the inherited tendency held sway, but all in South Africa know how rapidly it is becoming attenuated and dying away.

The circumstances have changed, and with it the attitude. Those Europeans who have known it in the past, and cling to it as the proper relation between white and black, will under the changed conditions have to modify the tradition. The rule of full and free discussion must needs apply here as in all other affairs of life. It is true that it may tend to unrest of the native mind. To some extent this cannot be avoided.

It is equally true that all who take part in such discussion should do so with a full sense of responsibility, and recognize the possibility of unsettlement that lies in it. The greatest tact and judgment are necessary, and more restraint than is usually used in political discussion. We must not obscure the truth or give a false impression, but try to put ourselves in the other man's place, remembering that what is obvious to us may not be clear to him, and do all possible to prevent misunderstanding. ˙ If this is the spirit that guides the discussion, not harm but good will be the result.

The Union of South Africa is ruled by the white electorate, they are responsible for the government of a people five times as numerous as they are. The majority of the governing group do not understand the question in all its bearings, nor have they time or inclination to study it. Their chief concern is with the economic development of the country, the part they are to play in it, and the reward they are to get for these activities. The native is of interest to them only so far as he assists to this end. Yet to any general line of native policy they must, as electors and members of the governing race, give their assent.

It is the first essential that they should be educated to and for this responsibility, and how can it be done without discussion? If that discussion is to be limited and hampered by considerations of its effect on the native mind, what is the education likely to be worth?

In the best interests of the native people, perhaps a benevolent despotism would be the ideal form of government, then discussion might be limited to the Chamber of the Executive. Instead of this we have the rule of a nominal democracy, in reality an oligarchy masked as a democracy. We must take the position with its limitations and drawbacks. One of these is full and free debate of the subject, ever conducted, we hope, with judgment and restraint, but open, impartial, non-partisan, without obscuration of the truth wherever it may lead.

However much it might be desired to limit discussion, the interests and relations of the races are so intimately interwoven, that they crop up at all times and on all subjects.

I write this in March, 1913. The Parliament of the Union of South Africa met last month at Capetown.

Internal dissension in the Government party gave unusual opportunity to private members. Notices of motion were given and the questions raised were those nearest to the hearts of the representatives. It was significant how the question of race relations came ever to the front. It entered into almost every subject introduced. Labour, immigration, the purchase of land, the sale of firearms, education, all inevitably brought in the native. And so it must and will be.

It may be considered that I am fighting a shadow, and that few in South Africa would openly favour a policy of limited discussion or discreet silence. This is probably true, but there is an undercurrent of doubt as to the desirability or wisdom of openly talking of the subject in all its bearings. Many would disavow the feeling, yet in subtle fashion it is part of their mental equipment, born of familiarity with the old idea of rule by the wise minority. Under present conditions it must go, and it is without hesitation or reservation that I add my contribution to the study of a question bearing so closely on our great South African problem, and which I would probably never have undertaken but for the belief that such an inquiry would be of value to us in our task in South Africa.

CHAPTER III.

SOME THOUGHTS ON RACE.

DURING a recent visit to Europe I had an opportunity of attending a memorable gathering—the first Universal Races Congress. Delegates were present from all the nations of Europe, from the greater part of Asia, from Africa, and America. They varied in type, colour, and appearance, from the Scandinavian to the Negro. The object of this notable meeting of such diverse people was laid down in the prospectus issued by the Council as " the discussion in the light of science and the modern conscience, of the general relations subsisting between the peoples of the West and those of the East, between so-called white and so-called coloured peoples, with a view to encouraging between them a fuller understanding, the most friendly feelings, and a heartier co-operation ".

The papers which formed the basis of discussion were wisely printed and circulated among the members before the meeting, thus giving all an opportunity of reading and familiarizing themselves with the broad outlines of the question under debate. Men of high standing and acquirements contributed these essays, and altogether they form a volume of great and permanent value to all students of race questions.

Eight sessions were held and the following are the divisions of the question for purposes of discussion, which will indicate the scope of the inquiry undertaken :—

1st Session.   Fundamental considerations.

2nd ,,   Conditions of progress.   General problems.

3rd Session.   Conditions of progress.   Special
                 problems.

4th   „   I. Special problems in inter-racial
                 economics.
                 II. Peaceful contact between civiliza-
                 tions.

5th   „   The modern conscience in relation to
                 racial questions generally.

6th   „   The modern conscience in relation to
                 the Negro and American Indian.

7th   „   Positive suggestions for promoting
                 inter-racial friendliness.

8th   „   The same subject continued.

In addition to other preliminary circulars issued there
was one containing a long list of questions, submitted
presumably to authorities who could not personally
attend the Congress. No indication is given of the
nature of the answers received, which if published
should be of more than ordinary interest.

Although the Congress did not adopt any platform
beyond stating their general object, which I have quoted,
a perusal of some of the questions submitted in the
circular referred to indicates preconceived opinions on
the question of race hardly in keeping with a strict
scientific inquiry into the whole question. What I mean
is shown in Question 5 which runs thus: (a) Is perhaps
the deepest cause of race misunderstandings the tacit
assumption that the present characteristics of a race are
the expression of fixed and permanent race characteristics?
(b) If so, could not anthropologists, sociologists, and
scientific thinkers as a class powerfully assist the movement for a juster appreciation of the races by persistently
pointing out the fundamental fallacy involved in taking
a static instead of a dynamic, a momentary instead of a
historic, a local instead of a general, point of view of race
characteristics?

I attended and listened with the greatest possible
interest to the discussions, which lasted several days.

It seemed to me, that while charging those who differed from them with making an assumption, the note of the majority of the speakers was that of assumption. They took for granted that the evident palpable differences between the varied races of mankind were not deep seated, much less fundamental. They argued that given the same geographical, economic, and cultural conditions, races apparently different would respond in the same way. That environment rather than heredity is and has been the great force in causing difference, and is and will be the power which will bring the peoples of the earth together with like aims and aspirations. Implied in this is the idea that the civilization of Western Europe is the standard of excellence, and to achieve this the nations of the world will gladly strive, successful as they attain in greater or less degree.

I have thus briefly given my experience at, and conclusions on, this distinguished gathering, because I feel the spirit of those present, and often the opinions voiced, are present-day expressions of a school with which I, and many others of actual practical experience with backward and alien races, join issue. I admire and would support the effort they make for a better understanding, for the extinction of unreasoning prejudice, for mutual respect in place of estrangement and hostility. I believe in the brotherhood of man, and I believe that, widely as the races differ, the resemblances are far greater than the differences, that human nature is much the same all the world over. If we could trace our descent far enough into the distant past we should probably find that European and Negro, Chinaman and Papuan, had a common origin. Experience also shows that even people so diverse as these respond in much the same fashion to the same stimuli, and under given provocation, love and hate, desire and accumulate, in much the same way.

This does not blind me to the fact that these resemblances vary enormously with different races, and become very much attenuated when we compare the Bushman, the Veddah, or the Andaman Islander with the Englishman or the German. Probably these resemblances become less or more in proportion to the length of time which has elapsed since they diverged from a common stock. Under the same circumstances the Englishman, German, and Scandinavian will act and react much in the same way, the Spaniard and Greek and Italian with some differences, the Persian and Hindoo will vary still more, while the Negro and the Papuan will respond in different measure and probably in different quality.

How many hundreds of centuries it may be since the Negro and the Englishman diverged no one knows, but it has resulted in a difference of colour, feature, and physique that is obvious to all, and many who know the races best believe that the physical differences are signs of difference in mentality and spirit that it were fatuous to overlook.

To assume that the results of geologic time can be swept away, or permanently modified, by a few years' special training, is to place the ephemeral before the fundamental.

Only a few of those who have lived their lives among a backward people, even one with so many admirable qualities as the Bantu of South Africa, are inclined to minimize the deep-seated nature of race difference.

To know a race one must live with them, and even then many of those whose whole life has been spent among a primitive people, and who thought they understood, will find, as many South Africans have done, that there are depths they never plumbed, and at some supreme moment deep-seated, hidden race tendencies become apparent, that make them wonder whether, after all, their knowledge is only of the surface, and wonder whether any white man will ever be able to understand the workings of the black man's mind and spirit.

The enthusiastic and altruistic supporters of the theory of the all-sufficing power of education and environment, are not usually those who have had this practical experience.

They have met members of an imitative race temporarily divorced from their natural surroundings, away from their fellows, under conditions tending to repress their inborn race character, and stimulate the artificial, acquired habits, and they have discovered that the shibboleths of the white man could be accurately pronounced by them. These isolated ones had been usually prepared for the test by formal and conventional education, often by practical divorce from those of their own blood. To the believer in the all-sufficient power of education and environment the case is proved by this evidence, knowing not that beneath the absorbent surface is the adamant of their race genius, formed by gradual accretion from thousands of long-forgotten ancestors.

The rapidity with which many members of a primitive race can, under favourable stimuli, absorb and imitate, is indeed marvellous, and it is not surprising that those who know only such aberrant members of a race, should judge all by these exceptional ones. I do not mean exceptional in their capacity but in their circumstances, for probably, given the opportunity, a considerable proportion of the backward race would similarly imitate the example of those who had acquired an outward and surface resemblance in manner, tongue, and carriage, to those of a more forceful and persistent group among whom they dwelt for a time.

The indwelling spirit it is that matters, and no amount of veneer will even in generations materially change it. Education may give it direction and opportunity, the final result will be the effect of the spirit moulded through the long past. Pressure from without, if long continued, may modify it, must have modified it in the past, but the recipient must fight hereditary impulse and desire at every step, and beyond a certain limited depth, outside influence will not penetrate. How deep this may be our present experience cannot tell us, but indications are not wanting ; and these point to the conclusion that we cannot predict how the inner nature, which has taken so long to mould, will react to alien outside influence and pressure, but we may be certain that no change of environment will materially change the spirit of a race in the short time many anticipate, and which is so disproportionate to the ages during which it has taken shape.

To see the free play of heredity and of environment in a given case on a large scale would be of the highest interest. For such an experiment a race should be given opportunity to imitate the arts, culture, and social life of a more complex group, and then left to work out its own salvation. I do not wish to dogmatize, but I feel that the result after some generations would be altogether different from the development of the race which had evolved the culture, and given them the opportunity.

All through individual and group life opportunities occur, temptations arise, choice is presented. On the choice at the fateful moment may depend progress, stagnation, or retrogression. Let us not forget that the acquired habits and characters are not transmissible ; each generation must begin at the beginning, the ancient germinal characteristics are all that the child inherits. A race may copy what is acquired, that is easy, but the Will which is the force behind the culture it is impossible to copy. In everyday life we are far too prone to judge by the superficial, though instinctively aware that there is a greater force beneath, and it is character after all that matters.

Race is deeper than culture. And so I would wish it. To mould all the diverse peoples of this wonderful varied world into one type does not seem to me to be desirable. We have our different gifts, and I would allow all such free play. In our estimate races have risen and declined, and given in the process something essential and of value to the world. From some it may have been little, as the folksong contribution of the Negro of the Southern States. Who can say what it may be in the future ?

This view has been voiced by one of the foremost of the Negro race, Dr. E. W. Blyden, who, though born in America, lived and worked among his own people in West Africa. At a dinner given to him in London in

August, 1903, speaking to the educated black men present, he said : "Now, gentlemen, you who have done me the honour to ask me to come here to-night are certainly among the leaders of your people. You have had access to European culture. You should be the leaders of thought, the leaders of action among them. My message to you to-night therefore is to school yourselves to look upon life from the standpoint of your own nationality. With your study of English history and institutions unite the study of the institutions and customs of your own country. I pray that you may be gifted with the moral and mental grace to see clearly, and pursue consistently, the path of duty, of preservation of prosperity, of dignity, and of genuine respectability for your people without any reference to alien theories, especially those which we are now too clearly discovering do not for us make for growth and usefulness, but are beset with perils and attended with weakness. We must all enter earnestly and intelligently upon the study of alien customs brought among us, comparing them with the customs of our fathers, with the view of resisting the one so far as they do not conduce to our permanent welfare, always keeping that one great truth in mind that the life is more than meat and the body than raiment."

The doctrine of race growth thus voiced was accepted by others of the race of the speaker, and there is a distinct movement among West Africans to strive to retain their national character and customs, and resist the tendency to follow and copy the civilization of the white man.

Our social system and civilization is not so perfect that I would impose it on all. The extremes of poverty and wealth, hardship and soul-destroying luxury, prostitution, physical degeneration, group war, social unrest, and nervous prostration from suicidal competition and emulation, are unknown to our simpler and often happier brethren. It may be that from them we may learn the lost virtue of content in the simpler things of life ; and a physical and mental balance making for happiness.

CHAPTER IV.

RACE PREJUDICE.

I THINK it well, in this early chapter, to inquire into, and analyse as far as possible, the feeling which goes by the name of race prejudice, which enters so largely into all questions of race, and is in particular so potent a factor in the question in the Southern States and South Africa. The terms race animosity, race hostility, or even race hatred, are often used loosely as synonymous with race prejudice. It is not however necessarily any of these, they are simple phenomena, while the feeling I want to try to understand is much more subtle and complex. It is necessary to a clear understanding of the attitude of white and black to each other, and of the practical results that follow from such attitude, that we take some pains to discover what this factor, which plays such an important part in the problem, really is and on what it is founded.

If we find that, wholly or in part, it seems part of our racial human nature, our conclusions will be fundamentally different from what they will be if it proves to be based entirely on economic grounds, or on selfishness or jealousy, or if again it is simply a dislike for what is unknown or unfamiliar.

To the majority of those whose lives have been passed in a country with a homogeneous population such as England, the matter seems simple enough. To them this feeling is what is implied in the term prejudice, an unreasoning and unreasonable dislike to those differing from ourselves, akin to that which is felt for some individual, and which is overcome, or changed to liking by further association and knowledge. It is by them condemned as unworthy in those accepting the Christian doctrine, or even in a broad-minded man of the world, and it should be fought against and overcome.

The average man, accepting the democratic political creed of Western Europe, which knows not race, nor colour, is strongly opposed to any political discrimination, and generally also to any social differentiation between those of different blood and ancestry. He would give equality of treatment and opportunity to all alike, whether white, yellow, or black.

The followers of the Churches go farther. To them all men are brethren, equally fallen from grace, equally entitled to salvation through the same Mediator. To emphasize differences, and advocate different treatment for those made of one blood, and for whom Christ died, is sinful and to be utterly condemned.

The freedom of social intercourse, even to intermarriage, between East and West, European and African, to be witnessed in England, is evidence that this disposition is common. It is not however universal even there. I know Europeans, men and women alike, who have never lived outside Europe, who have a strong distaste for any kind of intercourse with those of a widely different race, and who find it requires a strong effort of will to come into close contact with them. These are, however, probably in a minority, and the feeling of repulsion varies with different individuals.

This is strikingly different from what obtains in all countries in which white and black live together in large numbers, although there prejudice varies in intensity, and differs in detail very considerably. These variations seem to me to be due to—first, the amount of difference between the races; second, the relative numbers of each; and third, the relations subsisting between them.

In New Zealand, where about one million Europeans live in the same country as forty-five thousand brown-skinned, intelligent, exceedingly capable people of Poly-

nesian race, prejudice is at a minimum. The Maories
are not dispersed among the whites as are the natives in
South Africa, but are more or less segregated in certain
portions of the North Island; there are thousands of
white New Zealanders who have never seen a Maori.
This fact, together with their meagre numbers, their
high standard of capacity, their general abstention from
industrial competition with the whites, and possibly their
light colour, are factors which must be taken into account
when considering the tolerance with which they are
treated. Prejudice, especially in the districts in which
they are comparatively numerous, is not altogether
absent, but the visitor from South Africa is struck by
the practical equality of treatment that is meted out to
them. It goes beyond this in some cases, for I have met
European New Zealanders, who, when questioned, told
me that they regard the Maories as their equals in every
respect, and some, though I fancied there was an effort
here, said they did not object to miscegenation. From my
observations, however, it seemed to me that if the Maories
were more numerous, and more intermixed with the
whites, the good-natured tolerance which I observed as
the general note, would not stand the strain.

In countries like India where the ruling race is Western European with but comparatively few who are not
in the upper places, and where the higher caste of natives may be wealthy and intelligent, race feeling takes
a different phase. The line is not drawn as in the
Southern States and South Africa. There must be intercommunication, often ceremoniously elaborate social
intercourse, between the highly placed of both races, and
this often obscures what is really felt. Many of the
factors which go to make race prejudice obvious and
bitter elsewhere, and which I will mention later, are
absent. But though there are exceptions the unwritten
law makes the line of cleavage clear, and social intercourse
of the kind that leads to intermarriage is never permitted.

In the Southern States and South Africa race prejudice

2 *

perhaps reaches its maximum. In the former no person with the slightest trace of Negro blood may associate with whites, or be classed as a white man. I will not here enter into the practical, often harsh, manner in which this operates, much of what I say later will deal with this phase of the question. In South Africa the distinctions drawn, as shown in my book " Black and White in South-East Africa," are as clear and unmistakable as the colour of the races. Much of this treatment may be regarded as due, not to a considered policy, but to what is usually termed race prejudice. The anomalies to be observed are many, and may be, and are, legitimately used as arguments by those who minimize the real force of the feeling and urge that it is ridiculous and inhuman, not based on any fact in Nature, and should be overcome.

I give some of these.

While the strongest resentment would be felt and expressed at a native travelling as a passenger in a public conveyance—a post cart or the like—especially with lady fellow-passengers, no exception is taken to his presence as a driver, and indeed ladies will manœuvre to get the box-seat at his left hand rather than take an inside place. To eat at the same table as a native would be the depth of indignity, but to eat food cooked by him, and often actually handled in the uncleanest manner by him, is taken as a matter of course. We shrink at personal contact, and would shudder to take the hand of a black man, yet to his care, or that of his sister, we entrust our most precious living treasures in their tenderest years, to be washed, clothed, tended, often caressed. The presence of the cleanest native alive in the same railway carriage as whites is an offence which demands the immediate attention of the Government, the dirtiest may make our beds. A single case of marriage between white and black by Christian rites will fill the newspapers with columns of indignant protest, but illicit intercourse, even permanent concubinage, will pass unnoticed.

It is these anomalies which provide the ridicule in which the arrows are dipped which are drawn on this human feeling. They show how much of our fallen human nature goes to its composition, and yet indicate how complex a thing it is. They show that it is not contact, *per se*, that the white man resents, although the unthinking ones contend that it is, and allege dirt, odour, and general beastliness as the reason for their action. While this is a factor in cases, the underlying reason is their resentment at anything that savours of equality. So long as the black man is performing menial duties, and there is no attempt at, or suggestion of equality, contact often of the closest, is tolerated. A suspicion of equality and the choler of the white man rises and overcomes him. He does not consider the psychological basis for his resentment, nor does he care whether it is reasonable or not, he simply will not tolerate the assumption, and often any attempt at reasoned argument only fans the flame of his indignation. Consciously or unconsciously, rightly or wrongly, he conceives that once he grants equal social treatment of any kind, the logical end will be the demand for social equality of all kinds, including what he will never grant, the right of equal marriage. To the man who advocates a greater leniency and toleration he puts what he thinks and what really is the clinching argument : Would you permit marriage between your daughter and this man ?

I know, and in some cases he knows, the argument that equal treatment in public conveyances, houses of accommodation and entertainment does not imply equal social treatment in all the intimacies of life. Sometimes he knows, but generally does not, the statement that if a race is not lowered in self-respect by unnecessary differentiation and unequal treatment, it will feel a racial solidarity that will make its members too proud to force themselves where they are not desired. These arguments are of no avail— he will not allow the thin end of the wedge ; in all social affairs implying equality they must be kept apart.

It may be appropriate here to cite what William Archer, an Englishman, whose book "In Afro-America" shows sympathy and good feeling towards the Negro race, says. Speaking of a visit to the Mississippi delta he writes: "What I think about the colour question must be superficial and may be foolish, but there is a certain evidential value about what I feel. The whole question is intimately one of feeling, and the instinctive sensations of an observer, with the prejudices of his race no doubt, but without local Southern prejudices, are, so far as they go, worth taking into account. Well, that day in the black belt of the Mississippi brought home to me the necessity of the Jim Crow car. The name, the insulting contemptuous name, is an outrage. There are some Negroes—so called—with whom I should esteem it a privilege to travel, and many others whose companionship would be in no way unwelcome to me; but frankly—I do not want to spend a whole day in the Mississippi Valley cheek by jowl with a miscellaneous multitude of the Negro race. The permanent difficulty underlying the unpermanent ones that time, education, Christian charity and soap and water may remove, is that of unlikeness."

Of a somewhat different nature, but with links binding it to this form of the prejudice, is the economic factor. This is usually connoted with the skilled forms of labour, in South Africa, at present at all events, the prerogative of the white artisan, and some critics who pride themselves on their liberality of outlook blame the white artisan for his narrow-minded selfishness in that he will not allow the black man, however skilled and efficient, to have an equal opportunity with himself. Let no one make a mistake here. The farmer will not object to the industrial training of natives which will fit them to relieve him of the labour of putting up a fence, or of doing rough carpentry on his farm, he will encourage it, and pride himself that he is not as these town artisans. Once, however, let it be apparent that the native is going to adopt improved methods of agriculture, and become a competitor, and not a labourer, and his broad-minded sympathy will vanish. So with the learned professions. It needed only the admission of one or two natives, who had unquestionable qualifications, acquired abroad, to be admitted to the Bar of South Africa, to make the legal profession pass resolutions discriminating against all those not of pure European descent. All this seems selfish enough. If remonstrance is urged against it, the answer is, Self-preservation is the first law of Nature.

And there is much force in this, for if economic competition between the races in all walks of life is to be the rule, a struggle for existence would ensue in which race prejudice would be fanned into race hatred, and although the result would be doubtful, the existence of the white man might be imperilled.

It may not be clearly seen by the threatened ones, but I believe there is an instinctive feeling, akin to the one I have previously mentioned, that if the white man and the black struggle together for economic life, the weaker of the now dominant race would have to take their place with the higher strata of the black race, and they or their children would lose rank, become intermixed, and lose their race purity.

These are the more earthly and material component parts of this widely spread feeling, and if they were all it might seem that the contention of those who condemn it as unworthy, selfish, and base, of no value, but rather a hindrance to the race, to be thrust from us by the higher altruism, would be worthy our serious consideration. But is this all? I cannot think so.

A distinguished American writer, Professor Josiah Royce, of Harvard University, takes this view, and says this feeling is simply a variation of the unreasoning fear and prejudice we have against mice and snakes. Most people have a fear and loathing of the latter, and if possible kill them at sight. It may be argued that they are God's creatures and form a part of the wonderful scheme of creation, and have their uses in the plan of the whole. It may, however, well be that the instinctive feeling of dread which appears to be almost universal is one that has developed through countless generations, and has been and is of protective value to those having it. The simile does not seem to be a happy one, nor one that should carry much weight.

It may be worth while to consider in what races this prejudice exists in its greatest intensity, and against whom it is usually directed. It is commonly accepted that it is strongest in the nations of Northern and Western Europe, and it is directed with the greatest force against those of Negro and Negroid descent. With perhaps certain exceptions, which may be disregarded, these groups are the farthest apart, physically, mentally, and spiritually of any of the existing races of mankind. As races converge the prejudice, though often present, is less intense, is often due to temporary causes, and is not so deep seated as that between more divergent groups. The races usually termed Latin, darker in hue, and possibly with some strands of kinship with the darker races, have not this feeling in the same intensity as the more Northern races, though it is undoubtedly present in them also. Miscegenation is more frequent in French and Portuguese colonies than in those whose overlords are of Teutonic, Anglo-Saxon or Celtic stock, and although it generally takes the form of concubinage, legal marriage is not uncommon. Nominally also in these colonies the coloured man has the right to vote. Still this does not mean that colour prejudice is non-existent. Indeed it sometimes takes a virulent and dangerous form, as in the case of the riots of a few years ago in Mauritius. I am told by residents in the island that this very serious disturbance was the immediate result of race prejudice, race jealousy, and race hatred, and that it was essentially *Noir versus Blanc*. It is difficult to account for all the phenomena connected with it on the ground of economic jealousy, or desire for dominance, though these are indubitably factors of importance.

It is notorious that persons born and brought up in

England, in the traditions of race equality, are often more prejudiced when they come to live in a bi-racial country, than those brought up amongst a backward people. It is the rule and not the exception, that those from Britain, who have been associated with Church activities, who have been supporters of missions, and hold orthodox views on religious matters, who land in South Africa with these ideas undimmed, soon absorb the racial opinions current in the country of their adoption.

Those who have nothing to risk or lose often hold most tenaciously to the popular doctrine. Cultured women, sympathetic and kindly in all their dealings with natives, who treat their coloured servants with the greatest possible consideration, have a shrinking from personal contact. Is it not possible, even probable, that besides the easily understood elements, there is a deeper instinctive and protective one, akin to that which preserves species in the lower animals, which is of value to the races and prevents race admixture and possible degeneration ? Only on this assumption can I account for all the facts. If this is so, the airy yet dogmatic manner in which some writers treat it is likely to lead us sadly astray.

I know of no book on this subject by one who has actually lived among a primitive people in contact with a highly cultured race, and who has known from actual practical experience the atmosphere engendered under such circumstances. There is, however, one book by a well-known and distinguished author whose qualifications to deal with this subject I can only judge by his production, on which I would like to make a few remarks. When I first saw it announced I obtained and read it with eagerness, for this question of Race prejudice has been one that I have long thought deserved much more attention than it had hitherto received.

The work to which I refer is "Race Prejudice," by M. Jean Finot.

The whole of his argument is that there are no deep-seated or essential differences between the so-called races of mankind, and he caustically criticizes the findings of anthropology, and is particularly severe on the conclusions drawn from anthropometry or distinctions which are based on skull measurements.　Here he has a good case, for although size and shape of head is often a marked and persistent race feature, far too much has been built upon it.　That this is the case, and that the exaggerations of the anthropologists give an opening for the satirist, does not prove the case of M. Finot, though it gives him an excellent opportunity for sarcasm which is somewhat amusing to those whose practical knowledge enables them to check some of the statements he himself makes, and to analyse the evidence he often accepts in so simple and naïve a manner.

I give the following cases for the information of my South African readers, whose comments would probably be more incisive than mine.　M. Finot says: "The Griquas, mixed products of Hottentots and Dutch, or the Cafusos, are quite equal to pure whites, just as the cross breeds of Indian and Spanish are at least as good as the Spaniards themselves".　I have met many South Americans of mixed ancestry, but have never lived or even visited the countries in which these people live, and knowing how dangerous a little knowledge is, I (unlike M. Finot) refrain from dogmatizing.　On the other hand, the Griquas I do know, and am familiar with many Europeans who live among them, and have daily dealings with them.　It is utterly contrary to fact to say they are equal to Europeans; either physically, mentally, morally, as a whole, neither are they equal in any single character of value.　A more unfortunate example for M. Finot's argument he could not possibly have found, for the Griquas are a degenerate, dissolute, demoralized people, weak and unstable, lazy and thriftless.　They appear to be constitutionally immoral, far more so than either the European or Bantu people among whom they live.　The branch of these people with whom I am best acquainted live in Griqualand East, just south of the Natal border.　They came to this land, then unoccupied owing to native wars and thus called No Man's Land, under Adam Kok their chief, some half century ago. It is one of the best parts of South Africa, well grassed and well watered, with fertile arable land, a glorious climate, with good rainfall, and healthy for all kinds of live-stock. This goodly land was parcelled out to the Griqua families in farms of from 2000 to 3000 acres. Never had a people a better start in life. To-day the land has passed from them and they live miserably as squatters, as herds for Europeans, or without definite employment, and the farms they once held are owned and occupied by Europeans, who are prosperous and thriving, and constantly advancing in the amenities of life. The Griquas were not dispossessed by force ; excepting for one short-lived outbreak the country has been in peace. They were simply constitutionally unable to hold ; gin, immorality, laziness, debt, the lack of foresight and inability to forego present gratification for future well-being, are the reasons for their race failure. The methods of the incoming European were sometimes not justifiable, but the hopeless weakness of the Griqua was his undoing.

I have gone into this case somewhat in detail, because I feel that if the other instances given by M. Finot have no more foundation in fact than this one, which I am able to check from my own personal knowledge, his conclusions are not of much value. But I cannot refrain from one or two other instances which will arouse amusement or indignation in my South African readers according to their temperament ;—thus again M. Finot says : " It is ordinarily admitted that the Bushmen are descended from the Hottentots, as indeed their language shows. But the difference that separates them is considerable. The Bushmen are in the first place much darker than the Hottentots, and remind us of Guinean Negroes. But whereas the first live in the woods, the Hottentots are nomadic shepherds and live in the Steppes. . . . People have wished to see in the Bushmen a race quite apart, the most monstrous and almost intermediary link between men and monkeys. Their excessive thinness and the remarkable smallness of their height, involve no ineluctable fatality. It is all explained by hunger. It is enough to observe the rare specimens of Bushmen at the Cape, who are well nourished, and are changed in aspect and stature to see what a single element, viz., nourishment, can afford in the appearance of man." I cannot spare the time to adequately analyse this tissue of truth and falsehood. M. Finot desires to demonstrate the powerful and immediate effects of environment on race characters, and in this case assumes extreme thinness and, correctly, short stature, due he says to starvation, and removable by nourishment; and extreme dark colour owing to living in the woods, reminding him of Guinean Negroes. I never heard of extreme thinness being specially characteristic of Bushmen, and certainly their colour could not remind one, with any knowledge of the subject, of Guinean Negroes. They varied in colour, but a light yellow tending towards brown was the usual one, and all South Africans and all ethnologists know they did not live in the woods, but as Dr. Theal says, " on the arid plains and the bare mountain sides of South Africa ". I cannot imagine any authority believing that the characteristics of the Bushmen, short stature, kinky hair in tufts, triangular face, yellow colour, small extremities, along with certain peculiarities in the females, together with his extremely wild untameable nature, could be materially altered by any change of food and habits within any reasonable time, and although the races have probably intermixed to some extent, I have yet to discover the authority, unless trying to bolster up a preconceived theory, who believes these people were descended from the Hottentots.

M. Finot is an advocate of race admixture. His panegyric on the Griquas indicates his views on this subject. He cites Le Vailliant (an authority of doubtful value) to prove that race admixture promotes fertility. Le Vailliant states "that Hottentots, who generally give

birth to three or four children, have as many as twelve
when united to white men or Negroes, the crossing of
Negroes with white men and women produces similar
results ". One would have thought that a scientific investigator would have wanted far more evidence on this
intricate and difficult subject of intercrossing and its
effects, before drawing conclusions. My African experience of fully forty years does not enable me to say
more than that I know no facts to warrant such a deduc-
tion.

I do not think many Southerners would endorse the
following : " The Negroes before the War of Secession,
and those of our day, who have received a superior instruction, form a marked contrast in character and aspirations.
With the dignity of man which has been inculcated, the
vices which are considered as instinctive in them have
almost completely disappeared." If it was all as simple
as this the race problem would soon be solved.

Again, speaking of the United States, and apparently
the South in particular, he says " the number of coloured
men and women mixed with the whites and participating in their ordinary life is incalculable. If ever the
white portion could fall from the face of those who have
no right to it in the Southern States, their social life
would be singularly revolutionized." I made special inquiry about this alleged passing over to the whites when
in the United States, both North and South, and from
both white and coloured. The consensus of opinion was
that it was very small indeed, quite negligible. One
authority, himself a coloured man of high culture, who
has published most valuable monographs, said that in his
life-long experience he only knew of twelve or fifteen
such cases.

I have dealt at some length with M. Finot's work,
first because it is accepted as authoritative by many, second
because it is the only book I know purporting to deal
exhaustively and scientifically with this question, and
thirdly because he takes a view that is diametrically

opposed to what I believe to be true. He thinks race prejudice is a simple matter, and is what the name implies, a prejudice discreditable to those holding it, to be rooted out as altogether unworthy. To strengthen this conclusion he professes the belief that races are the result of their *milieu*, and may be modified rapidly and permanently by a change in their surroundings. I think that such races as we are dealing with are the result of long ages of separation, and no change of *milieu* will, in any reasonable time, permanently change the essential features which have been ingrained into the very nature through probably thousands of generations.

I also hold that race prejudice is not a simple, but a complex phenomenon, probably in part instinctive and protective and not to be utterly condemned, partly selfish and based at the desire to remain paramount, yet even here not altogether personal but strengthened by a desire for the welfare of future generations of their race.

As against the academic yet loose and inaccurate statements of opinion I have given, let me quote one who has actually lived among a backward people, who knows and loves them, and writes with sympathy, insight, and discretion. Edgar Gardner Murphy says : " The South has insisted, and insisted wisely, in maintaining the absolute distinctness of racial life. The wisdom of this insistence, the deep sociological value of what has been called race prejudice, despite its sometimes brutal and excuseless manifestations in every section, will have, I believe, an ever-widening recognition. But if human society is to establish its distinctions of racial life, it will find it can base these distinctions more securely upon intelligence than upon ignorance."

I have said that race prejudice is not the same thing as race animosity or race hatred. If I read the annals of my native country aright, it was considered the duty of an Elizabethan Englishman to hate a Spaniard, and at the beginning of last century an Englishman who did not

hate a Frenchman as he did the devil was unworthy of
his birthright.

Race prejudice as it exists in South Africa and America is a different thing to this. Individual Spaniards or
Frenchmen of those earlier times, on parole in England,
would not be made conscious of the wide social gulf which
separates white and black to-day. Many of those who
would not dream of permitting the first advance to a
common social life, and who would fight against political
equality to the last ditch, in practical life as we have it to-
day are among the best friends of the black man, and
have a sincere regard for the race. Many white women
who are kindly and considerate, and would sacrifice themselves rather than hurt the feelings of their native
servants, would shudder at anything approaching the
familiarity implied in social contact.

But unquestionably in the majority the gap between
prejudice and hostility is neither wide nor deep, and
untoward events will quickly fan the flames and cause
the fire to leap the gulf, and here is a real danger and a
very sufficient reason why the feeling should be carefully
watched and kept in check both by individuals and
Governments.

What in its milder manifestations may be a salutary
protection can easily become a cause of lamentable and unjustifiable oppression. Negrophilists (I use the term with
all respect), and those engaged in philanthropic work
among the natives, often express the hope—it can hardly
be a belief with many—that as the backward race becomes
educated and adopts the mode of living of the dominant
group, the latter will open its ranks and accept the Negro
as one of themselves, only requiring what they would
demand in one of their own, and disregarding physical
differences. If this hope were justified by the facts our
course would be comparatively clear, we should have only
to educate and develop character, and teach and enjoin a
high standard of living, to bridge gradually the difference
between us. I have long felt the importance of clear light

on this point, and watched attitudes, and listened to opinions, with the view of getting at the mind of the average man.   That some few individuals of exceptional temperament would accept the advanced black man is not the crux of the question, it is rather what the mass would do It is to me one of the saddest features of this apparently insoluble question that the prejudice of the white man is quickened, and becomes more alert and even bitter, as the Negro or native approaches his standard of life.   In the Southern States a " nigger in his place " is tolerated, even liked; in South Africa a raw Kaffir is in many cases preferred, and receives kindly consideration, that is not forthcoming when he becomes dressed, educated, and speaks English.

It will be apparent in what I have said so far in this chapter, that I regard this feeling as one chiefly animating the white man, and have dealt almost exclusively with it from his side.   We want, however, to know how the black man stands.   Many are trying hard to get at the back of the black man's mind, but not I fear very successfully.   This very difficulty, admitted by those who know him best, those who speak his language, and have lived with him all their lives, is an indication of the fundamental difference in which I believe.   It is almost impossible to analyse, weigh, and balance the emotions in one so far removed.   So far as I can do so I find there is little of permanent deep-seated prejudice in the mind of Negro or native towards Europeans.   In times of active warfare he may be filled with a fierce hatred, and willingly cast away his life to quench it.   When his life is made intolerable by constant interference and oppression, a similar but less active resentment takes possession of him, which may be fanned into revolt; but it is not in his nature to dwell constantly on his position in the scheme of things, and if his few wants are satisfied, and he is let alone, he will take things as they come with perfect equanimity.

It is due to his foresight and anxiety for his future

and that of his children, which helps to make the white man cherish the desire for solidarity and domination which enters into this feeling. This anxiety is unknown to the native, and he in the past has been quite willing and honoured that the white man should enter into marriage relations with his women. Their seduction and subsequent abandonment is another matter; this is a grievance to him as it would be to any race on earth; but honourable sexual relations are not objected to by him nor by those most interested. If secure in her position, I do not think the average native woman has any aversion to alliance with the dominant race. This feeling is, I believe, quickened in the case of mulatto women, many of whom desire white offspring. In the United States those of mixed descent have been forced back among their mother's kin, and perforce must accept it, and then they wisely disclaim any desire for white society and connexion. I do not think, however, there is any repugnance to it comparable to the race prejudice of the whites. On the other hand there is a distinct disinclination to unite with the darker side of their ancestry.

Judged by this test, which is, I think, the ultimate one, we must acquit the black man of race prejudice, or if it exists it is in a much attenuated form. His temperament is not congenial to such a growth. When not excited by fear, drink, or hatred, he is kindly, long-suffering, disposed to sociability, not peering into the future, but content with the present and his position in it, and such a character is not the one to harbour permanent prejudice, though he may easily be awakened to active hostility.

It may seem to some that this portion of our inquiry may be academic and out of place in a practical exposition. This is not the case. The fact of the existence of this feeling accounts in large part for the present position of affairs in large tracts of the earth's surface, and affects the happiness of many millions. The statesman must ever bear it in mind; in many of its manifestations it is a rock of offence to the conscientious, it may, if allowed or

3

encouraged to expand, mean oppression, or even war and desolation.   To attempt to get an accurate estimate of its component parts, and how far it must be considered a permanent factor in the world, should have a real value for the man of affairs.   At present, and as far as I can see into the future, the statesman cannot ignore it, he must always remember and at times reckon with it.   He must not allow it full sway, his attitude should be one of watchful control, for it is of its nature to change under slight provocation into unjustifiable repression and hatred. Realizing this, we may yet feel that it is in part based upon instincts that are fundamental, and which may tend to preserve to both races their essential nature.

CHAPTER V.

THE SOUTH LAND.

I VISITED the South land in spring and early summer, travelling from Washington, D.C., through Virginia, North Carolina, South Carolina, Georgia, Alabama, Mississippi, Louisiana, Tennessee and so back again into North Carolina and Virginia. I purposely never travelled by night, and chose by preference the slow trains from which I could see the country, and in which I had opportunity of meeting and conversing with the local people. These South-Eastern States formed the backbone of the old Confederacy, the land so fondly spoken of by its inhabitants as Dixie.

It is bounded on the west by the forest-covered and rugged Appalachian chain of mountains, in which are peaks 6000 feet above tide-water, and with considerable areas over 2000 feet. Eastward of these mountains is a high and rolling country called the Piedmont section, and from this eastward again to the sea a broad stretch of plain.

Coming from the open grass-covered lands of South-East Africa, it was the absence of grass and open country that first struck me. Day after day the train rolled through a tree-covered landscape, but it was not the forest primeval. Here and there the trees were of such a size as to warrant the term forest, but generally they were small and insignificant, with shrubs and scrub growing between them, not at all an impressive scene. It seemed to me to be a second growth, and I learned that this was the case. Often this scrub vegetation was insufficient to protect the earth from the elements, and the effect of weathering could be seen in soil exposure, in ugly dongas, and in full streams charged with the surface soil.

Much of it struck me as a land that had been ravaged, denuded of its natural covering, forced to yield till it could yield no more, and then left to be swept by wind and rain until it could protect itself to some extent by the thin woods it now bore.

Notwithstanding this, the general impression I got was that of a pleasant land. The fresh green foliage and flowering shrubs, the white flowers of the dogwood, conspicuous in the greenery, seen in the clear bright air and spring sunshine, was homelike and satisfied one, and when on some height of land the prospect of rolling wooded hills spread far and wide, I felt I could understand the affection of those whose homeland it was.

My estimate of its present condition was, I found, shared by many of the practical men I met. They admitted and deplored the mishandling and ravishment of the past. This was due, it appeared, first to concentration on one or two profitable crops, principally cotton and tobacco, then to the fact that there was virgin land in abundance, which led to overcropping and abandonment, and lastly to the system of slavery and big plantations. If this was all that could be said the outlook would not be an inspiring one. I discovered, however, that those who regretted the past were often full of hope for the future. It has been demonstrated that with proper culture, rotation of crops, keeping live-stock and soiling with leguminous plants, the weary earth may be restored to beyond its pristine fertility.

In all parts of the South this building-up process is in operation. Not perhaps on a large scale, little can be seen from the railway line, but when one gets into the country, the process can be seen in actual operation here and there, and examples of wonderful achievement are sufficiently frequent to stimulate the process of regeneration.

South Africans will gather from this general description of the land that it is not a stock country as we understand the term. I saw comparatively few cattle, and fewer sheep. The principal domestic animal is the hog, which often runs wild in town as well as country. Artificial grasses, lucerne, and other leguminous plants, however, can be grown, and undoubtedly there is a future for cattle raising. A far larger proportion of the land is arable than is the case in South Africa. It is a varied land, with mountain, plateau and plain, but nothing like so varied as South Africa. There are no such striking contrasts as between the sun-baked, shimmering, arid Karroo, and the green humid Natal Coast.

In South Africa we have huge stretches of country in which the rainfall is less than 10 inches annually, while I have known in other parts 28 inches fall in half a week, and a total precipitation for the year of 70 to 80 inches.

In the South land the rainfall is ample and far more regular. There are no droughts, and over vast tracts the precipitation averages 45 to 55 inches, well distributed throughout the year. The blizzards that devastate the plains of the West are unknown. I noticed that in one State the maximum force of the wind in a long series of years was only 48 miles an hour.

Between the Mississippi delta and the mountain districts of Eastern Tennessee, Western Virginia, and North Carolina, there are great differences, but nothing like so great as between the hot humid sugar belt of Zululand, the temperate well-watered grass lands of the high plateau of the Eastern Transvaal, and the desiccated areas in the North-West of the Cape Colony.

Before speaking of rural conditions I should briefly mention town life. The South is not a country of large cities. None are in the same schedule as the larger cities of the North or of Europe. The capitals of most States are country towns, and even the industrial centres, such as Birmingham and Atlanta, do not compare in size with those elsewhere. A decade or two ago, the contrast was still more striking, but gradually there has been an awakening to modern conditions. Northern capital, energy, and experience are taking up the opportunities. At not infrequent intervals along the railroads are small cotton-mill towns. These usually centre round one or two large factories of the familiar type, excepting that in many cases the power used is electricity, transmitted from waterfalls many miles away. The workpeople live in wooden cottages of cheap construction, detached or semi-detached, in the immediate neighbourhood of the factory. The labour employed is exclusively white, and is largely drawn from the country, and much of it from the mountain districts. Those employed were small farmers and their families, and though their wages as operatives came as a welcome addition to their incomes, their life and conditions in the factories have led to deterioration in health and physique in many cases.

The average town in the South—apart from the industrial centres—has reason for its existence in the rural industry of the surrounding country. As a rule these towns are, to the visitor, even more conducive to melancholy than the ordinary up-country dorp of South Africa. The houses are built of wood, and the yards, which should be gardens, are waste spaces littered with rubbish. The streets are quagmires rootled up by hogs, or dusty beyond description. The display at the ramshackle stores seems to be confined to huge posters of Northern manufacturers, and these centres of commerce serve as lounging places for loafers. Mention should, however, be made of the case of some towns which stand out as conspicuous exceptions, and demonstrate by shady parks and avenues, by homes with gardens full of loveliness, how much Nature would contribute if man only made the effort.

The chief crop to-day, as it has been for scores of years, is cotton. It is the staple and the standard of value of the country. Both white and black grow it, each race raising perhaps one-half of the total crop. To the lint the farmer looks for the cash to pay for his out-goings, and the seed and seed-meal furnish valuable food for such stock as he possesses. After cotton comes corn, the mealie of the South African, which furnishes much of the food of the Negro, and is a staple in the bill of fare of the white man, especially in rural districts. Cornbread and bacon are still, as in slavery days, the food of the South. In Virginia and North Carolina tobacco takes the place of cotton, and in Louisiana and Mississippi the sugar crop is of the first importance.

Travelling slowly through the country, and always with an eye open to discover how man was dealing with it, I was not favourably impressed with the methods of cultivation. It was the early spring, and the ploughing season was on, yet for hundreds of miles I did not see any mechanical agricultural contrivance more modern or specialized than a one-horse plough. Commercial fertilisers were used everywhere, the smell of them pervaded the land, but in most cases I found they were just used in sufficient quantity to ensure the annual crop. It appeared to me to be a country that needed building up, and my attention was directed to the question of the possibility of doing so, for in this lay the possibility of emergence from the present rather unsatisfactory rural condition. I found enough in my personal observations and in recorded cases, to prove not only the possibility, but the certainty of this growth to better things. I found that cotton, corn, tobacco, and sugar, by no means exhausted the possibilities of this broad well-watered sunny region. It was claimed that climatic conditions were so favourable that two crops of many plants could be grown, and that by proper cultivation and manuring, the land might be in almost constant yield. All along the coast-belt continuous crops of various vegetables—in America truck— could be grown, and the crops and profits were high, in some cases enormous, and the cities of the North formed accessible and profitable markets. Every kind of vegetable grown in the Northern States or Western Europe grew kindly, and others, such as sweet potatoes, requiring

sub-tropical conditions, could be added to the list.   In
the warmer regions oranges, lemons, grape-fruit; in the
cooler sections apples, pears, peaches, apricots, cherries,
grapes, and all temperate fruits, with nuts such as pecan,
walnut and others.   Corn is not the only cereal which
may be grown, wheat, oats, and rye, with proper cultivation and treatment, have proved quite successful.   While
with the ordinary cultivation, yields are not high, even
of the well-known staples, there are plenty of instances
proving that proper treatment and building up will increase them largely, and at the same time permanently
improve the soil.

I cannot even give a summary of all I saw and heard
with regard to this improved productivity; as showing,
however, the variety of produce and the large yields
possible, with proper conditions, I will mention a fifty-
acre farm in South Georgia which gave in one year :—

8 bales of cotton each 500 lb. from 4 acres.

7 bales of cotton each 500 lb. from 5 acres.

And of course the valuable cotton seed in addition.

470 bushels corn from 10 acres.

280 bushels oats from 7 acres; after the oats were
cleared these 7 acres gave 700 bushels of sweet
potatoes.

300 dollars worth of sugar cane from 1 acre; and in
addition 700 dollars worth of vegetables during
the season.

The general impression I got in travelling was that
by far the greater portion was uncultivated, and that the
cultivated areas were small as compared with those
under forest or semi-forest conditions.   This impression
I had to a certain extent to correct, for as it was spring,
and a rather late spring, the crops did not show up as
they would later in the season.   Still I find that in
Virginia one-half of the land is uncleared and uncultivated.   Only 35 per cent. of the area of North Carolina
could be called improved.   Out of 37,000,000 acres in
Georgia, 11,000,000 only was in occupied and improved

farms, and it is claimed there is still room for 100,000 families on the cleared lands, and for an enormous number on the larger area still unoccupied.

In all these States facilities for marketing produce are good, especially as compared with a country like South Africa, if it is taken as a whole.

I find that North Carolina with an area of 48,580 square miles has 5300 miles of railroad, that South Carolina with an area of 30,495 square miles has 3000 miles of railway, and Georgia with an area of 57,500 square miles has 7000 miles of railroad.

Just a few statistics as to climate :—

Virginia, 78° F. mean summer heat ; 33° to 40° F. winter ; rainfall 38 to 49 inches.

North Florida and South Georgia, mean annual temperature 66° to 70° F. ; rainfall 50 to 55 inches.

South Carolina, mean annual temperature 63° F. ; rainfall 48 inches.

Georgia, mean annual temperature 63° F. ; rainfall 51 inches.

I give the annual rainfall for Alabama by months.

January	February	March	April	May	June	July	August
5·02	4·63	6·60	4·84	2·90	5·86	5·22	2·82

September	October	November	December
2·30	2·81	2·78	4·46

This is a precipitation and distribution that many countries would like to experience.

Now as to land values. I do not include the most fertile and well-improved lands, but those which in my judgment are susceptible of improvement with proper treatment.

In Virginia with 4609 miles of railway, lands suitable for vegetable growing may be had from $15 to $20 an acre, and land suitable for apple and other fruits at the same price.

In Southern Georgia uncleared land may be bought at from $5 to $20 an acre, and cleared but unimproved land from $10 to $30 an acre.

In Northern Georgia fruit and grazing land runs as low as $5 an acre.

In Mississippi unimproved land suitable for trucking is purchasable at from $5 to $10 an acre.

According to the United States Census of 1900 land values for all rural lands in these South-Eastern States averaged out at $7·780 an acre, in 1910 it had gone up to $16·82 per acre.   This points a moral and has an application to my theme which will be seen later on.

In the whole South-Eastern States we have an area of 83,000,000 acres under some sort of cultivation or improved in some measure, 86,000,000 acres unimproved, and 120,000,000 acres in forest.   This forest land is valuable, in many cases very valuable, providing a source of wealth and a field for labour from the harvesting of forest products.

Notwithstanding the past ravages of man, these States may fairly claim the following not inconsiderable advantages.   Ample and well-distributed rainfall; plenty of sunshine, and genial and generally healthy climate; firewood and timber for building everywhere; plenty of land, which though often impoverished, may be built up, while at the same time yielding a living.   An immense variety of products both of the temperate and sub-tropical zones, fibres, cereals, fruits, nuts, and grasses; accessibility to profitable markets, railroad, river or ocean transport available for all sections.

It has been in the past a land of big plantations, of a caste system, of aristocratic and wealthy planters who monopolized the fertile lands, and a class of poverty-stricken, ignorant, and indolent whites who did nothing to add to the productivity of the country, the whole based on the slave system; the aftermath is visible to-day in the ravaged land and backward agricultural position.

Yet in all essentials it is a country fitted for mixed farming, farming which will improve the land, and where middle-class prosperous homes may be built up just as they have been in New Zealand.

The hindrances in the past have not been due to Nature, but to an artificial and maleficent social system, and though conditions have altered to-day, it is social conditions, and not the land nor the climate that stand in the way of the best development of the rural South.

I have thought it well to endeavour to convey a picture, sketchy but perhaps sufficient, of this South land, its present economic rural condition and its possibilities, for on these I base conclusions on the great social problem that faces the country.

CHAPTER VI.

THE PAST, SLAVERY.

IF we are to appraise justly present race relations in the South, the progress the Negro has made, the trend of present tendencies, and the possibilities that lie in the future, a short chapter must be devoted to the social condition of the country at the time of emancipation, and we must consider certain political movements which immediately followed the close of the Civil War.

Many years ago, in my early days in Natal, I came across several books which I found of engrossing interest. They were written by Frederick Law Olmsted and were entitled " A Journey through the Cotton Kingdom," " A Texas Journey," and " Journeys through the Seaboard Slave States ". In these were described his travels and experiences in these countries just before the War of Secession.

He travelled when practicable by rail, but railroads were not frequent in the fifties of last century, and most of his journeyings were by coach and on horseback. He valued comfort, and has much to say of the lack of decent accommodation, but this did not deter him from visiting the heart of the country, and associating, under rude and primitive conditions, with men of all classes and callings. He was a practical farmer, his home being in New York State, and he has much to say on land and cultivation. He seems to have been a Sociologist before the term was used, intensely interested in all social and economic subjects. His temperament appears to have been singularly equable, and he was certainly gifted with clear sight and judgment. His pictures of the country and people, and the incidents he encountered, impress the reader as being as truthful as they are vivid.

No formal history of the Southern States could be so illuminating, nor convey such clear pictures of the lives and surroundings of the people, both white and black, as the pages which describe the travels of this New York farmer.

Since that day I have re-read these books, and I find my early impressions fully confirmed. With a knowledge of what has happened and is happening in Africa, where the races meet under milder but not dissimilar conditions, one can visualize the pictures drawn by the author.

It is evident that the simple conclusion drawn by the ordinary man, generally from books written with a purpose, of the slave cowering beneath the whip of the haughty aristocratic owner, who lives in luxury on the debasement of the slave, is not the whole story.

Conditions varied very much, with climate, crops, local customs, the personality of the owners, and the particular work the slaves were called upon to perform.

In very many cases, as I should have expected, the Negro set the pace, and although task work was common, the standard set was not arduous, and as is so common in Africa, especially when the native has no incentive to effort, the strain of keeping him up to a high pitch of endeavour was too great a task for the master, and was abandoned for an easy-going routine.

Olmsted gives instances of white owners whose temperament was such, that without driving, they got what they considered satisfactory results from their labour, and who never had recourse to punishment. We find similarly gifted individuals in Africa.

Nevertheless, it is indubitable, that in cases the most abominable and hellish cruelty was practised, and this necessarily happens when despotic power is in the hands of a class.

Direct wastage of implements and material was enormous, and it was impossible to teach labourers, rendered brutish and inefficient under such a system, to exercise initiative or economy. New and improved methods were forbidden by the ignorance and inertia of the slaves; beyond a certain dull routine they could not be moved.

The social results which are directly attributable to the system were: A small number of rich planters, who when resident on their estates, lived in a sumptuous patriarchal style, and often treated their servants with consideration, but who, when non-resident, demanded returns which led to slave-driving in its worst forms. A larger number of slave-holders whose methods varied considerably, and the bulk of the white population, illiterate, poverty-stricken, passionate, and lawless, often living by illegal trafficking with the slaves. Then the Negro slaves of whom a few were skilled and highly valued, who lived in some measure of material comfort, the house servants, often pampered and consequential, with little of discomfort in their lives, and the mass, living like the working farm animals, sufficiently fed, and clothed in the coarsest manner, without initiative or hope, driven to their tasks under fear of the lash, giving as little labour as possible, adepts at shirking and malingering.

The economic results as compared with free labour, a subject into which Olmsted made special investigation, were miserably poor. Estimates and comparisons were made by many of those he met, it seemed to be a common topic of conversation. By some the result was considered to be not more than half what was achieved by free labour, and this even at work the Negroes were accustomed to do regularly. Some of those questioned considered four Negroes were only equal to one white labourer in the North.

The training in initiative, resourcefulness, and forethought, and the stimulus furnished by the willing labour of a free worker were entirely absent, and the Negro was forbidden the knowledge and elevation which come from education. His family life was that of the beasts, he was mated for purposes of reproduction, and his children

were not his own.   It was in 1619 that the first cargo of
African slaves was landed in the United States, and
although the traffic was forbidden by law, the last cargoes
to arrive did not long antedate the Civil War, so that
during this long period there were constant accessions
of barbarism to the ranks of the Negroes.

It is impossible to conceive any life or training less
calculated to fit them for the exercise of the privileges of
citizens of a country like the United States. Yet by
Federal edict at the close of the Civil War, every Negro
was given the same political rights as his late master, or
the most cultured citizen of Boston.

The effect of the slave system was at least as maleficent on the whites as on the Negroes.   The aristocratic planter looms large in pictures of the period.   He
is described as haughty, passionate, yet chivalrous, with
a high code of honour, and of great intellectual gifts.
Such could only have formed a mere fraction of the whole
population, for out of a total white population of eight
millions, owning four million Negroes, there were only
three hundred and fifty thousand actual slave-owners.

The mass of the whites had little cause to love either
planter, Negro, or the system under which they lived.
The best lands were taken up and monopolized by the
large planters, and cultivated by their slaves.   Such
skilled work as was necessary under the plantation system was undertaken by trained Negroes, the poor white
was denied the opportunity to learn or profit by skilled
callings.   It is apparent, too, that, as to-day, much of the
commerce, especially the retail distribution, was in the
hands of Jews.   Thus debarred, the majority of the whites
sank into lethargy and poverty, living shiftless lives, despised even by the slaves they were too poor to possess.

It has often been matter of wonderment to me that
this class ever took up arms in a quarrel in which they
had so little direct interest, and fought so long with such
valour and determination.   When we attempt to gauge
the present position of the two races in the South, we must

ever bear in mind their condition during the long years of slavery, and, in particular, when trying to assess the present state of the Negro, must retain a picture of what he was when a new horizon opened out to him with Emancipation.

A few words must first, however, be given to an intermediate period, the years of Reconstruction.

CHAPTER VII.

THE PAST, RECONSTRUCTION.

WHEN the war closed it left the South in chaos. The old planter families who had so long ruled the South, and to a large extent the Union also, were ruined, and many of the younger men fell fighting. Their wealth, which had consisted of land and slaves, was as regards the former ravished, and the latter lost to them for ever. They came back to devastated homes, with little immediate prospect of rebuilding them. The mass of the Confederate soldiery had neither homes nor work. The Negroes were a dark mass, bewildered and irresponsible, scattered over the land, or controlled in some measure by the Freedman's Bureau.

The position was not unlike what it was in South Africa after the last Boer War, and those of us who, from actual experience, know the condition of our country at that time, and the tremendous and patient struggle it took to set civil life on a sound footing, will have some conception of the state of the South. Yet not fully, for with us the question of the black man and his status did not increase our difficulties, but here it meant the entire reversal of the economic, social, and political position of one-third of the population of the South, and establishing the civic structure on a new and entirely different basis. Not as with us a rebuilding of the old, but literally a reconstruction.

Provisional State governments were soon established, and as such were recognized by the Federal authorities. Conventions were called which enacted new Constitutions, and under them new Legislatures were elected.

All this was the work of the white man, the Negro had not yet realized where he stood, but bewildered and gasping, he wandered or waited.

He was not allowed to remain thus for long, the newly appointed State legislatures rapidly set to work to formulate his position, and it became quickly apparent that the white man was not going to permit the Negro to choose his position in the State for himself.

Laws were passed which could have but one interpretation ; they were devised to place the Negro again in a position of servitude, as nearly like that of slavery as it was possible under the Thirteenth Amendment of the Constitution, which had been accepted by the States as they re-entered the Union.

In South Carolina an ordinance was passed at this time, making the provision that " no person of colour shall pursue the practice, art, or business of an artisan, mechanic, or shopkeeper or any other trade or employment beside that of husbandry, or that of a servant under contract for labour, until he shall have obtained a licence from the judge of the County Court, which licence shall be good for one year only ". The law went on to say that for a licence as pedler or shopkeeper a fee of £100 must be paid, while for the rudest mechanical calling it was £10. These licence fees were applicable only to Negroes and were not demanded from white men. The object was obvious.

A Bill was introduced into the Legislature of Louisiana under which every freed man or woman shall furnish themselves with a comfortable home and visible means of subsistence within twenty days of the passing of the Act, and any coloured person failing so to do shall be arrested by any sheriff or constable, and by him hired out to the highest bidder for the remainder of the year.

Similar laws were passed in other Southern States, and the North became alarmed, fearing that what had been won at the cost of a four years' bloody war would in this way be lost, and the individual States would still defeat the intent of the Federal authorities.

When Congress met therefore to consider the question of the permanent reorganization of the South, it was with suspicion as to the intentions of the late Confederacy, and resentment at some of their actions since peace was declared.

The Federal Government gave a fresh lease of life and more ample powers to the Freedman's Bureau for the control, guidance, support, and protection of the coloured people, independently of State action.

In June, 1866, the Fourteenth Amendment to the Constitution was passed which conferred the franchise, both State and Federal, on all persons born, or naturalized in the United States, irrespective of race, colour, or previous condition of servitude. The provisional governments of the Southern States, with the exception of Tennessee, rejected this amendment, which prompted Congress to pass in March, 1867, a Reconstruction Act, designed to provide for efficient governments for the insurrectionary States, and of course dispossessing the governments already set up by the white inhabitants.

The South was divided into military districts, each ruled by a General of the Federal Army.

State Conventions were elected under the supervision and control of these officers, and as the bulk of the whites were disenfranchised as rebels, those persons elected to the Conventions were sent thither by the Negro vote, the few whites who had remained faithful to the Union, and Federal office-bearers. The result was that Constitutions were adopted in all the States granting equal suffrage to all, black and white alike, but meantime barring all the leading whites on account of their participation in the War of Secession.

Thus the State Governments were given into the hands of the Negroes and those whites who were able and willing to co-operate with them. Few Southern whites would accept, or attempt to profit by, such a

4 *

position, but there were many from the North who saw the opportunity for power and plunder, and flocked into the South land, and for some years battened on the ignorance and venality of the Negro for their own profit. These political adventurers were contemptuously called carpet baggers, a term which, originating with this class, and specially applicable to their condition, has since been given a wider application.

For some years they exploited the opportunity and the Negro to the full. They robbed to their heart's content. In all the States the public debt increased enormously, and yet there was nothing to show for these vast increases, which went to the politicians and in a smaller degree to the venal voters.

A favourite method of plunder was to issue railroad bonds which were given to nominal contractors who shared them with the members of the Legislature, and never even started the work.

In North Carolina alone fourteen million dollars worth of these fraudulent bonds were issued, and no railway was constructed. Enormous salaries were paid to place-seekers, often utterly unfit for the posts for which they drew these emoluments. Public contracts at extravagant rates were the perquisite of supporters, and the profits were again shared with those in power.

The Courts of Law were suborned, and although the robberies and robbers were known to all, redress or punishment was impossible to obtain.

The enormous increases in the public debts of the several States are some indication of the corruption prevalent. During this time the State debt of Alabama rose from eight and a quarter million dollars to twenty-five and a half million dollars, that of South Carolina from five and a half to eighteen and a half million dollars, and in Louisiana in the short space of one year it increased four-fold.

The prerogative of the State Governors to pardon criminals was in some cases sold for cash.

This was all intensely exasperating to the educated and property-owning whites, who were for the time helpless, as the majority had been disenfranchised. But what made this period hateful beyond words to all Southerners was the sense that their former slaves, and their unprincipled and loathed parasites, were thus lording it over them. They might have submitted with some grace to the Federal officials responsible for the administration of the Freedman's Bureau, or those in command of the military organization, and there is no reason to think that these did not act with consideration and discretion, but to see low-born Northern reprobates in the seats of the mighty, and those who had been their servants members of the Legislature, was more than they could bear.

It was impossible that such corruption could last, it was inconceivable that the whites of the South should allow their illiterate ex-slaves, and those prompted only by the desire for plunder, to rule them. Gradually they banded together, and by force of character and intelligence, backed often indeed by physical force, took possession of the ballot and of the government.

Much was done that even the circumstances could not justify. If the Negro did not yield easily he was terrorized into submission.

The end came in the early seventies, by which time all political power was in the hands of the Southern whites, the carpet-bagger had fled, and the Negro had entirely ceased to be a political factor. Later, as I will show in the chapter on the present political position of the Negro, the power which was taken by force was legalized by enactment in all the Southern States, and though at variance with the Constitution of the United States, the position of the Negro now is that he cannot under State law attain to a voice in the management of public affairs.

In considering the present racial position in later chapters we must always bear in mind what I have tried to convey in this and the preceding chapter.

The new era in the South, begun in the late sixties or early seventies, counted about four million Negroes, utterly uneducated, without property of any kind, immoral, without any training in individual self-help or co-operation, helpless and childish ; and eight million whites, also ruined as far as material things went, but resolute to rebuild society, if not on the old lines, on a basis that meant that under no circumstance would they admit to equality those who had been their slaves, and who for a few short years had been their rulers.

CHAPTER VIII.

THE Southern white man is proud of his descent. He boasts that the South is the most truly American portion of the Union. Before the war the planter families traced back their descent to their British ancestors, and while inordinately proud of being Southerners, had an equal pride in being of undiluted British stock.

To-day they call attention to the vast stream of immigrants pouring into the North and West from South and South-Eastern Europe, and question whether these aliens can be absorbed and assimilated into the American people without grave danger of degeneration of character, morals, and ideals.

Some predict a time when the American people and American ideals may be in danger of being swamped by the incoming waves, and the truly American South will be the bulwark of National salvation.

It is true that from the first the tide of immigration never flowed south of Mason and Dixie's line. The Union has absorbed millions, first the Irishman, then the German, followed by the Scandinavian, and now come the Italian, Croatian, Ruthenian, Galician with the dwellers in Mesopotamia, all generically classed by the true American as Dagos.

New York, Chicago, and Philadelphia are no longer American but cosmopolitan cities. I visited Bronx Park, New York, on a holiday, Commemoration Day, and heard far more of foreign tongues spoken than I did of English speech. The zoological collections in the cages were

most interesting, but far more interesting was the ethno-
logical collection swarming all over that vast park.

Sections of these and other large cities of the North
and West are inhabited solely by these aliens; their
speech is all-pervasive, and their appearance and manners
are un-American. For miles on end the names over the
shops are those of the immigrant, not one of British
sound or origin. And although the present-day immigrant does not take up land in the country to the same
extent as his predecessors, large tracts are still exclusively
held by folk whose ancestors never saw Britain, and who
still talk in a foreign tongue.

Not so in the South.

I travelled many miles along country roads where the
small farm-houses stood back a little in the woods, and
noticed the surnames at the post boxes. All were
English, Scotch, or Irish, the first-named predominating
in most sections. The same does not apply exclusively
in the towns; here the signs indicate that the ubiquitous
Jewish race has seen and seized the trading opportunities
of the South. I found here one of the many parallels between the South and South Africa. In South Africa, the
proportion of Jewish immigrants to any of other non-
British peoples is very large indeed, the boat train at
Waterloo Station on any Saturday morning in the year
will prove that. They come, not to do any manual
labour, they neither do that nor engage in agriculture,
but to exploit those, who by reason of their environment
or race, have proved such a lucrative field, the Dutch-
speaking country population—the Boer—and the native.

A similar condition of things has attracted them to the
South, and I had many opportunities of seeing what a
firm hold they have on the Negro people and their trade.

Apart from these, and the population of a limited area
near the mouth of the Mississippi, where much French
and some Spanish blood is still in evidence, the Southern
people are of one race.

The indisposition of the immigrant to go South is not

due to any natural drawbacks. As I have shown, the South has a genial climate, abundant rains, a soil fitted to grow many valuable crops, abundance of wood and minerals, and good communication by river and rail. Above all, land is cheap and may be easily procured. If I considered natural conditions and advantages alone, there are many parts of the South-Eastern States in which I would far rather make my home than in New England or the Middle West. Yet the immigrant shuns them.

The reason is a social one.

The average immigrant comes to America prepared to make a living by manual toil, in the sweat of his brow, and willing to undertake menial tasks. By course of reasoning, or instinctively, he avoids a country in which social conditions are entirely new and strange, and not simply a development of what he has been accustomed to. Especially does he refuse to enter one in which he will have to compete with the black man, who is able and willing to work for a low wage, and is accustomed to a standard of living which, though perhaps not lower in some respects than that of the immigrant in his native land, is not the one he hopes for in America.

At times certain communities in the South, emulous of the rapid material advance of the North, due in part to abundant immigrant labour, made an effort to turn the stream in their direction.

In 1906, 450 Belgians, Austrians and Galicians were landed at Charleston, S.C. They were fêted by the city authorities and distributed through the State of South Carolina. They did not appear satisfied with their lot or prospects, and gradually drifted away. A commissioner, Mr. Gadsden, was sent by the State authorities to Europe to investigate conditions in the countries from whence these immigrants came, in order to get some light on the subject. He reports : " Our efforts have been almost entirely expended in inducing immigrants to come to the South, and we have thought little or nothing of how they were to be treated after they came into our midst. It

seems to me that we have entirely overlooked our industrial conditions, viz., that the wages scale of the South
is based upon Negro labour; our attitude through the
South will have to be materially altered before we can
expect the immigrant to be satisfied."

Probably the greater number of the Southern people
do not want the immigrant. Dr. A. B. Hart says there
are two reasons why he does not go to the South, one is
that the South does not like the immigrant, and the other
is that the immigrant does not like the South.

Perhaps the nail was hit squarely on the head by a
correspondent of the "Richmond Times Gazette," who
writes, "they will prevent the establishment of the labour
conditions that existed before the war, and will interfere
with the plantation system," and he especially deprecates
any attempt "to try any of the races that have become
inoculated with Union notions ".

Professor Kelly Miller, himself a Negro, writes : " The
white man avoids competition with the black workman
and will hardly condescend to compete with him on equal
terms. Wherever white men and women have to work
for their living they arrogantly avoid those sections where
they are placed on a par with Negro competitors, and if
indigenous to such localities, they often migrate to
regions where the black man and rival is less numerous.
For this reason European immigration avoids the black
belt as an infected region."

Among South African politicians there are those who
constantly compare the streams of home seekers who enter
the other great self-governing Colonies, with the almost
imperceptible trickle entering the Union of South Africa.
They point to our vast open spaces, and sunlit skies, and
ask why we cannot also attract them; why crowded
steamers call at frequent intervals and pass on with all
this bone and sinew to lands six thousand miles farther
from the homes they have broken up and left.

They blame the Government for apathy, or worse, a
deliberate attempt to discourage any increase of our

population from the surplus populations of Europe. They fail to see that sun and space are not all the immigrant asks; the vast majority hope to live at first by manual toil, and grow on from that, and they consciously or semi-consciously pass by any country in which they must compete with a backward race and live as they do.

I have met intelligent and educated Southern men who held that the American Union owed a debt of gratitude to the Negro, who by his presence had preserved to the American people a large section of the country, and in that section kept the original race free from admixture with immigrants. Whether this is desirable or not may be matter of opinion, certainly it is a fact that the immigrant avoids the South where the Negro is, and goes North where the Negro is not, and I think this fact and the parallel we see in our own country are worth thinking over by some of the South African politicians I have mentioned, who assume that immigrants may be had if only the Government will advertise widely enough, and paint the country in sufficiently gaudy colours.

I must return from the people who are not in the South to the people who are there. As would be expected after three hundred years of separate existence, with little renewal of blood, and under special social conditions, the type differs from the original stock, and in such a large country varies somewhat in different parts. In no section did I find common the accepted conventional type of Englishman, with his bright colour and vigorous fullness, though occasionally I came across an individual who in appearance would have seemed quite in place in an English shire. A sallow skin, and deliberate, even languid attitude, became more apparent and common as the far South was approached. In the country people a slack lounging movement was common ; this was seen in the general store, the social centre where much deliberate whittling, chewing, and spitting were in evidence. The women and children were often pale, even anæmic.

I was told that the hookworm disease, which is very prevalent, accounts in large part for this apparent lack of vigour. I was informed that fully half of the employees in the cotton mills, who are all whites, suffer from this complaint.

A high colour and fleshy redundancy are not, however, sure indications of strength, or even health, and notwithstanding their slack gait many of the Southern men showed signs of physical power.

I was struck with a certain hardness of physiognomy in many, an expression in the eye and the cut of the jaw and chin, that would deter the stranger from taking liberties. At times I was reminded in the physiognomy of some, of the theory that the modern American approximates in appearance to the aboriginal so-called American Indian, and wondered whether the lawlessness and cruelties to be mentioned later were connected with an actual strain of this blood. I did actually meet several who claimed partial descent from the red man. Few had the vacant expressionless look of many English rustics. A quiet watchfulness was a prevailing note. With the exception of habits resulting from an abuse of tobacco, which were all-prevalent and often disgusting, manners were generally good, and far more restrained than I had been led to expect. The inordinate curiosity and boastfulness which may have been characteristic of past generations of Americans, and which is to-day often attributed to them, I found conspicuously absent. Willingness to talk and exchange opinions were usual. Interest in and knowledge of their immediate surroundings were, however, joined to a dense ignorance of anything outside America.

Sitting one day on a barrel in a country store, having been introduced by a local man as an African, I was asked by one of those present whether the Negroes they had in the South were real Negroes or not. He said he had been told by one who claimed special knowledge on the subject, that the real African Negro had a

tail about four inches long and did not possess a soul.
Was this so ?

Another guessed that they had a powerful lot of
Negroes in North Carolina ; more niggers he reckoned
than there were in all Africa.

The portrait of a certain British Royal personage was
figured on a packet of tobacco I opened one day in the
train, and my fellow-passenger volunteered the information that the personage portrayed received a cent for
every package sold, for the use of his picture.

It was generally recognized that I did not belong to the
South, and conversation naturally turned on places and
affairs extra American, and the weirdest geographical
information was unfolded. Ideas about Canada and
China were given by one man I met casually in the
train which made me gasp.

General education is in a backward state, though the
South is rapidly mending matters both as to quantity
and quality, and State appropriations are being aug-
mented, and especially is this the case for agricultural
education. Primary education is not compulsory in the
South, the fact that it is not so is due to the presence of
the Negro ; the white man might be willing to apply
compulsion to his own race, but will not do so if the
Negro is to participate.

How far universal and compulsory education has ful-
filled the anticipations of its early advocates in Britain is a
moot point ; one thing is certain, that reading of a kind
is much more common than in the past. One can see
evidence of this in book-stalls, book-shops, on the trams
and in the trains, and in all places of public resort. Little
of the kind is seen in the South. Book-stalls are few and
ill supplied. In many considerable towns I never saw a
book-shop. Excepting for the daily papers, which are
not of a high class and which are much devoted to local
and personal news, no literature was seen in the hands
of the travelling public.

From those to whom I carried letters of introduction

I expected hospitality, and I received it in abundant measure. But I got more. On several occasions people I met on the cars, with whom I casually entered into conversation, asked me to their homes in the kindest and most spontaneous manner. Judging from appearances it would in some cases have been a tax on their resources. I could not but be touched with these offers of kindly entertainment.

Perhaps the most distinctive group of the Southern people are those living in the mountain section, principally the Western part of the State of Virginia, Western North Carolina, and Eastern Tennessee. Both country and people are poor, the mountains are covered with forest, often second growth, the inhabitants thinly scattered. They are generally of English, Scotch, and Scoto-Irish descent, and are notoriously addicted to shooting, blood feuds, and the illicit distilling of spirits. I had an opportunity of seeing them in their homes, and of staying at some of the institutions provided by Northern philanthropists for their education and uplift. From observation and information received I gathered they were a people having many fine qualities, and that the younger ones readily responded to educative influences. The physiognomy and physique of those I saw in the schools, and their general appearance, manner and carriage, indicated this. I met several teachers in these institutions who had also had experience in Negro schools, and they made a comparison thus. Here we have a fine basis of race character to build upon. If there is reversion they revert to something good, in the Negro we have constantly to guard against reversion to something worse. Many of these people have migrated to the small towns of the lower country to work in the cotton mills, some selling their farms, others retaining them and hoping to return. It seems a pity that this close, monotonous and unhealthy employment should be substituted for farm life. Attempts are being made to so improve their surroundings and prospects in their present homes as to lessen the drift towards the less healthy factory employment. I regard this as a sound philanthropic movement.

These people must not be confused with the class usually called poor whites mentioned in a previous chapter. The latter were more directly the result of the presence of the Negro, were prevented by his presence and the system of slavery from engaging in manual labour, and had their economic outlook and social environment changed thereby. They touched him at the lower levels of social contact, and their debasement was a direct result. The mountaineer, on the other hand, hardly knew the Negro then, and to-day in many parts hardly sees one. Their poverty is largely due to the sterile nature of the country in which they live, though their presence there is partly the result of the institution of slavery. The occupation of the fertile lands by large plantations worked by slave labour, forced a proportion of the whites into the mountain regions who otherwise might have found a better livelihood as small farmers in the richer lowlands. Whether it is a consciousness of this or not, it is a fact that, notwithstanding the Negro has little part in their present lives, they love him not, and I was told that if the route of a Negro teamster took him past their houses, he took care not to delay, but passed on quickly lest harm befall him.

The rise of the cotton mill is part of a general industrial awakening in the South. The traveller by train passes many of these large plain buildings, both isolated in the country and situated in the towns. As a rule the buildings and surroundings are nothing like so ugly and sordid as the cotton factories of South Lancashire or West Scotland. Many of the modern ones are provided with electric power, and the tall chimney-stack belching forth dark smoke, is fortunately absent. The workers are housed by the employers in wooden cottages, usually detached, forming a scattered township, and in some places, in the open country, there is opportunity for gardening or keeping a little stock. Hours of labour are long, and child labour is often employed under extremely unsatisfactory conditions. Organisation among the cotton-mill employees is still in the future.

The black man, however, is rigorously debarred from working in these factories. On this point the employees would unite to resent his presence, and one or two attempts to run mills entirely by black labour do not appear to have been successful. The Negro is at liberty to grow cotton but not to manufacture it. It seems to me he has been forced to take the better part.

In many other directions the natural resources of the South are being developed, largely by Northern energy and capital. Although Southern money and brains are also thus employed, the industrial sense, with all it connotes, and which permeates the North, is not yet fully awakened in the South. Though doubtless it is much attenuated, the visitor still senses the feeling born of slavery, and continued through the presence of the Negro, that the high-class Southerner is or should be a planter, lawyer, soldier, or legislator rather than a merchant or manufacturer, and that manual toil is for the Negro. Economic pressure, modern conditions, and patriotic emulation are rapidly changing this view, but a tradition born so long ago, and for long assiduously cultivated, takes time to break down entirely.

In the South the Negroes form only about thirty per cent of the total population, and this fact, and the ever-growing demand for labour, make it more difficult to follow the tradition in its entirety. Indeed, I was surprised, with my African eyes and experience, to see so much laborious work done by whites. About half the cotton grown in the cotton belt is raised by white labour alone. Although the number of whites engaged in toilsome jobs was small as compared with England, it was in marked contrast to South Africa, where, excepting in certain relief work, no white man is seen handling a spade, pick, or barrow.

Custom in the South seems to vary somewhat in

different places. For instance, at the Port of Baltimore I found gangs of Negroes discharging and loading cargoes under a white boss as in South Africa, while at New Orleans it is as common to see a mixed white and black gang handling the same cargo. Speaking broadly, this is quite exceptional, as a rule the black and white labourers doing similar work are kept separate. In some cities I observed the white men employed at road repairing, and in different streets of the same town a black gang laying down asphalt paving.

Skilled work is done by members of both races, and it is not uncommon to see both working side by side in the same workshop, or on the same building. To this point, and the probable future of the skilled Negro artisan, I will refer later.

Judged by the standard of Britain and the British Colonies, the Southern white man cannot be regarded as a law-abiding person. Homicide is a weakness peculiar to him. Few newspapers are issued without a report of shooting, wounding, and killing. And this seems to be lightly regarded. Although I never actually saw shooting going on, once or twice I was in the neighbourhood of gun-play, and heard the current remarks thereon. It was in each case between white men. The facts were stated by witnesses in an indifferent way, as casually as if they were speaking of an unavoidable accident. This in-difference would have been still more marked had the victim been a Negro. Had it, however, been a case of black shooting white, I saw and heard sufficient to make me feel that the attitude would have been quite different. Then one might expect race riot and lynching, and the actual perpetrator would not be the only one to suffer. In the case of white shooters, whether the victim be white or black, adequate punishment, according to our ideas, is seldom inflicted. Juries seem to regard the crime lightly, and even when punishment is incurred, the friends of the criminal often bring pressure to bear on the authorities and he is released. I have heard several theories given

5

to account for this phenomenon, but none seems to me to fully account for it.   The presence of a subservient race who may be imposed upon with comparative impunity, does certainly lead to an arrogant and masterful attitude on the part of the stronger race.   The popular election of those who administer the law, and the absence of rural police must also be taken into account.   The common practice of carrying weapons in many sections is alleged as a cause, and of course no shooting could happen if there were no guns.   But we in South Africa are accustomed to firearms, have during the past forty years used them in legitimate warfare far oftener than the Southern people, and yet homicide is not a favourite pastime with either Dutch or English.   And if murder does happen, we are content to let the law take its course, we do not desire personally to kill the offender.   I leave it at that, sure however of the facts stated, which whether satisfactorily explained or not, have a bearing on our inquiry.

All through the South one sees evidence of religious observance.   Wm. Archer in " Afro-America " goes so far as to say it is the most simply and sincerely religious community he ever was in.   In the towns churches are numerous, and often large and well built in proportion to the population.   In the country one passes little frame churches at frequent intervals.   Several times I met on the trains bands of young people wearing badges and rosettes, who belonged to religious organizations, Sunday School Unions and the like, who had been attending Conferences.   I attended many Church services, mostly of those belonging to denominations holding Evangelical views, which form the majority in the South.   In England and the Colonies at the present day one seldom hears sermons and addresses which denote an absolute acceptance of the Evangelical doctrine of our fathers, preached in its entirety, with full stress laid on punishment as on reward.   Modern criticism and latter day tolerance have modified it, and even if the creed or catechism be nomin-

ally accepted, the emphasis is not where it was when I
was a boy. I found the South had not departed so far
from the pure doctrine, and heard sermons there such as
I remember long ago, pressing home future punishment
in materialistic detail; the wrath to come, and the danger of
delay. The attendance was generally good, with a great
proportion of women, but with a larger number of men
than one usually sees in England and the Colonies in
these days. Once when attending such a service and
looking round at the staid and devout worshippers, I remembered the facts of a lynching that had taken place in
the neighbourhood, and could not help wondering whether
any of those I saw with bowed heads had been present,
and what their views on such an occurrence would be. I
felt the discords and antagonisms that everywhere go to
make up our human nature. But the contrast is not
often so forcibly brought home to one. I never saw a
Negro in these churches, they have their separate organizations, managed entirely by themselves, to which I
will give attention in a later chapter.

Before Emancipation the white churches in the South
supported the institution of slavery, and numerous clerical writers could be cited who attempted to prove from
Scripture that it was of Divine origin and had the Divine
sanction. To-day there are their descendants, Christian
ministers who condone if they do not approve lynching,
and who turn to the Scripture to prove that the Negro
is, and always will be, an inferior, and attempt thus to
justify discrimination and repression. To the Negrophilist and humanitarian of Western Europe this sounds
the rankest hypocrisy. But the Southerner is not the
only man who clips his religion to suit his peculiar sins
and environment.

Just as in South Africa no general conversation touching
on public affairs can be long continued without bringing in
the native, so in the South the Negro is never far below the
surface in the minds and conversation of all one meets.
Should the topic of conversation be agriculture, Negro

5 *

labour and Negro tenants crop up; if it is skilled labour and its organization, the question of the admittance of the Negro comes forward; should it be social betterment in cities, then the problem of the Negro dives and tender-loin districts is included; if it is the prohibition question, again the Negro and how he affects it. Direct questions on the part of the investigator are not necessary to bring up this topic, it is near to the top in the minds of all, and a little tact will elicit opinion and attitude. I found a firmly fixed, inexorable belief in the racial inferiority of the Negro possessed the minds of most, and opinion varied from a contemptuous tolerance to an out-spoken hostility. A nigger must be kept in his place, and that place was a subordinate one, industrially, politically, and especially socially. A watchful suspicion on all attempts which could be interpreted as claiming equality was al-most universal. It was expressed most strongly on two phases, a fear that the Negro would impinge on their source of livelihood, and a dread that he would attempt to claim social equality, which implied to them the destruc-tion of race integrity. On these two foundations was based the great mass of animosity, and it expressed itself in many practical ways, some similar to those we observe in South Africa, others somewhat different and curiously different. For instance, in South Africa the average white man never shakes hands with a native, excepting perhaps on occasion when he has something to gain, and then with a qualm, or it may be in the native territories and with a chief. In the South there does not seem to be the same objection to this act of courtesy, though it is not common. There seems, however, to be the strongest distaste to prefix Mr. or Mrs. to the name of a Negro or Negress. One Negro writer, in speaking of the con-temptuous attitude of Southern men to coloured women, states he has never known a white man to use this polite-ness to a coloured woman. Many of those I spoke to when asked as to the condition of the Negroes in their section would reply they were in good shape now, but some little time ago they got "bigotty"; shooting had however occurred, they had received a lesson, and all was well now. Several on different occasions expressed the opinion that at intervals, more or less frequent, it was necessary to give the niggers a lesson. Reference was often made to some outstanding occasion, such as the Atlanta race riots, which had been conspicuously success-ful in putting the nigger in his place, and men present at these scenes of violence often volunteered the informa-tion that on such occasions the casualties were greater than reported. I often wondered what would happen to a negrophilist who used the usual arguments about race equality if he began talking in a public place to these quiet, watchful, determined-looking men. I never ven-tured the experiment myself. I simply listened and questioned.

Quotations to illustrate what I believe to be the popu-lar attitude could be given in hundreds, one or two must suffice. Ray S. Baker in his book "Following the Colour Line" cites C. P. Lain who writes thus in the "Atlanta Constitution": "We the Southern people entertain no prejudice towards the ignorant inoffensive Negro. It is because we know him, and for him entertain a compassion. But our blood boils when the educated Negro asserts him-self politically. We regard each assertion as an unfriendly encroachment upon our native superior rights and a dare-devil menace to our control of the affairs of the State." Governor Hoke Smith, of Georgia, in a speech says: "The Negroes who are contented to occupy the natural status of their race, the position of inferiority, all com-petition being eliminated between black and white, will be treated with greater kindness".

Thomas Dixon, junior, in the "Saturday Evening Post" in 1907 : "Does any sane man believe that when the Negro ceases to work under the direction of the Southern white man, this arrogant, 'rapacious,' and 'intolerant" race will allow the Negro to master his industrial position, take the bread from his mouth, crowd him to the wall, and take a mortgage over his house ? Competition is war, the most fierce and brutal of all its forms. Could fatuity reach a sublimer height than the idea that the white man will stand by and see this performance ? What will he do when put to the test ? He will do exactly what his white neighbour in the North does when the Negro threatens his bread—kill him."

A correspondent to a Georgia paper writes: "Let me tell you one thing, every time you people in the North countenance in any way, shape or form any form of social equality, you lay up trouble, not for yourselves nor so much for us as for the Negro. Right or wrong the Southern white man will never tolerate it, and will go through the horrors of another Reconstruction period before they will permit it. Before we will submit we will kill every Negro in the South. This is not idle boasting or fire-eating, but the cold hard facts stated in all calmness."

John Ambrose Price in "The Negro Past, Present and Future," written in 1907, writes: "The elevation of the Negro by education is one of the greatest humbugs ever held up to the American people. Not for a moment do I think education can thwart God's purposes for the Negro in subjecting him to the service of the white man, but I do think it a waste of money to educate him contrary to his destined capacity or by a method that makes him less worthy. It is a great injustice to his race. The only permanent position open to the Negro is that of labourer in the Industrial South."

I read a book, "The Caucasian and Negro in the United States," by W. P. Calhoun. Space does not permit me to do more than give in a few words the impression it made upon me at the time, and I copy the following from my notes: "W. P. Calhoun is a Southerner and gives I think a true idea of the feeling of the average Southern white man. It is apparently not written by a maker of books, has no literary style, but bears evidence of first-hand knowledge of the subject, and also that the writer takes the popular view. In this it seems to me to have a value beyond that of many more pretentious volumes on the subject. He will not allow that the Negro is other than unutterably inferior to the white, and always will be. He writes crudely, without passion, but there is an inexorable force in it for that very reason. Nothing can alter the relative positions of the races, nothing is likely to soften the enmity and bitterness. It is Fate."

Hitherto I have been trying to convey the impression left on my mind as to the attitude of the mass of the Southern people towards the Negro, and I have cited some who have put into writing what I conceive that attitude to be.

Almost all I conversed with, whatever the particular shade of their opinion, admitted the gravity of the situation, and the strained relations between the races. The actual happenings day by day in the South, and every daily paper I read, evidenced this. We must admit a vast reservoir of prejudice, suspicion, and hostility, and the great question in my mind was : Is this prejudice and tension increasing or decreasing ?

The majority of those with whom I talked were of opinion that it was growing, and nearly all stated that it had changed during the last few years. Many attributed this to the passing away of the older generation, who came into closer contact with the Negro at a time when his position was more clearly defined, and who often had friendly relations with individual Negroes, and knew many personally. That the attitude is now a different one I fully believe, and it appears to be one of greater suspicion and less knowledge. I attribute this to several reasons : (1) the greater complexity of life due to the invasion of modern mercantile conditions demanding commercial results in the relation of employer and employed ; (2) the decay of personal and often friendly relations present in slavery days, and which continued for some time after slavery ceased ; (3) the advance of the Negro to a standard of living more nearly like that of the white man ;

(4) occasional assaults on white women which cause intense exasperation, continuing after the immediate cause is removed; (5) the probability of industrial competition, which was not so apparent in the earlier times.

The matter is of such vital importance to our inquiry that I append the opinions of several writers and public men, premising that I am now dealing with the attitude of the mass of the Southern people; of certain opposite tendencies I will speak later, and also in a chapter to come of the position in the North.

Dr. A. B. Hart, writing in 1910, says : " Here is the most difficult part of the whole matter, the two races so closely associated are nevertheless drifting away from each other. Time was when men like Wade Hampton, of South Carolina, and Senator Lamar, of Mississippi, expected that whites and Negroes would co-operate in political parties; time was when former slave-holders joined with former slaves in a confident attempt to bring the Negroes higher. The voices of encouragement are still heard, but there is in them a note of weariness."

A. F. Thomas, of Lynchburg, Virginia, in a booklet issued to the Constitutional Convention of Virginia says : "The Negro has progressed wonderfully, his relative position is nearer the white man's standard of civilization now than thirty years ago, yet the fact is apparent that the races are farther apart than they were the day the Negro was emancipated. The nearer the Negro approaches the white man's standard of civilization the less love there is between them."

Edgar Gardner Murphy cannot be deemed a pessimist, but in his book, "The South and the Negro," he makes it clear that in his opinion the relations of the races in the South have become increasingly difficult of late years. He attributes this to several causes, among others to industrial development, which has brought poor whites from their farms in the mountains to work in the factories, thus bringing the races into contact, and in some fields of labour into competition. He does not therefore despair, but thinks and hopes that this is a phase which will pass, and that the better thought and feeling of the South will ultimately prevail.

Governor N. B. Broward, of Florida, in his message to the Legislature in 1907, says : " Though no question has arisen to cause any disturbance, yet it is apparent, even to the casual observer, that the relations between the races is becoming more strained and acute. The Negroes to-day have less friendship for the white people, and the white people have less tolerance and sympathy for the Negro. It is my opinion that the two races will not for any great length of time occupy the same territory without friction and outbreaks between the two." He goes on to say that the education of the Negro will not postpone or prevent it, and he can only see any solution of the difficulty in sending away the Negro population to another territory.

Senator John J. Ingalls, in the " Chicago Tribune," over the title " Always a Problem," writes : " The great gulf between the races has widened and deepened since emancipation. If possible the barriers are more insuperable in the North than in the South, and the prescription more contemptuous and intolerant." This after a very kindly appreciation of Frederick Douglass, the gifted mulatto, who is spoken of by him as an eloquent, accomplished, and dignified gentleman.

From an address by John Temple Graves before Convocation of the University of Chicago the following is taken : " The races are wider apart, more antagonistic than in 1865. There is less of sympathy and more of tension than the races have known since the terrible days of Reconstruction made havoc in the South. Four decades after emancipation the Negro in point of fact is less a freeman and infinitely less a citizen than in 1868."

Thus John Sharp Williams of Mississippi : " More and more every year the Negro's life, moral, intellectual, and industrial, is isolated from the white man's life, and therefore from his influence. There was a kindlier and more confidential relationship when I was a boy than between my children and the present generation of Negroes."

Many well-meaning Southerners are hopeless, and this is the note struck in the following letter cited by Dr. A. B. Hart and written by a prominent citizen of Birmingham, Ala.: "If my heart did not go out to the Negro as a human being, or I cared less for my God, and an earnest wish to walk in His ways, I would kill the Negro or die trying. God must indeed intend that Time shall work out His ways and not the men of this generation, for, after a longer life than most, and all of it spent with and among the Negroes,—I give it up."

J. A. Price, writing in 1907 on the possibilities of Race War, says: "We have several reasons on which to base the liability of such an approaching danger. One is the growing race hatred between the young generations of white and black, another is the increased efforts of the Negro race to follow the instruction of their leaders, who tell them to arm themselves and assert their rights. If no remedy is found for this condition race riots will increase and become general, and thereby bring matters to a final understanding, which may be a surprise to the Negroes' supposed friends."

George W. Cable, in 1885, in "The Freedman's Case in Equity" and "The Silent South," speaks rather hopefully of the prospect of the Negro receiving his civil rights in the South; the right to vote, the right to an equal use of all accommodations; that in time there will be no civil discrimination on account of race or colour. Speaking of those days Cable says: "In Virginia they may ride exactly as white people do and in the same cars. In South Carolina respectable coloured people who buy first-class tickets on any railroad ride first class as a right, and their presence excites no comment on the part of their white fellow-passengers."

He finishes "The Silent South" with this passage:

"Nationalization by fusion of blood is the maxim of barbarous times and peoples. Nationalization without race confusion is ours to profess and procure. It is not a task of our own choosing. But our fathers unawares entailed it upon us, and we cannot but perform it. We cannot hold American principles in perfect faith and not do it. The good doctrine of liberty to all and licence to none thrusts itself inevitably into our hands. To make national unity without hybridity—the World has never seen it done and we have to do it. . . . We have got to build up a nationality free from all civil estrangements as from social confusion, yet wider than the greatest divergence of the human race. That is the meaning of the great revolution on us to-day." These words were written over a quarter of a century ago. To-day no coloured person dare ride in any public conveyance in Virginia, South Carolina, nor, indeed, anywhere else in the South, in the manner Cable describes as being usual in 1885. The building of a nationality without hybridity has gone on very, very slowly since those days, if indeed it has made any progress at all. The whole question of race admixture I will deal with in a subsequent chapter, I just now cite one witness whose evidence deals expressly with this point, and deals with it at an appropriate time. Dr. Shufeldt says: "In 1882 I watched some hundreds of children at noon as they poured out of one of the large public schools in Washington, D.C. The other day, 1890, the same sight was presented to my eyes at exactly the same place, but a most marked change was perceptible. In the first case the vast majority of the children were black, the mulatto being the exception. In the latter more than fifty per cent were mulatto."

The opinions hitherto cited have been those of Southern white men, I will now add those of some Negroes as an indication of how they interpret the present trend of white feeling towards them.

Professor R. S. Lovegood, of Wiley University, says: "The prejudice against the Negro is more severe than that against any other people and it grows stronger, even the Christian Churches are yielding to it."

Bishop Turner, of the Methodist Episcopal Church (Coloured), says bluntly : " I see no future for the manhood of the Negro in this country, and the man who is not able to discover that fact from existing conditions must be void of common sense. Our civil, political, and social status is degrading, and as degradation begets degradation the Negro must go from bad to worse *ad infinitum.* Neither wealth nor education can elevate us to the level of respectability."

Bishop Holsey of the same Church thus : " There is not now, and there never has been, the smallest possibility for the Negro race in these Southern States *en masse* to rise to the dignities and possibilities of his manhood. The more the Negro is raised in the scale of social and civil accomplishments, and the nearer he approaches the Anglo-Saxon standard of civilization, the greater will be the strain between the two peoples, and will produce explosions and intervening strife that must prove fatal to the weaker race."

So much for Southern evidence, both black and white, as to the tendencies now in force. I would still like to quote two Englishmen, one who writes of conditions twenty years ago, and the other the last word of to-day.

First from W. Laird Clowes' book, " In Black America," published in 1885, I cull the following opinion which would I feel sure be endorsed by many, possibly by a majority in the South : " My own impression as derived from a somewhat wide observation is that since Emancipation the distance between the races has really, as well as apparently, increased, and that it is still increasing. Whites and blacks have less in common than of yore, there is less chance than there ever was of them working together peacefully for good, and racial antagonism grows daily. And education by no means tends to lessen the friction. On the contrary it adds to it."

Although H. G. Wells has not so far as I know made

a special study of the coloured question in the South, the impressions of such an acute observer should be of value. In the chapter on "The Tragedy of Colour," forming part of his volume, "The Future in America," he sums up on the point we are now discussing: "If there is any trend of opinion at present on the matter it lies in the direction of a generous decision on the part of the North and West to leave the black more and more to the judgment and mercy of the white people with whom they are locally associated. This judgment and mercy points on the whole to an accentuation of the coloured man's natural inferiority, to the cessation of any other educational attempts than those that increase his industrial usefulness (it is already illegal in Louisiana to educate him beyond a contemptible level), to his industrial exploitation through usury and legal chicanery, and to a systematic strengthening of the social barriers between coloured people of whatever shade and whites."

To-day as I write several new attempts at differentiation, on lines suggested by new conditions, are being made. While I was in the South the first ordinances were being passed to prevent the races occupying the same sections in Southern cities—Baltimore taking the lead. Hitherto the Negro has been practically segregated in the lowest quarters, now the comparatively well-to-do naturally want better surroundings and have bought or rented houses in white neighbourhoods, and caused much resentment, and undoubtedly in some cases depreciation in the value of the adjacent property held and occupied by the whites. This is a condition of things bound to come as increasing numbers of Negroes desire a better environment, and it is responded to on the part of the whites by Segregation Ordinances. The example of Baltimore has been followed by many other cities, and legislation to effect this purpose has been introduced in several Southern States, backed apparently by a popular determination to bring the matter to an issue.

There are quite a number of coloured male and

female clerks employed in the public service. In proportion to the total Negro population the percentage so employed is very small, but in Washington, D.C., there are quite a respectable number employed in the various offices. There has recently been a deliberate and sustained effort to draw distinctions, devised to separate the white and black clerks beyond anything hitherto attempted. This has been controversially dealt with in some of the newspapers, and organized efforts have been made by the coloured people and their friends to defeat it. They may or may not succeed. The significant fact for us is that such attempts are possible, and are constantly being made to-day in many directions, entailing constant vigilance on the part of those whom they affect.

Serious attempts have been made of late to limit the State appropriations to Negro education. There seems to have been a recrudescence of opposition to the literary education of the black man, as unfitting him for his proper sphere. I met the principal of a State Normal Coloured School in the South who told me he had only just secured his annual appropriation by the most persistent and energetic lobbying, and others informed me that it would never have been obtained but for this special effort, and the personal respect of the Legislature for the principal. There have of course been times of violent opposition to Negro education in the past; it is nothing new. It is a burning question and sometimes the opposition blazes forth, again smoulders, or is quiescent. I cannot pretend to determine whether the present hostility is simply a temporary set-back, marking a passing phase, or not. It has, however, been causing some present anxiety to those who are friendly to better education, and seems to signify, with other tendencies, a disposition in some quarters towards renewed criticism of the value of, at least, *higher* literary education for the Negro.

Concurrently with this disposition to curtail opportunity, there has been a movement to introduce legislation to prevent any white person from teaching in a coloured school.   This is a distinct innovation, for hitherto much of the higher Negro education in the South has been in the hands of white organizers and teachers from the North.   It is true that such teachers have been viewed with disfavour by the whole South, and social ostracism has often been their portion, but there has hitherto been no law to prevent it.

Now I must state a paradox, but one which will be understood by South Africans.   Many Southerners told me that the Negro was an incubus on the South, that he held back the true progress of the country, and that his presence had demoralized their people : and yet—they could not do without him.

The most virulent nigger haters would often be the first to resent bitterly any attempt to remove him. Through his labour and by reason of his submissive dis-position, their lives are made easy for them, and while acutely jealous of any attempt on his part to advance, they will not let him go.

One Southern writer says: "I know of several counties, not a hundred miles from Atlanta, where it is more than a man's life is worth to go in and get Negroes to move to another State.   There are farmers who would not hesitate to shoot their own brother were he to come in from Mississippi to get 'his niggers' as he calls them, even if he had no contract with them."   Ray S. Baker in "Following the Colour Line," says: "One of the most significant things I saw in the South, and I saw it every-where, was the way in which white people were torn between the feeling of race prejudice and their downright economic needs.   Hating and fearing the Negro (though often loving individual Negroes) they want him to work for them, they can't get along without him."

I was told by a very intelligent mulatto I met in Alabama that in the neighbourhood in which he lived a Negro had been done to death by a white mob for preach-ing colonization to Africa.

Summing up the general position in the most conservative way, I would say that in the South, while race prejudice generally, and repression and differentiation in particular, may not be actually growing in intensity, it is in some respects changing, and it is certainly not decreasing. Among the mass of the people it is intensely bitter, and liable at any moment, and for causes that seem entirely inadequate, to break out in active hostility, race riots, shooting, and lynching. At best it is a banked fire, a sweep of suspicion and flame breaks out.

I have tried to give my impressions of the feelings of the average Southerner towards the Negro, without bias. It is essential that it should be understood. It is painful to have to record that a people of our own race should be so saturated with hostility to a weaker one, which is unable to defend itself, either at law, or by force of arms.

We have race prejudice and to spare in South Africa. It is very difficult for anyone, however experienced and impartial, to correctly assess the comparative depth and intensity of this feeling in the two countries. My impression is, however, that we are more tolerant and well disposed towards the native, as we are certainly more law respecting in our relations to him, than are the people of the South. What is happening there of subversion of right and justice with its maleficent reflex action on character should, I think, act as a warning to us to keep a close watch and firm hand on any tendency to exaggerated prejudice.

The Negro people of the South are but one-third of the total population. Ours in South Africa is overwhelmingly preponderant. Increase of our white population has been urged as a possible solution of the native problem. In the light of the experience of the United States it does not appear probable that any possible readjustment of the relative numbers of the two races in South Africa would necessarily have this result. We must still patiently study, we must still watch and wait ; the problem will still be with us.

This chapter would sound hopeless enough if this was

all. Thank God it is not. Even in the old, bad slave days there were Southerners who could think straight, and act justly. Some such, convinced of the unrighteousness of holding their fellow-man in bonds, set free their slaves and reduced themselves to penury, and their deeds do follow them. I had the privilege of meeting Southern men and women of tender conscience and high ideals who deplored the common attitude, and who I know dealt justly and kindly in all their relations with the weaker race. And such are not altogether isolated. They have begun to band themselves together to work for improved conditions, and to strive for the betterment of the Negro people. Great courage and infinite tact and judgment are required, and these are in evidence.

At the first Southern Sociological Congress held at Nashville, Tenn., at which I was present, there was a special section to study and discuss Negro questions, and the opinion of the better South was there reflected. Negroes were present at the discussions and freely joined in them. Reports were given of social work done among the Negro population by Southern organizations. Among others was an association of men from the various Southern Universities, formed with the special object of accurately studying the social relations of the races and working for betterment. It was also announced, to the surprise of some at a distance to whom I told it, that co-operation between the white girl students of the High School and the coloured girl students of Fisk University was in contemplation, to work to improve the position and life of Negro women and children in the city.

I attended this Congress as I was going North, and after an experience of the Black Belt, and an almost undiluted diet of the ordinary Southern talk on the nigger, his weaknesses and inordinate pretensions, and the necessity for keeping him in check, the sane and liberal tone in these discussions came as a hopeful and welcome change.

I might mention many names of those Americans who

6

have thought clearly, and felt deeply on this problem, but such mention would be invidious, as any list would be incomplete. I would, however, mention one name, that of Edgar Gardner Murphy, who in his notable books, "The Basis of Ascendancy" and "The Present South," which are read far beyond the limits of the United States, has lifted the question to a high plane, and I believe truly represents a minority in the South, whose influence is far greater than their numbers. I have cited the opinions of many Southerners whom I regard as expressing the opinions of the majority. As representing the others let me quote Mr. J. L. M. Curry, an ex-slaveholder, who at Montgomery, Ala., in May, 1900, thus spoke : "We have heard much and will hear more before we adjourn of slavery. It was an economic curse, a legacy of ignorance. It cursed the South with stupid, ignorant, uninventive labour. The curse in large degree remains. The policy of some would perpetuate it, and give a system of serfdom, degrading to the Negro and corrupting to the employer. The Negro is a valuable labourer, let us improve him and make his labour more intelligent, more skilled, more productive. Shall the Caucasian race in timid fearfulness, in cowardly injustice, wrong an inferior race and put obstacles in its progress? Left to itself, away from all elevating influence of contact and tuition there will be retrogression. Shall we have two races, side by side, equal in political privilege, one educated, the other ignorant? Unless the white people, the superior and cultivated race, lift up the lower both will inevitably be dragged down."

So much for the white man, now for the black man.

CHAPTER IX.

THE BLACK MAN, WITH WHOM IS THE PART WHITE.

In this chapter I want to try and convey a picture of the man whose presence makes the problem, to make an attempt to fill in his race character, and endeavour, as we did in the case of the white man, to discover how he regards those among whom his lot is cast.

What he does, how he lives, works and worships, and what his probable future will be is dealt with later on. But first we want an idea of the man in himself.

Since my visit to the United States I have often been asked, both by English and South African friends, how the Negro compares with our native Bantu people. My answer usually began with a long explanation. I had to make it clear that the term Negro is strictly speaking a misnomer. The name is applied to all those who have any, even the smallest drop of African blood. Some of these are actually lighter in complexion than white men who have never left England or Massachusetts, and who, back to distant ancestors, could prove freedom from any alien strain.

In conversing with such light-coloured people I felt a natural reluctance to refer to them and their like as Negroes, and hesitated or apologized when I used the term. I was told they accepted the name, and did not want it altered or modified. I have been rebuked by them for using the milder and truer term, coloured person, when speaking of the group.

May I interpolate here to say that this matter of nomenclature is not unimportant. I feel that whenever there is a choice of names, and especially when one connotes inferiority, or something unworthy, one should always consult the feelings of those concerned. It is a little matter to say Negro rather than nigger or darkie, or native rather than Kafir or nigger, but the courtesy expressed, and good feeling implied, would be a healing solvent and not an irritant.

The exact number having visible signs of white blood is variously estimated, and indeed it is very difficult to get satisfactory statistical returns. Some years ago the census officials made an attempt, and returned fifteen per cent as of mixed blood. Then for a time all were counted as Negroes in the census returns. Then once again discrimination was made and twenty per cent were counted as of mixed ancestry. My own observations lead me to think that this is not above the mark. Dr. W. E. B. du Bois told me that in his opinion thirty per cent of the total number bore visible traces of their white ancestry.

A few days after landing in the United States I attended a very large meeting of Negroes, probably one thousand were present, the majority almost or quite black. Here and there, standing out almost livid from the dark mass, was a white face, one that would not have been noted as peculiar in a white assembly. It gave me a queer feeling of incongruity at the time, which recurred on similar occasions later. So before making the comparison between the African in America and the African in Africa as desired by my friends, I had to explain that a Negro is often not a Negro and yet that these are Negroes.

Then came another explanation, or rather statement of fact, which though, of course, known to all educated persons, is not often fully realized, and it must be realized and kept in mind if we are to understand the position.

Our native people in South Africa have their own language, customs, and traditions, still for the most part unbroken by the white man. The land they live in is their own native land. River and mountain, plain and valley, bear the names given to them by their fathers, and are associated with the past of their race. The black man in America is bereft of all these racial supports. For nearly three hundred years he has been sundered from all that his race built up of social order, custom, and tradition, and has been forced to accept what he could adapt from the white man. Comparison under such diverse circumstances becomes very difficult.

I may say, however, that the undiluted black people of the South struck me as being more typically Negro than our Bantu. We have many who are a dull, sooty black, but also many of a bronze shade, a living colour in which the red blood seems to diffuse itself through the dark skin with a warm, healthy, soft glow, and which is always in my mind associated with the beautiful grassy hills and wooded valleys of the Natal Coast, with the little brown huts, and the wattled kraals full of cattle.

This Zulu colour I did not see in America.

In feature and expression too our people are more comely, and I should think have more native ability, as they certainly have more dignity. There is, of course, much in common both in appearance and character, both are Africans, but these distinctions were definitely impressed upon me.

In general physique, too, I think the South African native is superior. As a general rule the American Negro did not stand to me for physical strength. There are many notable exceptions; one sees extraordinarily powerful-looking, almost gorilla-like men, the sight of whom enables one to understand the despair of the pugilistic world to discover a "White hope," but the proportion of these is small.

It has been stated that the long residence of the Negro in America under different climatic and other conditions has modified the type, and even those of pure African lineage approach in appearance the features of the white man.

M. Jean Finot, for instance, states that the colour and

appearance of the Negro have changed in the United States with his *milieu*.   I carefully watched for any evidence of this, but could find none, nor did I meet any responsible person with long experience of the race who believed it to be the case.   The consensus of opinion was all in the other direction, that, apart from admixture of blood, the Negro in all essentials remained the same.

I do not wish it to be inferred that I think this would continue indefinitely through the ages.   Gradually, but very gradually, the race would alter in response to its changed environment.   Those who profess they already see actual visible results are I think anticipating what will take a vastly longer time to effect.

In our half-castes in South-East Africa—the result of union between a white father and Zulu mother—it is not uncommon to see a red and yellow complexion, the yellow clear, and the red suffusing it, that gives the impression of health and is distinctly attractive.   Among those of the Negro people whom I must call mulattoes for want of a better word, the colour was invariably a dull yellow of varying depth sometimes approaching a sallow white, which was often sickly looking.   A bright expression, especially in the children, was not uncommon among those of mixed descent, but good looks were not conspicuous, and the physique was, if anything, inferior to that of the all-blacks.

If race characteristics are deep-seated, as I believe, then in such a variety of blending as is present in the United States, varying from an unmitigated black man, quite indistinguishable from a present-day West African Negro, to a man who would pass without comment in a London club, there must be innumerable exceptions to any generalizations as to character and capacity.   The non-recognition of this most important fact makes many of the attempts to portray Negro character of but little value, and if I attempt it I do so conscious of the difficulty of the task and recognizing that there are many exceptions.

The two streams of mankind which in different degrees have gone to make up the modern American Negro, are so different, that I think it may be accepted as a general proposition that the predominant mental and moral characteristics of any single Negro vary with his colour; if entirely black they will be those of the African, and this will be altered and modified according to the proportion of European blood in his veins—in the extreme cases he will think, feel, and act as a black man, or as a white man.

The bulk are of course black; of these we may say that they are, under ordinary conditions, happy and contented, indolent, vain, long-suffering, kindly, intensely social, lacking foresight, unthrifty, imitative rather than constructive, with strong sexual and religious emotions, unrevengeful, with a distinct capacity for fidelity to those they trust. I may add a disposition to accept authority, and to submit to discipline, obedient to their recognized superiors, and evincing an esprit de corps when associated in a mass.

Some of these traits are indicated in their present position and past history. I have said they are unrevengeful and have a capacity for fidelity. Nothing shows this more clearly than their faithfulness as slaves to their masters during the Civil War. The whole white manhood of the South left their homes in charge of the despised black man, and in these words a great Southerner, Henry Grady, tells of it: "History has no parallel to the faith kept by the Negro during the war. Often five hundred Negroes to a single white man, and yet through those dusky throngs the women and children walked in safety, and the unprotected homes rested in peace. Unmarshalled, the black battalions moved patiently to the fields in the morning, to feed the armies their idleness would have starved, and at night gathered anxiously at the big house to hear the news from Marster, though conscious that his victory made their chains enduring. Everyone humble and kindly. The body-guard of the helpless.   The rough companion of the little ones.   The observant friend.   The silent sentry in his lonely cabin. The shrewd counsellor.   And when the dead came home a mourner by the lonely grave.   A thousand torches would have disbanded every Southern Army, but not one was lighted."

One of the strongest characteristics of the Western European, whether in his old home or oversea, is his foresight, which has been one of the greatest factors in his material advancement, and which, so often exaggerated and allowed to predominate, becomes the bane of individual life, destroying joy in the present for a future that may never come.   Not so the Negro : his lot must indeed be an unhappy one if he cannot enjoy the sunshine as it streams upon it, and only pressure from his strongest animal needs will force him to forecast the future, and sacrifice the present to make provision for it.

Many individual instances can be given of Negroes who,. alone and unaided, have apparently planned out a life's work and consistently striven to achieve it, and many who, by example and help, have raised the tone and character of the community in which they lived.   The case of Dr. Booker T. Washington will occur to all.   In proportion to the total number, and it must be remembered we are dealing with over ten million souls, such cases are rare.

Closely connected with a lack of foresight is the economic extravagance of the Negro.   Thrift is not one of his virtues.   On several of the many occasions on which I addressed gatherings of students, I emphasized the necessity of thrift, taking as my text, out of debt out of danger.   Once or twice I made an apology to the principal for dealing with such a trite and material subject, but excusing myself by saying that my observations led me to the belief that unthrift and extravagance were great failings of the race, and were directly responsible for many moral lapses.

I said I tried to suit my subject to the needs of my

audience, and would never have dwelt on this subject to, say, the last generation of Scottish youth. They quite agreed with this view, and one said : "If the Negro had been as a race as thrifty as the old Scottish crofters, ere now they would have owned the Southland ". I saw abundant evidence of reckless, wasteful expenditure. The dress of the city Negro congregations was more fashionable, with apparently more spent on gewgaws and frippery, than that of a middle class English congregation probably ten times as wealthy. The youth of both sexes were often adorned in ultra fashionable attire, often looking ridiculously bedizened, and obviously conscious of their finery. I have seen such emerging from a pitifully poor-looking home, leaving a mother dressed in rags. The drummer selling gramophones, harmoniums, buggies, and other luxuries on the deferred payment system, can always find customers or victims in the Negro cabins.

Thousands of tenants who by the exercise of self-denial could pay their way year by year, are hopelessly in debt to their landlords, who often unscrupulously take advantage of this trait to make unholy profits out of them. Shopping seems a mania with them. On market days and shopping nights they throng the stores, not to buy necessaries and depart, but to lounge about, feel important, and finally succumb to the temptation to buy some useless article they cannot afford. The same weakness may be seen in their homes. The guest chamber or public room is fitted up with conventional rubbish, the back rooms empty, untidy, and neglected. Miserliness is a great vice, but no one need be afraid that it is likely to become a besetting sin of the Negro, and those who know him best are unanimous in preaching thrift. The author of a monograph on the Philadelphia Negro and who is himself one of their own race thus writes : " Probably few poor nations waste more money by thoughtless and unreasonable expenditure than the American Negro, and especially those living in large cities like Philadelphia. First they waste much money on poor food and unhealthful methods of cooking. The crowds that line Lombard Street on Sundays are dressed far beyond their means, much money is wasted in extravagantly furnished parlours, dining-rooms, guest chambers, and other visible parts of the house. Thousands of dollars are annually wasted in excessive rents, doubtful societies, amusements, gewgaws, and frivolity." Alfred Holt Stone, a Southern writer, in a study which clearly shows much personal acquaintance with the Negro and some sympathy for him, says : " In the Yazoo delta, which is most fertile, the Negroes are extravagant and unthrifty. They could in a few years, if they were industrious, thrifty, and far-seeing, own the Delta. They are much addicted to gambling (crap), homicide, and loose living. They are unreliable and constantly moving. They spend large sums in aimless railway travelling. There are few drunkards, but there are few, men or women, who do not drink."

I have said that the Negro is long-suffering and kindly. Could any proposition be more abundantly proved ? His history in the United States since 1619, during and after slavery, demonstrates it. What other race would ever have submitted to be enslaved, to live at the whim of a master of another race, subjected to indignities, even to the continual debauchment of their women, and not have risen and died rather than submit ? To-day lynchings by white mobs, often accompanied by hideous bloody torture, and often of the innocent, happen every few days and not a single retaliatory lynching by Negroes has happened in the South. To a white man death would be preferable to submission, but though often affrighted, and sometimes defending himself in blind fear and fury, the Negro soon forgets, and is happy until the next time.

The strong emotionalism of the Negro is evidenced in his religious services which I will describe later on, and in which feeling and the social instinct play the principal part. He seems to be easily excited to sex emotions and this, together with a lack of will power and self-control, make for looseness of living and a disregard of marital and parental responsibilities which is regarded by many as the greatest danger to the race.

His personal vanity is often inordinate. If I saw a man dressed in clothes cut just beyond the current fashion, the coat a little longer, the waist cut in a little deeper, the trousers more deeply creased, and the ends turned up a little higher, I found he was coloured. American newspapers and periodicals are in many cases intimately personal, but the Negro journals excel in this respect, and are full of photographs with eulogistic personal articles, pandering to the vanity of those portrayed.

The chief characteristics of the Negro as I have outlined them will, I am sure, be regarded by South Africans as in the main very like those of our native people. There are differences in degree ; our people, though a long-suffering race, would not submit without protest and struggle to the conditions of life which have been borne by the Negro. And though imitative, the innate conservatism of the Bantu of South Africa makes them cling to their ancient customs. But on the whole a truthful picture of the characteristics of one would apply in large part to the other.

It would be possible from the writings of Southerners, Whites and Negroes alike, to cite opinions on each of the individual characteristics I have mentioned, and especially on the weaknesses, throwing them into a deeper shade than I have done. Out of the mouths of their own people a far harsher judgment might have been passed. In the "American Negro" by W. Hannibal Thomas, himself a Negro, a picture of the moral weaknesses and criminality of the Negro people is drawn, which, if true, would make one utterly despair of the future of such a race. But it is no more true than are the views of those who represent the Negro as being entirely the victim of his environment, and only needing equal opportunity to become exactly as a white man, acting and reacting in precisely the same way.

To an extent which in a general way represents the infiltration of white blood, the man of mixed origin shares these characteristics. Many of those classed as Negroes, who have successfully followed the example of the white man in his various activities, and particularly in those demanding practical efficiency, and who are cited as examples of Negro success, have been more white than black. I have spoken to white educationists, whose lives have been spent among Negroes, and who have not been able to note any great difference in capacity between the children of pure Negro descent and those of mixed origin. Others again claim greater ability for the latter, while I did not meet one who stated that the students of all-black descent were superior. Probably there is not a great difference shown during school age.

When the actual work of life begins, however, I think it is the case that a greater adaptability to the conditions of modern civilization, and greater power to secure a satisfactory place therein, is shown by the mixed blood. The higher general capacity and status of the mulatto parent also gives a better chance to his children. I visited many of the Higher Schools and Universities of the coloured people, and in nearly all cases saw the students gathered together. Those who know America will understand that I did not escape the usual penalty— an address to the students. Many times I have carefully scanned my audience, and am confident that the proportion of those of mixed origin present was far higher than that shown by the census. I met many Negroes who had prospered in material things, and many who were in the higher walks of life, professional men and others. Here again I am certain that the proportion of part whites was in excess of what it is in the general population. Anyone interested can easily procure Negro publications full of photographs of prominent members of the race, those present at notable gatherings, congresses, and the like. He will not, I am sure, be struck by the preponderance of black faces and negroid features : on the contrary he will probably be surprised that many of those pictured are classed as Negroes at all.

I was told by an intelligent light-coloured woman whom I met in Alabama, who was married to a well-to-do mulatto there, and who came from Charleston, S.C., that in her early days in that city she had no black associates, and that between the light coloured and black there was a gulf fixed similar to that separating the former from the whites. Later in life when she moved into Alabama she found there no such class distinctions between black and coloured. Her ancestors on both sides had been freed men for two generations, the family owned property, and had a recognized position in Charleston.

A gentleman responsible for the administration of an influential Society engaged in educational and philanthropic work among the Negroes, read me a letter received from an agent in North Carolina stating that the lighter coloured members of a congregation there had been causing anxiety by refusing to recognize their darker brethren as equals. These light-coloured ones called themselves Croatians, which is the local name given to a small community in the neighbourhood of mixed descent, probably partly Indian.

I have also been credibly informed that in parts of South Carolina the mulattoes have kept apart from the blacks, desiring to form a separate community calling themselves the Brown Brotherhood.

Cases such as these are, however, rare. As a rule all who share, in however small degree, in African lineage, consider themselves Negroes. It is clear to me that the action of the whites in refusing to recognize those of any shade of colour has consolidated all of African descent into one camp, and that the undoubted tendency of the lighter coloured to consider themselves superior and withdraw, has received a check, and is much attenuated by this attitude of the whites towards all those of colour.

I do not think that this superior adaptability of the man of mixed descent to his American environment need surprise us, nor need it raise any partisan feeling. I do not claim that the white man is in all things superior to the black : both have their gifts, but certainly the former is the stronger in practical efficiency, and he it is who has built up the civilization in which he and the Negro live together. It would be singular indeed if the mulatto, sharing in the blood, and presumably in the spirit and efficiency of his father's race, did not fit into it more easily and fully than one differing in essentials, and who had never, either in Africa or elsewhere, shown any genius in achieving a similar civilization. In the character of the black man there is much that is admirable, much that, if we possessed it in larger measure, would make us more lovable if less efficient, but it is folly to deny the difference.

I have tried in the last chapter to tell what the white man thinks of his black fellow-citizen. What the black man thinks of the white must now be essayed. I have spoken of the ever-present acrid hostility, the watchful suspicion towards the Negro, noticeable in many white Southerners. I never sensed exactly the same feeling towards the whites in the black man proper. He no doubt feels the disabilities under which he suffers, and when they are pressed home has a feeling of resentment, but I do not think this feeling remains when the immediate occasion is past. If his surroundings are tolerable he enjoys himself with his fellows and does not let his position in Society, nor the possible future of his race, disturb him. I heard many expressions of dissatisfaction with present conditions and a desire to have them righted, but they did not imply a hatred of the white man who made the conditions.

The same cannot be said of the mixed population. I felt that the iron had entered their soul, and hatred akin to that which the white man feels for them, was ever present in the minds of many. I met many whose sole topic

of conversation when with me was the degrading position
of their race, and this often among those who had been
successful in their callings. One can well understand
their bitterness. Many of them are only nominally
Negroes; their main line of descent and their appearance
are that of a white man, and they have the white man's feelings and ideals. Yet they must not attempt any intercourse with the people of the race to which they really
belong, and whose achievements are those on which they
would naturally set their ambitions.

The white man is responsible for them, and yet the
white man disowns them. It is a cruel position, and
though they may have achieved a measure of success in
material things, the contemptuous limitations placed on
them must ever chafe their souls. Speaking to them I
often found that they disclaimed any desire to mix socially
with the white man; they were, they said, proud of their
own people, proud to be Negroes. But they did resent
all the injustice and differentiation heaped upon them,
they resented being branded as inferior. They claimed
equal opportunity and equal treatment as provided for
them in the Constitution of the United States, and yet
denied them both North and South.

A man, they said, should be treated according to his
conduct and ability, and judged by no other standard.
We are not even distinguishable by the colour of our
skin, and yet, because an ancestor sinned, the men of his
race deny us the common rights of citizenship. We cannot walk with head erect, but must always go warily,
looking to right and left, lest we give cause for offence,
and insult, contumely, or death be our portion.

No man with a sense of justice could hear all this
without the saddest feelings. In one respect, however, I
felt they expressed themselves as they did not really feel.
The line of cleavage drawn by the South, thrusting all
those with one drop of African blood among the Negroes,
has made for race solidarity. Had the gulf not been
fixed so wide, so deep, I feel that those whose blood and

mentality are mainly white would never have remained in the Negro camp. A black man may be proud of his race, but it is unnatural to expect a white man, forced among blacks, to remain there unless the force is inexorable. I feel that if the gulf was bridged, those who now express themselves as proud to remain where they are, would crowd into the white ranks, even though they stepped with the lowest there. The tragedy of the South is not the black man whom God made black, but the coloured man, begotten by the lust of his white father.

It is not difficult to understand that such a people as are the American Negroes in the mass, could in a primitive state of Society, fulfil themselves, and weave a social state sufficient for their needs. One can conceive that, even when ruled by a stronger race under conditions approximating to their native state, matters might go tolerably for them. It is much more difficult to imagine them forming an integral and valuable part of a State in the van of modern capitalistic progress, and adapting themselves to the rapid march of events therein. The qualities which have made and carry on the modern state, and make for success therein have in large measure been denied to them. Under present conditions of change and competition, that man, be he white or black, who lacks the qualities required for success therein is trampled underfoot. Millions of our own race in Western Europe and America are the victims of twentieth-century conditions of life. I was told, by some of his more sanguine well-wishers, that the Negro only needed a fair chance to prove himself fitted to take a permanent and honourable place in modern life. The South has hitherto been in a backwater. Life there is rapidly approximating to that of communities in the van of industrial progress. The Negro has to prove himself therein. Can he do so?

Half a century has elapsed since he had freedom thrust upon him. In the next chapter I propose to examine how far in this period he has justified himself in the modern sense, and wherein he has failed.

CHAPTER X.

WHAT THE NEGRO HAS ACHIEVED.

At the close of the Civil War in 1865 the Negro had all his way to make. It is true a few were skilled artisans, a few who had been freed had acquired a little property, but the vast mass had nothing, neither land, house, nor implements.

No people on earth ever had a harder task set to them. The children of Israel despoiled the Egyptians before they set out for the promised land, the white man of the South took care the Negro did not despoil him. Illiterate, without self-reliance or self-control, accustomed to obey and not to think, weak and timid and without material resources, they had to find a place in a civilization built up by a stronger race; they had to fight a fight unarmed, and not understanding the terms of the conflict.

It is claimed by their advocates that no such progress as they have made has ever been achieved before by any people in the like short period of time. When we remember their hopeless position, and the fact that, though they had many influential friends and well-wishers both North and South, the mass of those they lived among were coldly critical or openly hostile, one feels inclined to agree with this finding, notwithstanding their comparative failure along many lines of civilized endeavour.

For to-day there is not a calling in which the Negro is not represented by more or fewer members of his race, and in some he has been very successful, but not uniformly so. In certain spheres he has fallen back in comparison to his numbers and the increased extent of his opportunities as compared with the early years of freedom. I want in this chapter to assess these achievements, and try to account for some at least of his successes and failures.

The great bulk of the Southern Negroes live on the land and are primarily producers. Cotton is still king in the South, and of this staple it is computed that one-half is grown by the Negro. His agricultural activities are exercised as wage-earning labourer, as tenant, paying his rent in cash or in a share of the crop, and as freeholder.

The price of land in the South has been low, and to-day it is cheap, and the Negro has had opportunity, and still has opportunity, to become a landowner. No obstacle has hitherto been put in his way to purchase as much land as he could pay for. The right to acquire land, without which no people is economically free, and the economic ability to do so, have been the privilege of the Negro since he came out of slavery. He has been shorn of his rights in many directions, but here, in the right to make a home on his own freehold, perhaps the greatest right of all, he has had as full liberty as the most aristocratic Southerner in the land.

Fortunately indeed for the race he has taken advantage of it, and the figures in the last Census show that he is acquiring in a higher ratio than ever in the past. To a great extent in the immediate past, and still to-day, though his friends hope in decreasing measure, like all peoples under modern influences, the Negro has felt the lure of city life, and more than most he has yielded to it and suffered grievously therefrom. His best friends have warned him of the dangers of this course, urged him to remain in the wholesome healthy country, and there build his home, and build it under the best conditions. It almost seemed as if these voices were raised in vain, and that the drift into the city was going to continue to the undoing of the race. Now there has been a pause and a reaction, to the great delight of those who, like

Dr. Booker Washington, have consistently preached the doctrine that the hope of the Negro was on the land.

This gratifying change is reflected in the last Census returns. Comparing 1900 with 1910 the Negro population has increased barely 10 per cent, but those engaged directly in agriculture have increased 20 per cent. In every Southern State east of the Mississippi, the Negro is a dwindling ratio to the whole population, but he is an increasing ratio on the farms, with the one exception of the State of Louisiana. These rural Negroes total 2⅓ millions, and with their families represent more than four-fifths of the total Negro population of the South, and they cultivate in all approximately one hundred million acres. Of these 2⅓ million people, no less than 890,141 are either farm owners, or rent the farms they till.

In Mississippi, Alabama, and North Carolina, the farms cultivated by white owners increased during the decade by 12 per cent, those cultivated by Negro owners increased by 17 per cent. In Georgia the white farmers owning their own land increased by 7 per cent, the Negro owners increased by 38 per cent. In the country as a whole the Negro farmers increased much more rapidly than those of the white race, the respective percentages being 19·6 and 9·5. In the South alone, the number of coloured farmers increased by 20·2 per cent during the decade, as compared with an increase of 17·4 per cent in the number of white farmers.

The acreage of land in farms operated by white farmers decreased somewhat in each geographic division of the South, while the acreage of farms operated by coloured farmers increased in all divisions, the percentages ranging from 7·7 to 13 per cent.

In the South as a whole the value of farm land and buildings operated by white farmers increased 122·6 per cent during the decade, as compared with an increase of 137·6 per cent for farms cultivated by Negro farmers.

Taking the South throughout, the average size of

7 *

white farms was in 1910 one hundred and forty-one acres, and was nearly three times the size of those owned by coloured farmers, which was 47·9 acres. The average value of land and buildings per farm was for whites $2923, and for coloured $1011, but the percentage of increase in the decade was somewhat greater in the case of farms owned by coloured farmers than on those of white farmers.

The total value of farm property owned by coloured farmers in the South increased from $177,404,688 in 1900 to $492,898,218 in 1910.

It may be said that in all probability the Negro farms were heavily mortgaged, and this should be taken into account. This was in fact urged by some Southerners with whom I discussed this question. In the abstract of the Census dealing with mortgages the owners of the mortgaged properties are not distinguished by race. I notice, however, that the percentage of farms mortgaged in the South-Eastern States is low as compared with the whole country, which seems to point to a general freedom from indebtedness in this section. In a detailed study of the position of Negro farmers in certain counties in the South freedom from mortgage is specially noticed.

During the years now under review the value of domestic animals owned by Negroes has increased from 85¼ million dollars worth to 177¼ million dollars worth or at the rate of 107 per cent; and the value of land and buildings from 69½ million dollars worth to 273½ million dollars worth or 293 per cent.

It will not be necessary to labour this point further. The Negro in the South as a farmer is, in American phrase, "making good".

The great bulk of the Negro people are, fortunately, thus engaged in agriculture; domestic and personal service claim the next largest number.

The main classes of occupation are thus given :—

	Persons Employed.
In agricultural pursuits . . .	2,143,176
„ domestic and personal service .	1,324,160
„ manufacturing and mechanical .	275,149
„ trade and transport . . .	209,154
„ professional callings . . .	47,324

Domestic and personal service is regarded in the South as the sphere proper to the Negro. There is little desire on the part of the whites to supersede him, and his or her position therein remains much as it was. Nearly all the household work for which wages are paid is done by coloured women. Waiters, bootblacks, elevator attendants, porters are in the main Negroes. Wages are low, general conditions of service inferior, and there is little progress among this class.

The number of those engaged in mechanical and manufacturing pursuits is, in proportion to the total Negro population, but small. The demand for really skilful and trustworthy men is greater than the supply, and wages are high. Skilled coloured workers can command a wage but little lower than that of the white man. There is little colour preference, and a Negro will be engaged to work alongside a white man. It is doubtful, however, whether he is holding his own in these skilled callings. There is an increasing demand for a higher class of workmanship, and the average Negro artisan has not had the requisite training to undertake it. In a later chapter I will deal with the Negro artisan in more detail.

In the numerous semi-skilled occupations which come under this head, and bearing in mind the general industrial advance of the South, it seems doubtful whether he is holding his own. I am informed by a Negro publication that in the following occupations Negroes have made substantial gains in the decade 1890-1900.

	1890.	1900.	Per cent gain.
Miners . . .	15,809	36,568	132
Masons . . .	9,647	14,387	49
Dressmakers . .	7,479	12,592	65·3
Iron and steel workers	5,790	12,327	112·7
Stationary engineers	6,326	10,277	62·4

In the following fifteen trades they have lost ground : carpentry, plastering, brick and tile making, marble and stone cutters, blacksmithing, wheelwrights, boot and shoe making, harness and saddle making, leather tanning, trunk and case making, engraving, hosiery knitting and woollen mills.

It should be noted that the largest increases are in mining and iron working, both of which have made great strides in the South.   Both are very laborious callings, to which probably the white man does not cling as to some of those demanding more skill and less muscular effort.

Professor Walter C. Wilcox, the statistician, thus sums up the position for the decade ending 1900 in skilled and partially skilled work : "The Negro has lost ground in the South in the following skilled occupations : carpenter, barber, tobacco and cigar factory operative, fisherman, engineer, fireman.   He has also lost ground in the following occupations : laundry-work, hackman or teamster, railroad employee, housekeeper or steward.   The balance seems not favourable, and suggests that in the competition with white labour to which the Negro is being subjected he has not quite held his own."

In the issue of the "North American Review" for December, 1904, Professor W. G. Brown inquires into the industrial position of the Negro, and is inclined to think he is losing ground, and that his position would become precarious if there was a large influx of labouring whites.

In the schedule I have quoted on the previous page manufacturing is linked to mechanical occupations.   Few indeed of the Negroes included in this column can be manufacturing anything on their own account. They may be employed in some capacity in manufacturing establishments belonging to white men or companies, but I saw no evidence of their owning, or holding controlling positions in, such concerns. Even as a skilled operative he has little part in what may strictly be called manufacturing. I do not think he has any genius for it. Modern manufacturing, and all it implies, demands abilities for which the Negro is not conspicuous. It requires inventive powers, organizing ability and commercial aptitude. Of the last named I will speak presently. Of invention or in the adaptation of improvements to his work there has been little sign given by the Negro. He has been content to follow precedent and run in a groove. Patents for inventions have been registered by Negroes, but they are few and unimportant as compared with the enormous number scheduled by whites. Much has been said of those due to Negro ingenuity, but a comparison and summary will show little evidence that he is likely to excel either in invention, organization or on the commercial side of manufacturing.

In Negro papers I often noted a long list of business and financial undertakings in which the people were engaged, often with a computation of the capital invested, and the total turnover. It sounded impressive when thus given in the total. When I came actually to see these commercial concerns the contrast between the description and the real thing impressed me once again with the fondness of the race for high-sounding phrases, and their inability to judge accurately of proportions.

Banking has been specially mentioned as one of the commercial activities which has been successfully managed, and which is cited to show the aptitude of the Negro for such pursuits. I find, however, that there are about sixty-four such Negro institutions in the United States with a total capital of $1,600,000 or £320,000, giving an average capital in each of $20,000 or £5000. When we consider that there are over ten million Negroes in the United States this seems pitifully small. A single financial institution with the capital of all these put together would hardly aspire to the name of Bank in Britain or the British Colonies.

The ordinary grocery, drapery, drug, or general store owned by a Negro I found to be usually of the poorest type, and hopelessly out of date. Often necessarily in a poor district, it was also small, badly and insufficiently stocked, dirty, and unattractive, yet all these are classed and numbered as Negro commercial concerns. The amount of capital invested in the majority must be miserably small. Occasionally one saw a comparatively up-to-date establishment, but they were few, and were always pointed out as something phenomenal. Compared with the stores owned and run by Europeans they were pathetically poor. In the higher walks of commerce, importing, exporting and wholesale business, the Negro appeared to me to be entirely out of it. Indeed the wholesale trade seemed to be altogether in the hands of Americans and aliens. In commenting on this I have been met by arguments which became very familiar to me. They run thus : The Negro is only fifty years removed from slavery, he has had no education, he has no opportunities to learn business methods, he has no capital and cannot command it, and so on. I know something of commerce and commercial men, and know that some of the largest and most successful concerns in all parts of the world have been built up by men with little book education, no original capital, and no special advantages beyond native ability, energy, and integrity.

There are ten million Negroes in the United States, and they are reputed to own wealth totalling $700,000,000, a vast field for the commercial activities of men of the race if the ability and aptitude were present.

To show how little they seem to appreciate or force the business opportunities undoubtedly present, and which are so apparent to one with an eye to see, I quote Professor Kelly Miller, a Negro, who says : " In communities in which the Negroes constitute one-half, one-third, or one-quarter of the population, and where their educational facilities are practically as good as those of the whites, we find they do not conduct one per cent of the business ".

I could not help contrasting the meagre results of the Negro business man with what has been achieved by the Jew in this field.   There are only about two millions of the Hebrew race in the United States, and many of them are poor indeed.   The majority probably came as immigrant aliens to the United States without a penny, illiterate, and unable to speak the language of the country. The Jew in the United States has also, like the Negro, though not to the same extent, to contend with race prejudice.   Yet I found him everywhere controlling huge financial and commercial interests.   It appeared to me that the whole of lower Broadway, New York, was monopolized by firms whose names ended in 'ski or 'vitch. In the South they have a large share in the retail trade, and their customers are Negroes.   I often strolled about the streets of Southern towns on shopping nights. The white (and Jewish) stores were crammed with Negroes, full of importance, pricing and buying.   The Negro stores were empty of customers.   Their purchases were not limited to the necessaries of life, they were spending their hard-won money on luxuries and frippery, and making the fortunes of Americans and aliens— principally aliens.

In my book on " Black and White in South-East Africa " I point out, that though our native trade is large, and most lucrative, both wholesale and retail, and though the natives know their own requirements best, and often have actual knowledge and experience of costs and profits as paid salesmen in retail stores doing a native trade, and though this has been going on for over sixty years, they never open businesses, but the whole trade and its profits are in the hands of Europeans and Asiatics. It seemed to me that the same racial incapacity for commerce is shown by the American Negro, and the same lack of racial solidarity in backing up their own, as against the alien trader.

There is in existence an American Negro business league, which is intended to encourage the Negro in business pursuits. This is good, and I trust it will succeed in inducing Negroes of capacity to take advantage of their opportunities, and at the same time help the race. The Southern white insists on racial distinctions, and a measure of racial separation. I think this is wise, but such separation should carry with it the advantages as well as the disadvantages which appertain to it. At the same time, I confess I am doubtful whether any great measure of success will result from this organization. Racial aptitudes differ, and I do not think along the line of commerce the Negro will become great. His salvation lies in what is natural to him, the cultivation of the soil he owns.

According to the figures given, the number of professional men and women of Negro race is 47,324. Again a small number for ten million people. The great majority of these too are preachers and teachers. I met Negro doctors and dentists in good practice, who told me they were not supported by their own people to the extent they should be.

I want to see the Negro people sufficient unto themselves, as far as their natural aptitudes and their acquirements will carry them. The white man is determined that the black man shall never be accepted as a full equal. Even among the friends who are striving to obtain justice for the Negro, there are many who are set against race admixture, who want him to value and preserve his race integrity, and who counsel a measure of race separation. Racially speaking this has been a great gain to the Negro people, hardly a single drop of their blood has gone over to the white side, while every single drop of white blood entering Negro veins is retained by the Negro race. Discrimination makes for—nay forces—solidarity, a solidarity that a weak race would never have achieved by its own efforts. But as I have shown, even with this constant pressure on the part of the white man, Negro solidarity in the practical affairs of life, where it should be strong, is weak. I believe, however, it is growing, and I hope it is. It is no menace to the white men if they band together to help each other, and there is a great field of prospective wealth and advance open to the Negro when he realizes it. Whether he can effectively seize it I do not know. It is perhaps the best plan to wait and see.

The total advance of the Negro people in material things since Emancipation has been indubitably very great. Any inquiry into it, if it is to be of value, should be directed not only to the sum total, but to its distribution among the members of the race. Here monographs dealing with special communities have a high value. From such a one, compiled by Professor W. W. Elwang, and entitled " The Negroes of Columbia, Missouri," I glean the following economic data. In this town the Negroes form 33·90 per cent of the total population, and hold 4·48 per cent of the real, and 3·42 per cent of the personal property. Nearly one-half of this property is in the hands of thirty-one persons. Of this half, valued at $37,265, nearly three-fifths, or $22,315, belong to eight persons. Still further, of this $22,315, no less than $10,500 is the property of one man and his ·wife. It seems rather a hopeless case for the majority. My impression is, that if Negro holdings were carefully analysed, a similar state of things would be found in many communities. Even to a greater extent than among whites, the few exercise foresight and thrift, the great bulk live from hand to mouth, careless of the morrow.

The nett result of what I have said of the economic position of the Negro may be thus summarized :—

In agriculture, great progress has been made and there are immense possibilities.

In domestic and personal service, little progress and no great prospect.

In manufacturing and mechanical pursuits, progress in certain directions, less in others.

In trade and transport, little fitness has been shown, and it is doubtful whether much progress will be made in the immediate future.

In professional pursuits, progress is being made, and more is possible.

I do not think those friends of the Negro who claim that he has shown ability to fill all the many activities of American civilized life as well as the white man, and who often exaggerate what he has accomplished, are doing the Negro a service. I have tried to analyse these statements, and I find, as might have been reasonably predicted, that his advance has been much greater and more solid in some directions than in others. Races, like individuals, have their limitations, and it would be unreasonable to ask a backward race, like the Negro, to prove itself fit and able to compete in a civilization so complex as that of the United States in the nineteenth and twentieth centuries. He has done much in certain directions, and I hope I have given him full credit for his successes: to do more, and praise indiscriminately when comparative failure is apparent, is to pander to his vanity, and feed a complacency to which he is too prone.

I have shown by figures the hope that lies in agriculture and the progress that has been made. I am such an enthusiastic believer in the opportunity for the Negro on the land, and his fitness for this first of callings, that on this subject I shall probably often repeat myself. It is of the first and most vital importance that the race should find what it can do of value to the State, should find an opening in which it shall have opportunity to develop its latent powers, that those who believe that on the land this will be found need not apologize for constant reiteration of this doctrine. A further reason for pressing home the value of this opportunity is that it will not remain open, and one of the tests of the race will be how far they are able to see and take advantage of it.

A visitor travelling slowly through the South as I did

gets ample opportunity to see how the rural Negro lives. I understand he has improved of recent years, vastly improved in many sections, but there is plenty of room for further improvement. His dwelling is usually a log cabin of small size, consisting of one or two rooms without verandah, and the outbuildings, if any are present, are of the very poorest. As a rule there is no attempt at beautifying the house or making it hygienic, and I very seldom saw a flower garden attached to the Negro cabin. There may be a vegetable plot, but the assortment of produce growing in it is meagre. The cultivation of the fields is usually primitive, although on much the same lines as that of his white neighbour of similar means. I was travelling in the ploughing season, and for hundreds of miles I saw no more modern implement than a single furrow one-horse plough. We could show a larger variety of modern implements on many farms in benighted Africa. The cultivation was shallow, the ploughing following the contour of the field to prevent soil wash. Both Negro and white farmers seemed to follow the same methods. It may be that for their main crop—cotton— this apparently slip-shod method is suitable, but it is not good cultivation. I am convinced that modern scientific methods would result in great improvement. Too much time and attention was given to cotton, which is still king in the South, still the crop that brings in the cash and pays the rent. Too often it monopolizes everything, and land that should be growing varied crops, food for man and beast, is occupied by cotton. The land is impoverished, and those tilling it have to buy the food they should raise themselves. It may be that the invention of a cotton-picking machine, which I was told is likely to prove a practical success, will reduce the disproportionate time now given to this crop, which is at present stated to be three-fourths of the whole year. This would to my mind benefit both the Negro and the community, and give time for attention to other matters of the first importance in the rural economy of the South.

Attention should be given to scientific manuring, the rotation of crops, green soiling, the care of live-stock, and the utilization of their manure, which would work wonders in the South. This land should be covered with smiling homes. Too long the plantation system, with its economic and social evils, has reigned. The country is adapted to mixed farming and comparatively close settlement, with co-operation and all the social and material advantages it brings. This applies not only to the Negro but to the white man. Some far-sighted enthusiasts and philanthropists are working to this end, not the least Dr. Booker Washington, and all well-wishers of the South must hope their efforts will be crowned with success.

Meantime, though Nature holds out ample promise, the aspects of the Negro rural home and its surroundings are poor and sordid, and to those who can only see the present may seem hopeless. It gives material for the sentimental writers of novels and essays, who picture the dull dark cabin in the noisome swamp, with the poor impoverished cotton fields, the inmates living in the direst poverty, deeply in debt, dreading the fatal day of reckoning, but with souls above their sordid surroundings, with deep longings for communion with other souls in brighter spheres, and so on and on.

After seeing the Negro in his actual surroundings, in his log cabin in the South, after assessing his real position and his possibilities, I felt little patience with this sentimentality.

The surroundings of the rural Negro are not ideal, they are often dirty, untidy, and unhygienic; his food, though abundant, is coarse and often monotonous, but there is nothing in it all to shed tears over, whole classes of white rural workers elsewhere in the world are in infinitely worse circumstances, and with far less to hope for in the future.

I say it emphatically, and will say it again and again, that if there is dirt, if there is overcrowding, if there is debt, if there is exploitation on the part of the white man, it is largely the fault of the Negro himself, and that man or that woman who weeps in sympathy with him, bewailing his condition, is not his friend but his enemy. That man is his friend who tells him plainly that dirt, disorder, unthrift, and laziness, are his besetting sins, and that if he does not overcome them he deserves all he gets both from Nature and the white man.

Dr. Booker Washington is right, emphasize the opportunities, and what opportunities ! Would to God the rural labourer of my own race in my native land had such a chance. Imagine it—a land of sunshine, not too hot nor too cold, abundant rainfall distributed through the year, timber for all purposes, firewood at the door, and streams of clear water running through the land. I shall show elsewhere how the Negro may get a home of his own in this land, meantime I ask my readers to take my word for it that any able-bodied, intelligent, industrious, thrifty Negro may have a home of his own in these surroundings, and what a home he could make ! Seeing the opportunity standing out so clearly—even I, just a visitor, felt my fingers itch to grasp axe and spade and make a beginning.

The log cabin, despised by the sentimental and morbid novelist, now dirty and unhealthy, might with little effort and no expense be made a bower of beauty. The novelist and essayist dealing in the tragic, shudderingly point to overcrowding, and the disease and immorality attending it. Why on earth should there be any overcrowding, why any disease ? If there is any chance of it let the overcrowded come out and sleep under God's stars. I said these cabins had no verandahs. The first thing they should have, with timber in abundance all round, is a wide deep verandah which could be put round each cabin, and every male occupant, at least, sleep in the open, sweet air all the year round. Overcrowding is the Negro's own fault, and if he will hermetically seal up all access to the fresh air, and the family sleep like pigs, of course he will have to bear the consequences.

And as to dirt. Why dirt? Soap, which is cheap, and water, which is everywhere, are necessary, and so is elbow-grease, which the human element should supply. Pathetic laments have been made over mud floors. I have lived in houses with mud floors which were perfectly clean and hygienic. No native kraal in Africa has anything else, and the inmates are splendidly healthy. If the superstructure is allowed to rot, and the floor to become uneven, and rain enter and mud-pools form, of course they become deplorable, but the cause for this is one and removable—laziness. Eliminate the laziness, and the floor will soon be all right.

Now for food. If it is monotonous, again it is the fault of the Negro. This generous earth and glorious climate will grow variety and abundance. Vegetables, fruit of all kinds, only need ordinary attention. Pigs and fowls thrive and are within the reach of all. Cattle do well, and most Negro cabins could have a cow or two. I have gone into the financial side of the matter, and I will take my reader into my confidence on this aspect of the question later on, but I say now that industry, foresight, and thrift, will enable the Negro in the log cabin to sit at a table amply provided with varied food, with cereal, dairy, vegetable and fruit products in abundance.

And for the ugliness of the log cabin of which so much has been made? After seeing the possibilities I feel sick of much of the stuff I have read, pouring pity on the poor Negro who has to live in a log cabin! I say it again, weighing my words, that every log cabin in the South could easily be made beautiful, surrounded by beauty. I saw an untended Marshal Neil rose climbing over the porch of a cabin, which was carrying hundreds of lovely blooms that ravished the sight. I know the profusion of flowers, and flowering and climbing shrubs, that can be grown in Natal, and all that is possible in Natal is possible in the South. I have seen enough to make me certain of it. Even in a despised log cabin, with wide creeper-covered verandahs, vegetables and fruit in plenty, a cow, pigs, and chickens, firewood for the collecting, and sunshine over all, I cannot feel the material elements for a wholesome, healthy, hopeful life are lacking. But effort is required. The Negro has not arrived at it yet. I believe he has advanced and is on the way to better things. Many helpful agencies have been established as I will relate, and the Negro is responding. Stimulus and sympathy he may require, but stimulus comes first, and the sympathy that finds expression in wails over his present economic short-comings by picturing the misery of his surroundings is of the kind that the Negro should not get, and those who proffer it are not his true friends. He is all too ready to sit down on his mud floor and pour out wail for wail. The true sympathy is to pick him up, and, roughly if necessary, set him to putting things straight. And I say this because I know it can be done, and I know that along this line is the true path for the Negro. Booker Washington is perfectly right.

CHAPTER XI.

NEGRO ORGANIZATION—CHURCH AND LODGE.

In somewhat singular contrast to the lack of effective business organization and cohesion among the Negroes for purely commercial ends, are the results achieved in Church matters, and more recently in the building up of friendly and secret societies. The strong religious and emotional nature of the African has in America found in the Church its satisfaction.

Around the Church as a centre are aggregated all that goes to make up the social life of the Negro, and social life means more to him than it does to the more self-centred white man.

Until quite recently all the Negro people, men and women alike, were Church members, and the great majority took an active part in religious observance. Even those who were not regular in their attendance, or who were backsliders, were not antagonistic, and might always be won back to an ideal they had never abandoned.

To-day I heard from the older Negroes who had grown up in the faith, and whose lives were closely knit to Church associations, many laments that the younger ones were lax, indifferent and fond of pleasure, and too often put pleasure first, and religious observances second. This note of disappointment is not of course peculiar to this generation, it was no doubt the plaint of the elders in the days of the Ark of the Covenant, but it is probably truer to-day than ever before. With the decay of old custom, with the invasion of the South by modern ideas and practices which is bound to come, will also come indiffer-

entism, love of pleasure, and the chafing at control, which
are so peculiarly characteristic of the present day.

Anything of the nature of philosophic doubt seems
foreign to the Negro character.   I asked an intelligent mulatto who dwelt on the tendency to forsake religion whether
it is due in part to this cause, and his reply was in the
negative.   They did not, he said, think enough to become
atheists or agnostics in the usual acceptance of the term.
It is reported that a similar question was put to an old-
time Negro and he answered: "Golly no, it takes some
sense to be an atheist and niggers hasn't enough sense ".

The common charge against Negro manifestations of
religious feeling is that it begins and ends in emotion, and
that this emotion is of a sensuous kind begotten of his love
of rhythmic, musical sound, and worked up to fervour by
the contagion of the crowd.   His nervous force being thus
drawn upon, it exhausts itself, and there is little left for the
works that should go with the faith.   It is charged against
him, that even among the elect, a high standard of morality does not accompany emotional fervour, and that even
gross immorality is frequent, and too frequently condoned.

Notwithstanding many theological colleges, the standard of learning and conduct demanded by the congregations from their ministers is not high, and lapses in one
who may be otherwise acceptable, are looked upon lightly.
It is not difficult to find in the writings of Negroes themselves these weaknesses emphasized much more strongly
than I have done, indeed some charge the admittedly low
standard of morality among the people as a whole, to the
absence of high moral ideals among those holding the
most influential positions in Negro religious life.

Granting all this, I have no doubt but that the Negro
Church has been an enormous power for good among the
people, and has probably been the one force that has kept
the race from utter stupefaction and degradation.   Unable
to find their satisfactions in the usual secular channels,
finding little but hardship and restriction in their everyday
life, and yet bursting with emotionalism, they grasped at

8 *

the compensations of a life to come, when all toil and sorrow should be done away with, and everlasting joy, of a kind they could understand, would be the portion of all believers. No wonder the songs that dwelt on the golden streets, the harp and crown, and eternal rest, appealed to them, and that their prayers are full of yearning for this glorious hereafter.

Not only for his religious emotions, but for his social satisfactions has the Church been the solace of the Negro. I attended many services, and found in Sunday school and church, as well as the many other activities which clustered round them, an obvious satisfaction at the mere pleasure of being together; chatting conversations, a purring satisfaction in moving among their fellows, a personal importance in occupying recognized official positions, were obviously very pleasant to them. I found that debating societies, tea-parties, guilds, class-meetings, benevolent societies, and similar activities, filled up the week, while almost the whole of Sunday was taken up with services, the necessary intervals being largely occupied with sociability,—in meeting, walking, and talking.

Poor and naked indeed would the Negro have been had he not had his Church to fill in his life. While as compared with the nervous force he puts into his praise, prayer, and exhortations, the moral side is weak and often stumbling, still the Church does stand for morality, and the doctrine is preached that works should accompany faith. It cannot be doubted but that the Church has been in all respects a force for the uplifting of the Afro-American people. Unsatisfactory as are the results in many ways, still the imagination is shocked, when one thinks what this people might have been and become, had they not known, or been bereft of, this force of betterment and satisfaction.

The principal denominations favoured by the Negroes are of the Protestant Evangelical type, Baptists and Methodists of various kinds being in the ascendant.

Some of these are nominally the same as the Northern bodies of the same name, Congregationalists, Wesleyan-Methodists, Presbyterians and others.   These, however, include only a small portion of the total Negro worshippers; the majority belong to independent organizations, of which the principal are the Baptists, with about two and three-quarter million communicants, and the African Methodist Episcopal Church with over half a million members.

It is noteworthy that neither the Episcopal Church, as we understand it in England, nor the Roman Catholic communion has attracted the Negro.   One would have thought that the more elaborate ritual, especially that of the latter, would have specially appealed to him, but such is not the case,   In 1906 there were only 38,235 Negro Roman Catholics in the United States.   In that year there were 3,685,067 Christian communicants of all sects, and the value of Church property owned by all the Negro Churches was $56,636,159.

Practically the whole of this vast organization is in the hands of the Negro people, and is altogether managed by them, the whites evincing no interest in it.   Probably the Negroes would resent interference with the management, although they would doubtless accept monetary assistance.   This yielding to the black man in the domain of religion, is in marked contrast to the demand for white supremacy in all spheres of secular activity.   A Negro says : "In politics, education, business, the white man manages and controls the Negroes' interests, it is only in the Church that the field is undisputed ".   It seems to me this is an illustration of the practical and material nature of the white temperament, the white man takes all that leads to power and wealth, and leaves to the black man the culture and control of his materially unfruitful emotions.

I could not learn, nor do I believe, that any of the various Church activities have a political trend.   If they have they are singularly barren in results.

This utter indifference of the white man in the South

as to what takes place in these organizations into which he never enters, contrasts with the somewhat nervous attitude of South African politicians and people with regard to the independent religious movement among the Bantu people, which is usually called Ethiopianism. Our people, like the Negro, seem to feel a measure of restraint in religious matters if controlled and supervised by whites. It may be they are consciously or sub-consciously aware that their emotions and aspirations, while in part met by the white man's religion, are not fully satisfied by his presentation of it. At all events a movement towards independence has received considerable support among the natives of South Africa, and it is likely that it will increase, and possibly take form and force by the uprising of some leading personality.

The suspicion with which Europeans in South Africa, laymen and missionaries alike, have viewed this movement is to some extent due to the allegation that it has, at least in part, a political colour, and that the doctrine of Africa for the Africans is held and preached. In view of the position in America and the evident desire of the Negro to control his own religious activities, may we not have been needlessly suspicious and nervous about this movement, which, taking the character of the African into account, seems not unnatural.

The absolute separation of white and black in religious life in the South is illustrated by the following incident related by the Rev. J. Snyder in the Forum: "Some years ago there was a great revival in one of the churches of my own city. The Evangelist was fervently inviting all kinds of people to come to the 'anxious seat'. Tramps, drunkards and beggars were among the number. At last it was announced to the church officials that a Negro upon one of the back seats was under conviction. Here was a problem of serious import. The officials held an anxious consultation, and it was finally decided that the Negro might receive salvation in an inconspicuous pew." Revivals like this one are quite out of fashion in South

Africa, our English-speaking people are in intimate contact with the modern currents of life, consequently such
an embarrassing incident could not happen. If it did, I
think the black man with us would also have to seek salvation in a separate and inconspicuous pew.

My experience of Negro churches was chiefly in the
towns, though I did visit religious gatherings in the
country. Many of the churches in the cities are very
large and well-built edifices. They are, naturally enough,
copies of those belonging to similar denominations among
the whites. I found that architecture, furniture, order of
service, and all that went to make up the church organization were copies. I noticed that the preponderance of
women over men, which is so apparent in English and
Colonial churches to-day, was not so marked in the Negro
churches. Considering their positions in life, the congregations were remarkably well dressed, both men and
women often attired in the extreme fashion. I have little
doubt but that the love of display enters largely into the
attractiveness of church attendance.

In these large Negro city churches the emotional
displays, common in smaller and less conventional gatherings, were subdued, though interjections were much
more frequent than in white churches. The singing was
a special feature, and when the congregation warmed up
to it, was distinguished by power and rhythm. In one
church the choir wore surplices and college caps.

Most of the discourses I heard were conventional,
and did not bear the impress of deep thought, or even
feeling ; personal feeling, and in one case personal grievance at an alleged slight at Convocation, were introduced.
One sermon, however, stands out as an exception. It
was a powerful, restrained address on the duty of the
race. It contained rebuke of apathy, and a plea for
higher morality, and especially denounced prevalent
drinking habits, and the supine toleration by the coloured
people of the evils inflicted on them by the whisky
dealers, and the lack of public spirit when an attempt

was made to obtain prohibition. It was delivered by a striking personality, a light-coloured mulatto, and was admirable in matter, delivery and earnestness.

In smaller communities, untouched by the reticence or indifference in religious matters which is the spirit of the times, there is much more freedom of expression, especially in revival services. Here emotion has full play, and sways the congregations. It is easy to level criticism at such, they offer targets to ridicule, but there can be little doubt that, taking the nature of the Negro and his racial wants into account, they are of value to the race.

The Negro gives generously of his substance to build up and support his Church. The spirit of personal emulation is brought into play, and offerings are made in public. Members of the congregation come forward bearing their gifts, and as the warmth and emulation waxes, they often repeat or increase their donations. I met a man, a Southerner engaged in Evangelical work and the distribution of religious books, who contrasted their openhandedness with the niggardliness of the whites among whom he travelled. In one small town I find that, although the real and personal property of the Negroes only amounted to some $80,000, the Church property belonging to them cost nearly $28,000! I should think that of all people on earth professing the Christian religion they give more of their substance to Church work than any other, not even excluding the Roman Catholic population of Ireland. It is in marked contrast to what obtains in Britain and South Africa. If the white Christians of the Union of South Africa, especially those of British descent, gave the same proportion of their wealth to their Churches, we should have cathedrals fit to compare with Cologne and Milan instead of the present-day poor dingy edifices which are in such marked contrast to our palatial governmental and municipal buildings. Other days, other aspirations.

At times when they were lamenting the comparative indifference to Church matters, I found some Negroes who considered it due in part to the remarkable development of friendly and secret societies. These are generally local societies, formed ostensibly for benevolent purposes, to ensure relief in sickness or unemployment, and burial at death. They have increased in number of late years, and not only provide for distress and unfortunate contingencies, but meet certain wants of Negro nature, his desire for personal importance and social gathering together. They generally have high-sounding names, provision for numerous officials with bombastic titles, a formal ritual and regalia, and they hold frequent social meetings. I doubt very much whether any society would succeed, however solvent and well established, which made economic advantages the sole claim to the support of the Negro population.

Even in small towns there may be several societies which in a sense are hardly rivals, for I was told that individual Negroes often belonged to different associations and held office in each. It is quite common for members to fall behind with their payments, in which case they forfeit their privileges, and the moneys previously paid in go to swell the capital of the society, or they pay heavy fines to retain full membership.

In a small city in Missouri the position of the members of one society is thus given by the Secretary: "Of the whole number admitted during the past six years 38 per cent never made a second payment, 72 per cent lapsed during the first year, and 5 per cent more after paying through the first year". It seems certain that a very considerable proportion of the members fail to meet their obligations, and the societies and officials benefit thereby. The cost of administration must be very heavy in proportion to the capital, and charges of peculation on the part of officials are not uncommon.

Their phenomenal increase seems due to the fact that they fill a want in Negro life, though at an extravagant cost in time and money. Excepting from the view of social satisfactions, the time consumed in the demands of ritual, the numerous gatherings for trivial ends, and the putting on and off of regalia is largely wasted. On the other hand, if the Negroes were not present at lodge meetings, they would probably be on the streets or in low dives, and gatherings for mutual help are far preferable to these. Individual thrift would probably result in more substantial financial results and save much unnecessary expenditure, but the Negro needs the support of his fellows, and the glamour of personal importance as inducements, before he can make the sacrifices which foresight and thrift demand. Take it all in all, I think the societies are a distinct benefit to the Negro people.

Many of the societies are secret, and it is possible that in some of them the benevolent side is not the most prominent. It is said that political and race issues are discussed under this cloak of secrecy. It may be so, but no practical results can be observed by outsiders. Few white men know or care what is done or said in these secret lodges, but many would be ready enough to take action if they thought that race assertiveness was the outcome of these meetings.

There has been some protest against the Negro societies taking the same names as white organizations, but, speaking generally, the white man ignores this movement, or if friendly, regards it as a good thing that niggers should make provision against misfortune.

I think it likely, if similar societies were formed among the Bantu people in South Africa, there would be a great deal of suspicion directed against them, and possibly efforts would be made to suppress them. Favouring as I do a measure of separation between the races for the good of both, I feel that organizations such as these, unless of a clearly seditious character, make for race solidarity and a proper race consciousness, and give an outlet for feelings and aspirations that are natural and should not be discouraged, though under present conditions in South Africa they should be watched, and perhaps unostentatiously and quietly guided, by the authorities.

CHAPTER XII.

EDUCATION, PRINCIPALLY THAT OF THE BLACK CHILD.

ONE of the surprises of my visit was the extent to which the Negro has responded to the opportunities for education he has had. Another was the facilities for education provided for him, from primary school to College and University, both by State appropriations and by the philanthropy of Northern friends. These efforts have converted the Negro race from an entirely unlettered people in 1865, when it is estimated that 5 per cent only could read and write, to one in which only 30·5 per cent are illiterate.

During the administrative year 1908-9 in the sixteen former Slave States and the District of Columbia, 1,712,137 Negro children were enrolled in the public schools, and these formed 56·34 per cent of the total coloured child population. In the same area, during the financial year 1910-11, the total public expenditure on Negro education was $13,061,700. This large sum seems small however when compared with the amount spent on common schools for the whites in the same area, which amounted to $75,863,931. The primary coloured schools of the South, particularly in the rural districts, are often in an unsatisfactory condition. I visited several typical ones, and found the buildings poor in construction, lacking in equipment, and as far as I could judge the teaching left much to be desired. The length of the school term is often not more than a few months in the year. Negro apologists urge that the Boards which handle the State appropriations, being invariably white, favour the white schools to the detriment of the Negro schools, and I think this is often the case. With the Negro a negligible quantity in politics and State management, one would expect this to be the case, and undoubtedly the South has in many instances withheld or curtailed the reasonable educational opportunities of the Negro.

This is one of the complaints which I heard everywhere voiced by the militant section of the Negroes. White public opinion on the question seems to vary with the years, sometimes there is a wave of dissatisfaction leading to curtailment, and again a period of greater liberality. Of late the former feeling seems to have been predominant in some sections and States, and I heard of great difficulty in obtaining appropriations, especially those for higher literary education. In the case of some Colleges the grant for purely academic subjects had been reduced, and an attempt been made to foster a more practical, and generally an industrial training. Again the title of some of these institutions had been changed to denote this alteration. This may be, probably is, a desirable reform, but by one section of the Negro people, who are jealous and tenacious of their rights, it is regarded as another attempt to deprive them of benefits they now enjoy. This section views all that makes for distinction of the races with suspicion and disfavour, and is not disposed, even for practical benefits, to condone action which savours of further relegation to an inferior status.

In support of the contention that Negro education was often starved for want of funds, a well-to-do mulatto, living in a country district, told me that while he was assessed at $40 a year for school rate, the amount voted for his district was only $60 in all. At the same time it must be only in very remote and backward districts that the Negro child is denied the opportunity to obtain a common school education.

It was, however, the facilities for higher education that most surprised me. There were in 1910, 141 public

High Schools for coloured persons in the South, with a total of 10,935 students. In addition to these there are 540 institutions engaged in the secondary and higher education of the Negro. Many of these are devoted to the ordinary literary curriculum, but there are others giving special industrial and vocational training. There are Colleges and Universities which grant degrees in all the ordinary subjects, and also schools for medicine, dentistry, and law. Between 1900 and 1909, 1613 Negro College graduates passed through these Universities, besides a very large number who did not take a degree. These higher seats of learning vary much in size, from Howard University, Washington, D.C., with an annual income of $134,000, to those which have a precarious revenue of only some $5000. Some are entirely State supported, others receive a grant in aid, while others again derive their funds from Northern sources. During 1910-11 the expenditures for Negro higher and secondary education in the United States were, by States and Municipalities $756,972, by the Federal Government $299,267, and from other sources, largely of course philanthropic, $3,519,615, or a total of $4,415,854.

The vast bulk of this was of course expended in the Southern States. It is estimated that the total value of the property owned by coloured educational institutions amounts to about $16,000,000. As compared with this the value of property owned by all such institutions in the United States for secondary, higher, and industrial training, amounts to $740,000,000. Endowments to Negro Colleges and Universities amount to $2,062,966, and to Normal and Industrial Schools, $3,983,819. In ten years these Negro institutions increased their endowments by half a million dollars. All institutions for higher and special learning among the whites in the United States in the same period added to their endowments a value of $9,761,122. It is reckoned that the direct contribution of the Negro people towards education, apart from taxation, amounts to about $1,000,000 per annum.

The discrepancy between the amounts spent on all branches of Negro education, as compared with the amounts devoted to the instruction of whites, seems very great, and my experience showed that in buildings, equipment, and the efficiency of teachers the white institutions were much superior. It must be remembered, however, that even in the South, the Negro population is below one-third of the total population, and if we take the expenditure in this ratio, and the ratio is a decreasing one, the disproportion, although large, does not seem so excessive. According to a Negro publication the Southern States have since 1870 expended $160,000,000 on the Negro common schools. During the same period about $1,200,000,000 was spent by the Southern States on all their common schools. Taking the Negro population for this period as one-third of the whole, multiplying 160,000,000 by 3, thus making the appropriations apply to an equal number in each case, it would appear that $480,000,000 is the ratio of the Negro appropriations, and $720,000,000 that of the white population. Certainly a great disproportion, but nothing like what the visitor would imagine when listening to the complaints of a section of the Negro people.

It may be interesting to compare the position in two of the provinces of the South African Union, Natal and the Transvaal, premising that the *per capita* amount spent in the Cape Colony is higher, and in the Orange Free State lower. In Natal we have about a million Bantu people and approximately 100,000 whites. An average of the last few years would give about £15,000 spent on native education and £150,000 on white education. This £15,000 represents $75,000. During this period it would be quite fair to average the Negro population of the South as 8,000,000, it certainly would not exceed this. Yet on these 8,000,000 was spent in 1910-11, from public funds $8,645,846, and from all sources $13,061,700. We may safely say that on each million of the Negro population in the South a million dollars of

public money was annually spent for education. In Natal
the million natives receive $75,000 worth! In the
Transvaal the position is not so good. Here in this
Northern province of the Union of South Africa it is
computed that the native population contribute £1,500,000
to the State Exchequer, and yet barely £15,000 is spent
upon their education. It is well sometimes to make such
comparisons when one is told that the position in the
South in this regard is without parallel, for discrimination
and injustice, in the civilized world.

I said that primary education was within the reach
of the great majority of Negro children in the South. I
would also say that a special industrial course, or a University education, may be obtained by any intelligent
Negro boy or girl, however poor, if endowed with grit
and character. Many of these institutions for higher and
vocational training make special provision for such cases
by allowing students to work out their fees, which are
never high, and often extremely low.

For many years the education given in most of the
higher Schools and Colleges was entirely literary, and
those passing through them became teachers and preachers. Often it consisted largely in an exercise of memory,
was on the surface, having little depth or value to
character. Many of the Negro preachers thus turned
out were vain and pompous, darkening counsel by long
words, and with a low standard of morality. There appeared to be a failure in linking on education to life.
Edgar Gardner Murphy says : " We have been giving the
Negro an educational system which is but ill-adapted to
ourselves. It has been too academic, too little related to
practical life for the children of the Caucasian. Yet
if this system is ill-adapted to the children of the most
progressive and most efficient of the races of mankind,
who shall measure the folly of that scholastic traditional-
ism which would persist in applying the system to the
children of the Negro. If the weaknesses of the Negro
have made him run to the bookish and decorative in

knowledge, we must remember that the schooling we have provided for him has at least been bookish if it has not been decorative."

In some of the cities in which there has been a large permanent Negro population, such as Washington, D.C., educational facilities have been excellent for many years, on the whole as good as they were for whites, yet it does not seem to have had the effect in bettering their worldly positions; few attained positions of trust and responsibility. It is true they were handicapped by their colour in competition with whites, but there was a wide field for personal advance and social usefulness among their numerous kinsfolk. Prof. Kelly Miller says on this point: "There is perhaps no place on earth where so much culture runs to seed, and so much intelligence goes to waste, as among the Negro element in our large cities. The younger element of the race, at least, is practically as well educated as the whites, and yet they count for almost nothing in the higher business and industrial life of the community. The fact cannot be disputed."

The predominance of literary education is now, however, being challenged by industrial training, including scientific and practical instruction in agriculture. The movement may be said to have been initiated by General Samuel Chapman Armstrong, the founder of the Hampton Normal and Industrial Institute in Virginia.

Trained in this Institute was Dr. Booker T. Washington, who carried the spirit and methods of Hampton far to the South, and built up a daughter institute at Tuskegee in Alabama. Widespread and deep have been the results. Now all over the Southland the Negro is looking for, and getting, education in the practical affairs of life, which will react on character, and will have, I believe, a far-reaching effect on the race.

Large bequests have been made by Northern men and women to this end. Federal appropriations and organization have been given, and the States are assisting. The position differs in different parts of the South; in some districts the whites stand aloof, but in many sections Southern men and women are taking part, both officially and unofficially, in this work. In Virginia supervising teachers have been appointed, who visit the rural Negro schools, and advise, assist, and encourage to more zeal and better methods, and especially to foster industrial and agricultural training. In this State there are travelling instructors in agriculture, who visit the farms, and call meetings of farmers, giving advice, encouragement, and demonstration. One branch of this work is that of agricultural demonstration agents, whose work is to superintend the actual growing of crops by improved methods as an object lesson, on land belonging to the farmer himself. As the work progresses local farmers are invited to watch and criticise the various operations, and test the results. Many instances could be given in which these actual practical demonstrations have resulted in almost fabulous increases of crops. It is stated that in some cases the yield of corn has been raised from 5/15 bushels per acre to 30/60, and lint cotton from 150/200 lbs. per acre to as much as 300/600 lbs. per acre. Annual conferences of farmers are called by these officials. In 1912 one was held at Tuskegee, and it was shown that at that time 451 demonstrators were working, 1400 landowners carrying on experiments over 3000 acres of land, and 4069 Negro farmers also co-operating in experiments.

Other organizations also assist, and Farmers' Conferences are becoming quite a feature of the South. At these meetings mutual help and co-operation are preached; yet the personal note is struck, and individuals give their experience, showing how difficulties have been met, and advance has been made. I could fill pages of testimony from white and black alike as to the beneficial results in individual cases and local areas of this interest taken in the people, and the value of the teaching and application of new and better methods; the difficulty is to choose and condense them. I must ask my reader to take my

9

word for it, and to anyone who desires further information, I would refer them to the publications issued by the Hampton and Tuskegee Normal and Industrial institutions, the two largest and most widely known institutions for Negro education, and which I briefly describe in the next chapter.

The value of this work is not only in bettering the material condition of the Negro, but in giving him hope and interest in life, a wider outlook, and a vista before him of increasing prosperity for himself, and greater usefulness for his race.

CHAPTER XIII.

EDUCATION LINKED TO LIFE—HAMPTON AND TUSKEGEE.

I HAD the pleasure of visiting both these places, and the deep impression they created makes me feel that they must have a chapter to themselves, even though a short one. I here again experience the difficulty of condensing. Scores of pages could be filled with statistics, showing the magnitude of the work done, and the results achieved at these institutions, but they would probably only tire the reader. I must quote figures, but I will be as sparing as possible, and in preference will give my impressions.

Hampton in Virginia, situated on a beautiful coast, is the mother institute. It was founded by General Samuel Chapman Armstrong in 1868. This far-seeing and devoted man, the greatest benefactor to the Negro and American Indian peoples, was born in Hawaii of American parents, and commanded a corps of Negro soldiers in the Civil War. A man of unusual insight, he was convinced that for the true uplift of these people, an education should be given that would form character, and at the same time be calculated to help them and fit them for their work in life, and make them worthy men and citizens. And so Hampton was founded, and from small beginnings it has gradually grown to the great undertaking I found. It is now presided over by Dr. Hollis B. Frissell, who is carrying on the work in the spirit of the founder. What that is may be expressed in his own words: "To train selected youth who shall go out and teach and lead their people, first by example by getting land and homes, to give them not a dollar that they can earn for themselves, to teach respect for labour, to replace stupid drudgery with skilled hands, and to these ends to build up an industrial system, for the sake not only of self-support and intelligent labour, but also for the sake of character ".

I found on my visit a large park-like area of 185 acres, beautifully kept lawns shaded by forest trees, and in this park numerous isolated substantial buildings, 113 in number, suited to the numerous and varied requirements of such an institution. The students are both male and female and are all resident. They number over 1600. The faculty, instructors and officers, are for the greater part white, and number about 200, and the policy pursued is laid down by a Board of seventeen Trustees, including prominent men from both North and South.

Every year a larger number of students apply for admission than can be accepted, but they are not necessarily denied because of poverty; they may, by working during the day, learn and work at a trade and thus earn their board and academic instruction, which in that case is given in the evening.

There are thirteen Trade Courses, including all the principal handicrafts, which are practically taught in thoroughly equipped workshops. All male students must also take a course in agriculture, as well as manual training. In the same spirit girls must learn housekeeping in all its branches, gardening and hygiene. This training is of course linked to an academic course. In addition, at a distance of some six miles is a farm of 587 acres with 175 head of cattle, 31 horses and mules, 300 hogs, and 1000 fowls, with 400 acres under cultivation, and with 22 houses and farm buildings. At both places the greater part of the buildings have been erected by the students, and all repairs are done by them.

All this and much more may be gleaned from the admirable catalogue issued annually, but it does not exhaust by any means the activities which centre in Hampton. Annual conferences are held to discuss subjects of interest

to the Negro people, when such matters are on the
agenda as " The Negro labourer in his relation to Trades
Unions," " The progress of Education in rural communities," and the like.   Twice a year a Farmers' Conference
is convened on the lines I have previously indicated.   A
mass of literature is issued by the publication department,
including an excellent monthly, "The Southern Workman," and a large number of educative leaflets which are
distributed free of charge, or at nominal rates.   I select
a few of the subjects dealt with in these pamphlets :
"Sheep, their care and management," "Dairy cattle,"
"Drainage," "Mosquitos," "Milk and butter," "Seed
planting," "Rotation of crops," "Farm manures,"
"Patent medicines," "Proper use of certain words".

Very wisely, as I think, the male students are organized
into a cadet corps, and wear neat uniforms made at the
place.   The Negro is peculiarly susceptible to mass
movement and discipline, and this establishes an esprit
de corps and mutual feeling and action that could not
otherwise be provided for.

After all, it is the spirit that matters, and though
I was deeply impressed with all my eyes saw, I was still
more moved by the underlying spirit that pervaded and
actuated the staff, and which must be communicated to
the students.   A spirit of social helpfulness was present ;
they were training themselves to help their own people.
I find from the accurate records kept that 83 per cent of
those who learned trades either followed them or taught
them after they left Hampton.   The authorities keep
touch with the students who leave, and it is clear that the
great majority carried the spirit of Hampton into the
world of life.   I went carefully through all departments
and was struck with the close and careful thinking that
had been devoted to all details ; the final result was always
kept in view, and the methods most carefully thought
out to attain it.

As an instance—I found the girls did not wear a uniform as did the boys.   When previously visiting a State

Normal School for Negroes in the far South, I found all the girls wearing a plain uniform costume, made by themselves, and costing very little. I asked the principal the reason, and he told me the tendency was to dress in showy, unsuitable garments, and he insisted on the uniform to encourage thrift and discourage display. I mentioned this to the lady teacher at Hampton. She did not agree with this policy. She felt there was a greater value to the students if they were shown how good and necessary it was that they should choose suitable clothes for each occasion. A girl might come overdressed, and the tone of the community would induce her generally to cast her unsuitable finery. If not, the teacher would quietly talk to her and explain. The result was that they learned to select and wear what was suitable. If uniformed, this value would be lost, and as soon as they were free they would blossom out in extravagance. This is an example of the thought given to the problem.

I have said elsewhere that the Negro has had the assistance of the biggest brains, the warmest hearts, and the heaviest purses of the North, and Hampton goes to confirm this.

I conclude with an extract from my rough notes written while the impression of the place was vivid: " The staff here seem splendid in their trained enthusiasm and devotion, and in the brain they have put into their work. It is magnificent."

It was here that a boy of mixed descent came, poor and without friends. He went through the courses with enthusiasm and finally left, saturated with the spirit of Hampton, resolved to make another Hampton in the South. This boy was Booker T. Washington, now known the world over as the great and wise leader of his race. I visited the Institution he founded at Tuskegee at an unique time. He had determined to hold there a Conference on the Negro and his problems, and sent invitations to Governments, Societies, and individuals. Eighteen foreign countries or colonies, and twenty-five missionary societies and other organizations were represented at the Congress. Both black and white attended. Many interesting and valuable papers were read, and the discussions were most informative. A Committee appointed to consider future work recommended that a similar Congress be held triennially.

One of the most striking features of the proceedings was to me what was not said. There were many papers read on what the Negro had accomplished in different countries, the best educational methods to suit his circumstances, the civilization of Africa by missionary effort, and the like, but I did not hear a word publicly said about his disabilities in the South. Of course at such a gathering one came into contact with Negro men and women from all parts of the South, and from them in conversation I heard much of social conditions. In this way I met men, gained information, and heard opinions that would have been impossible but for this gathering, and I feel I owe a debt of gratitude to Dr. Washington for such an unique opportunity.

That social and political disabilities had no part on the public agenda may have been due to the fact that the meeting was held in the South, and the discussion of such topics have been deemed, by general consent, to be unwise, or it may have been that the atmosphere of Tuskegee is not one for dwelling on what is being suffered, but on what has to be done.

So the tone was a hopeful one, much had been achieved, very much more was to be accomplished in the future. Meeting at Tuskegee, and seeing what has been done, it would have been difficult to strike the pessimistic note. In contrast to Hampton the staff here are wholly coloured, but the plan of the place is modelled on that of the older Institute, in Virginia. I found the same well-kept lawns, shady trees, and beautiful and suitable detached buildings among these surroundings. I went through all departments, including the farm, and what I saw is much like what I saw and have related of Hampton. I may just give a few figures to show the magnitude of this daughter Institute.   The estate consists of 2345 acres of land, with 113 buildings of all kinds, and these, together with the stock in trade, equipment, live-stock, etc., are valued at $1,279,248.   In 1911 there were 1702 students, 1600 of whom boarded and slept at the Institute.   As at Hampton these students are compelled to learn a trade, they cannot attend for purely academic instruction and, as there, the poor student gets a chance of working out his fees.   At first entrance all must do their share of manual work, whether they pay for their course or work it out, they must undertake janitor's work, scrubbing floors, cleaning windows and the like.

The work and influence of Tuskegee extends beyond the school grounds, large as these are, and every year sees an increase of this outside extension work.   An annual Negro farmer's Conference is held on the lines I have previously described.   This was established twenty-three years ago, and was then only attended by the local farmers of Macon County, now they gather from all over the South.   A Farmer's Institute was formed in 1897, and the members meet monthly at Tuskegee in the large Agricultural Buildings.   A short course is given which consists of two weeks' concentrated observation and study.   When it was started eleven attended.   In 1911 the number registered was 1900.   This work has proved of the greatest value as a stimulus and encourage-ment.   These are only a few of the extension activities which radiate from Tuskegee.

In going round the workshops I made inquiries from instructors and pupils alike as to the prospects of the latter when they left school.   Many told me they intended to be teachers, and that there was always a demand for Tuskegee graduates as instructors.   I was informed that others, more energetic or ambitious, did not seek openings in established schools, but that they themselves started new work in virgin ground.   Many others said they in-tended to work as journeymen at their trades, and would be able to get full journeyman's wages when they left, and that on the average they would earn $2·50 to $3 a day. In one department the teacher in charge said they had fifty applications for every competent man they could turn out. Although this may be exceptional, it is not extraordinary, for the training the students get is far more complete and thorough than is obtainable by the ordinary apprentice in a workshop. They not only handle the tools of their trade, but the principles underlying their use, and the reasons for the various operations are explained. They must be good executive workmen, skilful with their hands, and they must also be designers, planning and working to plan. Those engaged in the building trade take their places in the drawing office, and have an opportunity of learning and practising what is denied to the ordinary apprentice, and they thus become fitted for the higher posts in the trade.

The authorities here claim that the average earnings of the 9000 students who have passed through the Institute are $700 per annum. Their average earnings before they entered were $100 a year. They also say of adult students, of whom there are a considerable number, that before entering their earning capacity was from $5 to $10 a month. After remaining at the Institute from one to three years such are in demand at wages ranging from $1·50 to $3 a day with prospect of increased pay as experience is gained. The exceptional ones are able to command almost at once from $4 to $5 a day.

The Institute commands the respect of the better South, though I felt in converse with many who may be taken to represent the average man, that they view the work with at most a watchful tolerance. I feel sure that any points of weakness would be carefully noted, but it is significant that I heard little that was definite in the criticism that was sometimes directed at it. The students were admitted to be well behaved and well taught, though some said the Tuskegee trained artisans were at first slow. The upholders of Tuskegee make a claim that they furnish no inmates to the penitentiary, and I never heard any serious doubt cast on this significant statement.

I again make a verbatim extract from the daily notes I made at the time. As far as I can judge, the behaviour of the students here, boys and girls alike, is exemplary. They are quite free from any awkward self-consciousness, are courteous and helpful, not in the least prim, but rather, among themselves, full of bright fun. I can hear the girls now talking and laughing among themselves, without roughness or undue noise. Each evening a meeting was held in the vast chapel, all the students attended, the audience probably numbered nearly two thousand. Their singing of the old plantation songs, the rising and falling of the waves of melody, the perfect rhythm, I will never forget. The way this audience enjoyed the jokes of the Negro speakers was delightful. One evening a little jerky speaker fairly danced about the platform, performing heroic gymnastics and acting the comic at the same time. He told of a preacher who read his address, and who placed his manuscript on the desk in a draught, while he rushed backward and forward along the platform. This was acted by our speaker, who ran to one end of the stage and shouted, "Hence, my brethren," saw nothing on the desk, and off to the other end and shouted again, "Hence, my brethren," back again and, "Hence, Hence," and then in despair, "Oh, my brethren, Hence has gone out of de window". A pause, and then laughter began to lightly ripple, and then fairly broke over the audience in a storm of swaying laughter. It was glorious.

I find at the conclusion of the notes written day by day during my visit the following : "I do not think I have laid sufficient stress on the beauty of this place. It is all planted with shady trees, and large lawns separate the buildings, which are substantial and in excellent taste. The bedrooms are large, well lighted and ventilated, and some are furnished with bath-rooms attached, and all the dormitory buildings have large airy sitting-rooms. It would be considered a very well-appointed high-class school in England. The system of eye and hand training, and the actual training for a vocation, along with academic learning ; the learning of principles, then applying them in practical work, and then describing what has been done, seem to me admirable. The idea of a military corps with drill, uniform, and band is excellent, and is shown in the esprit de corps, the physique, manners, and bearing of the students."

CHAPTER XIV.

GRIEVANCES. THE JIM CROW CAR.

On 1 March, 1875, the Congress of the United States passed a Civil Rights Bill in which it is declared that, "all persons within the jurisdiction of the United States shall be entitled to the full and equal enjoyment of the accommodations, advantages, facilities, and privileges of inns, public conveyances on land and water, theatres, and other places of public amusement, subject only to conditions established by State law, and which must be applicable to citizens of every race and colour regardless of any previous condition of servitude".

Yet in every Southern State with the exception of Missouri, laws have been passed and are now in operation, requiring that separate compartments or coaches shall be provided on all railways for persons of African descent, who shall not travel in the same coaches as whites. It should be noted that these ordinances explicitly provide that such separate accommodation shall be of equal comfort and convenience as that provided for whites, and that the fare shall be the same.

The earliest of these laws was passed in Tennessee in 1881 and the last in Oklahoma in 1907.

By State or Municipal ordinance the races are also separated in street cars in most of the cities of the Southern States.

This is in marked contrast to the position in slavery days when, as F. L. Olmsted shows, black and white travelled together.   He says in one place, "Among our passengers inside the Stage Coach was a free coloured woman, she was treated no way differently to the white ladies.   My room-mate, a Southerner, said this was entirely customary in the South, and no Southerner would ever think of objecting to it."   There seems to be no doubt but that here, as in many other ways, discrimination is clearer and harder than it was in the past.   G. W. Cable, writing in 1885, says, "In Virginia they may ride exactly as the white people do, in the same cars.   In South Carolina respectable coloured people who buy first-class tickets on any railroad ride first-class as a right, and their presence excites no comment on the part of their white fellow passengers."   Neither in Virginia nor South Carolina would this be possible to-day.

This universal separation is one of the grievances constantly voiced by those who demand equal rights irrespective of race or colour.   While many claim that there should be no distinction, but that the Federal law should be carried out to the letter, the majority are not so insistent.   These say they do not demand to ride in the same cars as the whites, they would scorn to go where they are not wanted, but they do demand equally good accommodation when they pay the same fare, and they say this is in practice denied them.   They complain that the coaches provided for coloured passengers are old and dirty, that sufficient accommodation is not supplied, and that they are consequently often overcrowded, also that disreputable white men use them, and act insultingly to the proper occupants, and all this is in marked contrast to what is provided for whites.

I travelled several thousands of miles in the South by ordinary trains, always by daytime, and preferably by mixed and stopping trains, both on the trunk lines and on branches running to remote country towns.   I was much interested in this question, for it is a live one in South Africa.   It also seemed to me to be an excellent opportunity for actually testing and checking the common statements made, by my own personal observations, so I took full notes of what I saw.

I found the distinctions were rigidly carried out. I never saw a coloured person in a white car, though on one or two occasions I did see a white man in a coloured car, usually this person was the purveyor of candy, fruit, tobacco, and nuts, who served white and black alike, and who most frequently occupied a couple of seats in the white car.

On one occasion, being at the Depot some time before the train started, I inadvertently lit a pipe in a compartment I took for the white smoker, and which was really the coloured car, and was told abruptly by an official to go where I belonged, which I humbly did.

In most cases the black and white sections were compartments of the same car, built at the same time, and the upholstery, fittings, etc., was identically the same in both cases. Both appeared to be cleaned before starting by the same officials, and both, occasionally— very occasionally—cleaned up during a long day's journey.

The number of white travellers was almost invariably far in excess of the Negroes, but the actual accommodation provided was often the same, not that the railway authorities favoured the latter, but they could not give them less. My notes show that on many occasions the white compartments were uncomfortably crowded, while the coloured were almost empty. I will give two instances. I copy verbatim from my notes made the same day. "Left New Orleans for Birmingham, Ala., and arrived there at 7 p.m., filthy beyond description. Chunks of hard biting coal struck one's face, and yet it was so hot that the windows must be open. Our carriage was uncomfortably crowded and looked like the steerage of an emigrant ship; dishevelled women, men, in shirt sleeves, many hot and tired children, among the dirt and discomfort I've mentioned. Twice I looked into the coloured compartment, the first time it was not filled like ours, the second time there was plenty of room." Again, "Left Asheville, North Carolina, for Danville, Virginia, the train was uncomfortably full, and near me was a party of Greeks, two women and a bunch of children, not poor, I should judge, but excessively dirty. The women were small, almost dwarfish, and of a low, coarse-featured type, the children were noisy and ill-mannered, and spankings and yellings were frequent. Later on more passengers entrained, several men being obliged to stand, and the smoking car was crowded and filthy. I looked into the coloured car, there was seating accommodation for between thirty and forty, and the sole occupants were three women, two by the way wearing University caps. It was infinitely cleaner than the smoker, and I think cleaner than the white general car. No white person attempted to invade the coloured section, though they could easily see the vacant space, as the door opened frequently to admit the passage of the officials."

It is true that on some of the branch lines the accommodation for coloured is inferior. If there are two separate coaches the older one is for the Negro, but, take it all through, I found that the whites were more frequently incommoded by the distinction than the coloured.

There are, however, disabilities in railroad travelling that in occasional cases press home more hardly. No Negro could enter the Pullman car, or have a meal on board a train. No Negro would be allowed a sleeper. It was pointed out by coloured people that if one of their people travelled from the Pacific to the Atlantic by the Southern routes, he could neither eat nor sleep on board the train, however willing to pay for it. This disability will of course only affect the few, the merest percentage of the total number.

Discrimination on the street cars is present in almost every Southern city, but there are local differences in practice. In Baltimore an extremely dirty Negro came and sat beside me on a seat constructed for two, though there was an unoccupied one farther up the car. In a city in Alabama, contrary to the usual custom, the six front seats in the car were reserved for Negroes. If racial effluvia is one of the objections to indiscriminate seating this is curious, for I saw white ladies taking the seats immediately behind the Negroes. In one Southern city I went out by tramcar to a park in the suburbs. It was a holiday, and the cars were crowded, especially on the return journeys in the evening. The whites took up the whole of the seating accommodation, and coloured people were deprived of what was specially reserved for them, and I presume they had to return by late tramcars after all the whites had got home. Here was occasion for justifiable complaint, and similar cases are bound to happen at exceptional times. On the other hand I have seen white men standing, and seats in the coloured section vacant. I have pointed out all this to Negroes and they have replied by giving cases of undeniable hardship. Still the observations of an impartial traveller should be of some value in a case like this, and my observations go to show that the disabilities are not in a practical sense of so serious a nature as some would have us believe. Undoubtedly the very fact of discrimination rankles in the minds of some, and these principally the educated of mixed blood. One can understand and sympathize with these feelings which have been thus expressed by H. G. Wells in 1906: "There are gentlemen of education and refinement, qualified lawyers and doctors whose ancestry assisted in the Norman Conquest and they dare not enter a car marked whites, or intrude on the dignity of a rising loan-monger from Esthonia; for them the Jim Crow Car ".

I do not think the ordinary Negro has any feeling of resentment to this separation in travelling accommodation. He recognizes he is different, and would not feel happy in a white car, and he accepts his own without

complaint.   And again, in the tense state of racial feeling
in the South, if no official discrimination was made,
and the races mixed and jostled in travel, it would result
in continuous quarrelling and frequent loss of life.   As it
is, though the position is felt to be humiliating by some,
it must perforce be accepted by all, and this prevents
occasion for active hostility.

Although the Civil Rights Bill explicitly lays it down
that hotels, theatres, and all places of entertainment and
amusement shall be equally free to all, the position in
the South is that these places, as usually understood, are
for whites only.   The black man has of course his separate
places, for he does travel, he must be fed, and he demands
amusement.   But he must find his own.   There is, so
far as I know, no State law prohibiting him these places,
but the custom is stronger than any law, certainly
stronger than the Civil Rights Bill of the United States.
It would be almost like committing suicide for a person
who is obviously coloured, or who was known in the
neighbourhood to be of African descent, to enter any
hotel or restaurant in the South, and insist on his
privileges under this law.   The risks are so obvious that
not a single Negro attempts it.

Although, as I have said, all these deprivations of the
ordinary civil privileges of citizens, and discrimination
against the race, are accepted by the mass without vocal
protest, and are not in my opinion considered a ground
of grievance by them, they are intensely disliked and resented in the hearts of the educated, and especially those
of mixed descent.   As I have pointed out, however, the
rigid application of these laws and customs makes the
position of the race quite clear, prevents misunderstanding and conflict, and has compensations.

This view is taken by many friends of the race who
strive to attain a fair view of the situation.   The reasons
for and the results of race separation have been elabor-
ated in the works of Edgar G. Murphy, from which many
eloquent and truthful passages might be cited dealing

10

with this phase of the question, but it may be summarized in the following short quotation : "The South in establishing the dogma of race integrity has not done so in order to enforce a policy of degradation, but simply to express her own faith in a policy of separation. Her desire is not to condemn the Negro for ever to a lower place, but to accord to him another place. She believes that where two great racial masses, so widely divergent in history and character, are involved in so much of local and industrial contact, a clear demarcation of racial life is in the interest of intelligent co-operation, and in spite of occasional hardships, is on the whole conservative of the happiness of both."

In discussing remedies or palliatives for the present strained position, Professor A. B. Hart writes : "Race separation would give greater opportunities to the Negro, and reduce the contact with the lower class of whites out of which comes most of the race violence in the South. It is substantially the method applied in the Northern cities, though nowhere to any such degree as in the South. It is a method which, with all its hardship to Negroes of the higher class, comes nearest being a *modus vivendi* between the races."

CHAPTER XV.

THE 15th Amendment to the Constitution of the United States passed on 30 March, 1870, specifically guarantees to all those born in the United States equal electoral privileges, both Federal and State, and explicitly states that there shall be no discrimination against any person or class on account of race, colour, or previous condition of servitude. In order to make this effective in the States and Territories an Act was passed immediately afterwards which states, "All citizens of the United States who are or shall be otherwise qualified by law to vote at any election by the people in any State or Territory, district, county, city, parish, township, school district, municipality or other territorial division, shall be entitled and allowed to vote at all such elections without distinction of race, colour, or previous condition of servitude, any constitution, law, custom, usage or regulation in any State, Territory or by or under its authority to the contrary notwithstanding". The intention of these enactments is obvious.

As I have shown elsewhere, from this time on for several years, say till 1877, many of the Southern whites were disenfranchised by reason of their participation in the Civil War, while the Negro, under the 15th Amendment, got and exercised the vote, and he and the carpet bagger ruled the land. These were the bad days of Reconstruction, still remembered and hated in the South.

The North, tired of the war, perplexed by the tremendous issues and responsibilities raised, eager to

10 *

repair the economic loss due to years of death struggle, and wearied of the Negro, took the easiest course, gave the franchise to the Freedman, and told him to look after himself. In this frame of mind, and wedded to the tradition that the way to attain and retain true freedom is to exercise the vote, this seemed the only path open to the conquerors. They had no actual experience of what happens, and must happen, when two races of unequal strength and equipment are placed in a position of nominal equality. To-day, after nearly fifty years' experience, few Northerners will claim that this plan had in it the germ of a permanent and satisfactory solution of the question. It is easy for us, with the experience of this half century, and some knowledge of similar conditions elsewhere, to denounce the futility of what was done, and point out a better course ; it is not difficult to be wise after the event.

Yet without claiming superior wisdom, it may be well to indicate a different, and what seems to me a better way. Instead of being forced into a position of nominal equality, for which he was totally unfitted, the Negro should have been adopted as the ward of the Federal Government. A special department of that Government should have been established for his guidance and protection, for the study of race relations, and to advise the Government thereon. Land should have been set apart, and as the members of the race became qualified, they should have been established on it under kind but strict control. Meantime work should have been provided for them, and they should have been made to work. Only as they became fitted should they have been allowed to take part in public affairs, and this should, for a long time, have been simply the management of local affairs. All this would have meant the expenditure of a very large sum of money by specially qualified men, and probably neither men nor money were available. Something in this direction, it is true, was done even before the conclusion of the war, as in March, 1865, the

Freedman's Bureau was established, and under it the immediate needs of the freed people were supplied, and the beginnings of an educational system created. But it was always hampered, its efforts were only considered provisional and tentative, and in 1870 it ceased to exist.

During the years of reconstruction and after, the white man of the South did not sit still under the rule of the Negro and his self-seeking white colleagues. No one who could adequately gauge the forces at work could have expected it. Even Northern and Western States, after the ratification of the 15th Amendment, restricted the vote to whites, and among these States were California, Connecticut, Colorado, Indiana, Kansas, Michigan, Nevada, New Jersey, Ohio, Oregon, and Pennsylvania. The question of granting the suffrage to Negroes was submitted to popular vote in the fall elections of 1865 in the States of Connecticut, Minnesota, Wisconsin, and Colorado. It was defeated in each, though they were all in the undisputed control of the Republican party.

Alfred Holt Stone says: "There is not a State in the Union from Massachusetts to California, which, through some element in its population, does not discriminate against the Negro race. We are fundamentally alike in our attitude towards the Negro, however much we may deny it, on each side of the line. And this truth will be more and more realized as our Negro population becomes more distributed, and political and economic conditions gradually tend to greater uniformity between different sections of the country."

In the South the opposition took violent forms to prevent the Negro from exercising the rights conferred upon him by the Federal Government. White organizations, secret and open, were formed to keep him from going to the poll. The notorious Ku-Ku-Klan terrorized him, and when it was considered expedient used the gun, the torch, and the rope. The whole South was solid in its grim determination to prevent, and make im-

possible in the future, not only Negro dominance, but
Negro equality in any form.   They succeeded, and in a
few short years the Negro was as effectually eliminated
from politics as if his short spell of dominance had never
been, and the 15th Amendment had never been passed.
Yet it still remains as part of the Constitution of the
United States.

Then came a time for the consideration of the position,
and many attempts were made by Southern State Legislatures to clinch by law what had been secured by force.
Tests were established of various kinds, educational,
property, character; tax and understanding qualifications
were demanded.   It is not too much to say that underlying these laws, in the minds of those who framed them,
as of those who were subjected to them, was the idea
that by them all white men should attain the vote, and
only such black men obtain it as would be negligible in
politics.

I quote the following from the Democratic State platform of North Carolina in support of this opinion : "We
can congratulate the people of North Carolina upon the
successful operation of the Constitutional Amendment
regulating the elective franchise.   The adoption of this
measure has permanently solved the problem which has
so long agitated the public mind, and been a menace to
peace and good government.   In its operation the assur-
ance made by the Democratic party to the people, that
no white man would be disenfranchised thereby, has been
fully verified, and the prediction of the Republican party
to the contrary, proved false."

In the State of Georgia for example, a voter must
have 40 acres of land or 500 dollars worth of property in
the State.   He must, unless physically incapacitated,
be able to read and write the Constitution of the United
States, and if physically unable to do so must understand
and give a reasonable interpretation of the Constitution
to an appointed Board.   With such a Board, altogether
white and nominated by whites, it is easy to understand

how few Negroes would be able to interpret and give a reasonable explanation, and how few whites would fail to do so.   These clauses might, however, conceivably debar some white men and admit some Negroes.   The mesh of the net was made smaller.   Although a person (white person of course) may have neither property nor education, he may be permitted to register if he is of good character, and understands the duties and obligations of citizenship under a Republican form of government.   This might have been thought sufficient to make white domination secure, but to give another opportunity to the white man, the grandfather clause was passed, under which any uneducated or impecunious person may register who is the lineal descendant of a voter of 1867, or of a soldier who was enrolled in the forces of the United States.

In Mississippi there was no property test, nor did they attempt to provide for all contingencies by the complicated laws of Georgia.   They achieved the same end by demanding that every voter shall be able if called upon, to reasonably interpret any portion of the Constitution of the United States.   Those called upon, if of African descent, found some difficulty in satisfying the examiners.

In many States before a voter can be registered he must have paid his poll tax, which is not collected with any great regularity.   Few Negroes would pay a tax which would remain uncollected if they did not register, and this no doubt is the motive for making this proviso.

We must remember also that behind all these elaborate legal provisions is the gun.   Before the South had begun to legalize the position, the Negro had practically relinquished the rights conferred on him by the Federal Government.   He had been made to see quite clearly that if he persisted in claiming and exercising the right, he would be killed, and at the present time if he cannot be kept out by legal enactments he will be kept out by force, which would not, if necessary, stop short of murder.

W. P. Calhoun gives an instance of a Southern white

man in South Carolina who "injudiciously attempted to push a Negro forward and make him vote ".   He was waited upon by a mob with guns, and shooting happened. He fled, leaving home and family.   In order to be able to return he made an abject apology, promising not to offend again, and if necessary he would change his politics !

The Negroes know all this, and are forced to accept the position.   Some few are on the register, and are allowed to vote, but if the issue became such as to really matter to the white man the Negro would never be allowed to decide it.   I spoke to several registered Negro voters, and they said they did not trouble to cast their votes, it was no good, they did not count.

W. Laird Clowes wrote his book "Black America" in 1891.   Over twenty years have elapsed and this book is of value as the record of what a clear-sighted and impartial Englishman noted at that time, and specially is it of value for purposes of comparison with the present. Then most of the State legislation, designed to consolidate and define the position secured by force, had not been passed, though of course the Negro had practically ceased to be a factor in politics.   Mr. Clowes gives the number of registered white and coloured voters in the three States :—

	White	Coloured
Louisiana . . .	108,810	107,977
Mississippi . . .	108,254	130,278
South Carolina . .	86,900	118,889

and yet at that time, in all these States, the white man ruled indisputably.   Writing of the franchise position in that year, so much closer to the times of the Ku-Ku-Klan than now, he says : "Indeed there is no conceivable scoundrelism that is not or has not been practised in the South to neutralize the Negro vote ".

And yet the Negro, voteless and voiceless in political affairs, is the one force that makes Southern politics what they are.   There is only one issue in the South, and that one is the nigger, who, apparently, does not count. The man who is unsound on the race question is politically dead in the South, if such a one voices his opinions too freely, he may be, in very rapid fashion, physically dead. A visitor of course finds it difficult to judge in ordinary times of the political spirit of a country, but I was told by some who spoke mournfully, that this attitude meant the extinction of political thought in the South. There is no clash of opinion as in the North and in Britain, and on questions which should awaken keen interest and discussion, there was only a torpid indifference. The Southerner boasts of the Solid South. This Solid South is politically a block of ice, inert, immovable, without thought or life. What the South wants is not political solidarity, but thought, discussion, the clash of different opinions, the warmth, yet the light which comes from free expression on any subject under the sun. It is the Negro who has made politics in the South what they are; speechless and voteless he yet prevails.

This political apathy on all subjects but the one, means that the South is all of one political colour, all belong to the Democratic party, and the result is that the control is in the hands of the party bosses. This indifference is shown in the proportion who take the trouble to record their votes. In Mississippi, in 1906, one vote out of fifteen was recorded, in Georgia only 33,341 polled out of a registered total of over 500,000.

The Negro for many long years regarded the Republican party as his friend, and pathetically looked to it for assistance. I gathered from conversations with Negroes that this long held faith was being at last shaken, and some told me the Negro should make the best bargain he could, either with his traditional friends or foes. Certainly any hope he had of help from his old time friends has become hope deferred, and it is not surprising that he feels hopeless.

Every now and then when it seems desirable to the political manipulators, a show of affection is made, and the parties string out platitudes and pass them off to the Negro in return for such voting power as he possesses.

Both parties in their declarations insert paragraphs of fine-sounding phrases intended to placate the Negro, but the politicians know perfectly well it all amounts to nothing. Alfred Holt Stone is quite right when he says: "A glance at the record shows that not one platform has ever been framed by that party which has been almost unbrokenly in power since the Negro was emancipated that has not contained its Negro plank. Almost invariably the other great party has answered in kind. And in each case it was mere *brutum fulmen*, an opera-bouffe affair with the Negro occupying the centre of the serio-comic stage."

On occasions the white man does let the Negro have a run when the issues are confined to the party or are non-important, and then, politically uneducated, he is at the mercy of the political machine, as shown in the following extract from the "New York Times" of 17 August, 1903 : "Baltimore, August 16, 1903. In the Republican faction fight between Senator McComas and the Anti-Organization Combine at the primary election in the Counties yesterday there was wholesale bartering of votes. About $25,000 was spent in one county alone in buying Negro votes. At Upper Marlborough all kinds of ruses were worked by Negroes to obtain funds from both sections, and they were mostly successful. At least two dollars each were paid for the black votes, but as a rule they brought from five to twenty-five. One Negro got fifty dollars for voting twelve members of his family. As soon as the polling window was raised a rush was made for it, but they refrained from voting until supplied with the long run. The men with the cash stood opposite the window and offered the money. The scene has probably never been equalled in Maryland politics."

CHAPTER XVI.

SEPARATION IN SCHOOLS AND PLACES OF PUBLIC RESORT.

ONE of the grievances voiced is the inferior education given to the Negro. This question I have dealt with elsewhere, and have shown that though the appropriations towards Negro education are small as compared with those received by the whites, the opportunities for primary education for the Negro child are greater than in many other civilized countries, and the number of institutions for higher learning are surprising to one who had imagined that the opportunity of the Negro ended with a poor elementary education.

The separation of the youth of the races in the schools is of course absolute. To the great mass of the Negroes proper, this is not regarded as a grievance, but to the man of mixed descent, who holds the doctrine of equal rights, irrespective of colour, such differentiation is regarded as a wrong inflicted on the race.

In some mixed communities outside the United States, in which race differentiation is not so marked, in which the backward race may exercise the franchise, and in which there is no discrimination in public conveyances, as for example in the Western province of the Cape Colony, the separation of the youth of the races in schools is yet insisted upon.

We may regard as narrow-minded, supercilious, and unjust the demand for separation in places of amusement, public conveyances, and even hotels; but many who would grant an equal place to the coloured man here, decline to allow their children to mix with those of his race, and they approve legislation to secure separation. Even when the sexes are kept apart, and the children are physically clean, these argue that the moral atmosphere in which the majority of the coloured children live is so different, that the close association in school life at an impressionable age, may weaken the moral fibre of their children, and lower their standard.   Their objection is much stronger when both sexes attend the same school. In the present temper of the South it is unthinkable that in any section the common schools will be open to both races alike.   Even the liberal and thoughtful South accept the doctrine of separation in school life as one that should not be questioned, and if pressed would probably in all cases stand for it equally with the average man.

Edgar G. Murphy, who is an educationist by profession, in his essay on "The Schools of the People" thus states his view : " But the social and educational separation of these peoples has created the opportunity and the vocation of the Negro teacher, the Negro physician, the Negro lawyer, the Negro leader of whatever sort.   It has not only preserved the Negro leader to the Negro masses by preventing the absorption of the best Negro life into the life of the stronger race, it has actually created within thirty years a representation of Negro leadership which is worthy of signal honour and sincere and generous applause.   The segregation of the race has thrown the members on their own powers and has developed the qualities of resourcefulness.   The very process which may have seemed to some like a policy of oppression, has in fact resulted in a process of development."

If two races of different traits and in a different stage of culture must live together, then I feel that the stronger should be animated by a sense of race dignity which will not only be apparent in a righteous scorn to take unfair advantage of their strength, but on all occasions prompt them to act with sympathy and tolerance.   To stand on a false dignity and demand exceptional treatment for ourselves and servility from the weaker, is much more likely to breed irritation and aggravate race hostility, than a considered apartness in certain spheres in which grave moral issues are raised.   If by some spiritual change the whole white South could act with uniform courtesy and kindliness it would do far more to smooth the asperities of present race relations and make for peace than the removal of the present colour distinctions in schools. No people on earth are more susceptible to kindly treatment, to a gentle, courteous, yet dignified manner than the African, no people will submit with less resentment to distinctions that are not insulting. If the South as a whole could follow the lead of the awakening best South, take an interest in the Negro school and make effort to uplift it, I feel that the cry of the militant section against a separation that makes for race sufficiency and race pride, would fall for the most part on unheeding ears.

What is true of the schools also applies to all other educative agencies, even those of a religious character. The Negro cannot enter those organized by whites, though he is at liberty to form his own. I was much struck with the wide organization and beautiful and complete buildings of the Young Men's Christian Association in the South. I went through some of their branches and saw and admired the manifold arrangements for the physical, mental, moral, social, and spiritual needs of the members. But no coloured man, however near white, could attain membership. W. P. Livingstone says : " The Y.M.C.A. is an important organization in every town of the United States, but the coloured element is never admitted to it. This is as true of the North as of the South. Were a Negro allowed to register in any association all the white members would immediately resign."

Equally with the whites the Negroes are municipal tax-payers. The amenities provided by these taxes are not for them. Neither municipal libraries, gymnasia, swimming baths, nor newsrooms are open to them. They may be seen in the public parks, and visiting such open-air places as zoological gardens. I found, however, that on holidays, when the parks were crowded and picnic parties much in evidence, the Negroes resorted to a part not frequented by whites.

CHAPTER XVII.

THE NEGRO BEFORE THE COURT.

IF there is a happy country in the world in which rich and poor, illiterate and learned, influential and obscure may feel certain of getting absolutely equal consideration and justice before the law, I do not know it. At the best we do but approximate to it, and though the approximation may be close, it is never perfect. If to the illiteracy, poverty, and obscurity be added the further handicap of race, a race practically without a voice in the government of the country, then, without any deep search into the Annals of the Courts, we may be certain that absolute impartial justice is far to seek.

We must remember also, that in the United States the administration of justice is not, as in Britain and the British colonies, in the hands of impartial officials chosen for their probity and ability by the Government; but these are elected directly by the people. And in this choice the Negro has no voice. Too often sordid political motives are what actuate the Electors, and the administrator of the law is absolutely unworthy. Let us still remember, as we must always do, that the Negro is devoid of political power and is largely inarticulate, and we can see that the primary conditions of absolute justice in the Courts can hardly be said to be present.

Many specific cases were related to me of cruelly heavy sentences passed upon Negroes, and comparisons were made with extremely light punishment meted out to the white man for the same class of offence; of abrupt treatment that prejudiced the accused, and, more particularly, of the impossibility of a Negro getting proper satisfaction when he brought a charge against a white man.

Many of my Negro informants also told me that men of their race suffered violence and injustice and never dreamt of bringing the cases into Court, feeling that they would not obtain redress, and would probably direct popular resentment against themselves.

Judge W. H. Thomas of Montgomery, Ala., says: "I have observed that juries have not hesitated to acquit the Negro when the evidence showed his innocence. Yet honesty demands that I say that justice too often miscarries in the attempt to enforce the criminal law against the white man. It is not that the Negro fails to get justice before the Courts in the trial of the specific indictment against him, but too often it is that the native white man escapes it."

I attended the Courts, but could not in the time at my disposal follow the full hearing of a sufficient number of cases to come to a conclusion on my own actual observations. I may say, though, there was a marked difference in the attitude and behaviour of the Court officials to white men and to Negroes—the latter were certainly not treated with any marked deference.

It is stated by Negroes that they are arrested for minor offences and irregularities for which the white man goes free, and this is likely to be the case. On the other hand, I have heard whites say that as no one expected high standards of conduct or behaviour from Negroes, breaches of such are condoned and arrests are not made, when, if the offender was a white man, he would be treated more severely, in that he had fallen below his natural standard.

From a careful reading of cases appearing in the newspapers, from talks with whites, and many conversations with Negroes; after hearing the recital of many special cases, and bearing in mind the social and racial conditions in the South, and making comparison with what I know occurs under similar conditions in South Africa, I would say :—

That in the higher Courts the Negro indicted gets justice.

That in the lower Courts his punishment is often excessive.

That the same may be said when the case is one between Negroes.

That when the case is between white and black the latter does not get impartial justice.

Finally, my judgment is that the Negro does not get equal treatment before the Courts and that here he has ground for legitimate complaint.

CHAPTER XVIII.

PERSONAL INJUSTICE.

IF a race is socially weak, politically powerless, discriminated against each day, unable to obtain equal justice before the Courts, and is faced by another race, strong, effective, grasping, and with all the machinery of government in its hands, it must be clear that it places in the power of the baser members of the governing race opportunities which, if they are not to be abused, must come to the heel of a tender conscience. We know that the majority of men are governed, not by conscience, but by greed and desire.

In the very nature of things there must be many cases of individual oppression in the South. Whilst I met many Southerners who I know would scorn to cheat or oppress a Negro, the tone of many others indicated that such methods were not condemned, but rather rested lightly upon them.

As a rule the industrial field is open to the Negro in the South, but many instances could be cited to show that he has often to walk warily, and is sometimes tripped up by the way.

A coloured doctor of medicine in New Orleans told me the case of a friend of his born in a town on the banks of the Mississippi. He left home for College, graduated, and returned a qualified medical man. He opened practice in his native town, his clients being those of his own race, as custom would not allow him to treat white patients, although the white practitioners had no scruple in treating Negroes. He heard rumours of trouble which culminated in him receiving notice to quit from the practising medical men of the town. He was given to understand he would leave the town without a stain on his character—they had nothing against him personally, but they would not have a Negro doctor in the place. He had no alternative but to go, and seek to make a living elsewhere.

Another medical man practising in a large town, told me that he began his career in a country district, and would have been glad to have remained there, it was his home, but it had been made clear to him that it was not safe for him to remain, and he abandoned his practice and came into the city.

An instance is given of a progressive Negro who saw an opening to hawk meat through the country-side. He built up a good business and was prospering. The white butchers became jealous, and told him he must stop, and he had no alternative but to do so. He then opened an ice-cream business in the summer months, and again received notice to relinquish it, and finally had to leave the section. This is, I think, true; my informant was a trustworthy person who spoke from first-hand knowledge, but I think it must be an extreme case; had such been frequent I feel sure more would have been brought to my notice. It is possible that this particular Negro may have been in some way, apart from business, an objectionable person, but it is extremely unlikely that, however objectionable, the same treatment would have been meted out to a white man.

There are many authentic cases of bodies of Negroes getting peremptory notice to leave a town or district within such a short space of time that they have to abandon or sacrifice their homes and belongings, and make a fresh beginning elsewhere. Sometimes this is ostensibly because the Negroes are a menace to public health, but generally simply because they are Negroes. The former would probably be given as the reason for the clearing out without any notice at all, of all the Negroes, men, women, and children, in Lake Charles, Louisiana. This is reported to have taken place one night in 1906 when several hundred armed white men invaded a low district in the town called locally " Holeinthewall," and rounded up all the Negroes and, "without giving them time even to dress, took them under guard to the train and sent them out of the city and section ". This seems to us a summary way of cleaning up the slums, and a method that must have meant grave hardship to many of the evicted.

As I have pointed out, the distribution of the races varies greatly in different parts of the South, and those in which whites greatly predominate are often extremely jealous of the intrusion of Negroes, and force is often employed to eject them. The following I quote from W. P. Calhoun : " A despatch from Birmingham, Alabama, says : 'The white farmers residing in the vicinity of Cordova, Walker County, where is located the million dollar cotton mill of the Indian Land Co. of Boston, Mass., and some of the mill operatives have rid themselves of the few Negroes who ventured to settle and work at the mills and on the railroad. The farmers formed a band of fifty and went from Negro cabin to cabin and ordered the head of each family to vamoose the ranch on pain of death, saying that Walker County had always been a white man's county and it was going to remain so.'"

From the " New Orleans Times Democrat " of 20 March, 1907, the following is taken : "Lawton, Oklahoma, 20 March. Negroes beware coppers. We, the sixty sons of Waurika demand the Negroes to leave here at once. We mean Go, leave in twenty-four hours or your life is uncertain. These were the words on placards which the eighty Negroes of Waurika, forty miles south of Lawton, saw posted conspicuously in a number of public places this morning. Dispatches from here to-night stated that the white men were in earnest, and that the Negroes will be killed if they remain."

Although the Negro people form 11 per cent of the total population of the United States and nearly one-third of the population of the South, although they have consistently supported the Republican party since emancipation, since which time the party has had almost uninterrupted control, although both great political parties have declared for equality, the Negro has never been permitted to hold any office of emolument under Government, excepting in a few isolated cases, invariably minor and poorly paid posts. These few exceptions go to prove the rule, that Negroes are never considered when the legitimate spoils of office are distributed. A Negro constable or postmaster is never seen. Promises have been made in plenty during election times by the party who had their support, but they have been forgotten—or rather they were intended to be forgotten—when the votes were cast. It is stated that this determination to exclude the Negro from office is more marked of late years than it was in the past. Whether this is the case or not the hostility to Negro office seekers or office holders now amounts almost to fanaticism.

Thus W. P. Livingstone, speaking on this question in his book "The Race Conflict," says : "Notwithstanding President Roosevelt's statements, he appointed fewer coloured people to positions in the South than any other President"; and again : "It is not the official treatment of the black man that has changed, but the state of public feeling in the South. The right to aspire to Federal office, unquestioned a few years ago, is now challenged and opposed with a vehemence and bitterness impossible for one to realize unless he has lived in the South, or come into touch with its people and newspapers."

J. Ambrose Price, a Southern writer, voices this sentiment thus : "We can never really claim to be one of the greatest Governments on earth while the Negro holds positions in the different departments of the Government. This is a disgrace to white intelligence and the claim of an honest Government. The United States Government was founded on intelligence, virtue, and natural distinction, and it must stand upon these principles, or it will suffer the disgrace which comes from Government positions being filled by Negroes."

Not a very sound argument, but it serves to show the temper of some. It certainly requires courage of the highest for a Negro to accept a public position of honour and emolument in the South. W. P. Calhoun says: "No white man, especially in the rural districts, will submit to any Negro holding office of trust, honour, or profit. In the large Southern cities this is submitted to, but the assertion is ventured, that if any national administration should make too many appointments of Negroes to office in any of these large cities, the repetition of Lake City, South Carolina, lynching may be looked for. It is considered a crime even for a Negro to apply for a Government position in the South. He seldom gets it in the North. In the city of Atlanta, Georgia, a Negro, H. A. Rucker, is in charge of the Customs. He has not been molested, but much grumbling was indulged in at the time of his appointment, and the grumbling is still going on, and not because he does not properly attend to his duties, but because he is a Negro. The Caucasian will never permit the Negro to take too much part in politics; as the years pass the feeling will be more intense, and the feeling between the races will grow apace till the climax is reached."

Wm. A. Sinclair, in "The Aftermath of Slavery," published in 1905, gives an instance which fully bears out the opinion of W. P. Livingstone. He says: "The house of postmaster Baker of South Carolina was surrounded at night, oil was poured into the house, and it was set on fire. When the family attempted to escape the mob fired at them. Baker was shot carrying his young baby, which was also killed; his wife, two daughters, and a son were shot. His offence was holding a Federal office as postmaster."

CHAPTER XIX.

BLOOD GUILTINESS.

No reader of Southern newspapers can go far through their columns without finding many records of shooting and killing between white and black. Sometimes it may be a case of quarrel between individuals and may only involve those immediately concerned. Always, however, when open hostilities commence between white and Negro there is a serious danger, that for purely racial reasons, others join in who are in no way connected with the original cause of dispute, and general shooting takes place, which may spread until it becomes a race riot, in which many lives are lost, and much cruelty inflicted. Once the ever-present, but it may be latent, race animosity is fanned into flame and takes possession of the mob, fiendish atrocities are often committed, and the lives of hundreds may be sacrificed, as in the notorious Atlanta riots. And the Negro invariably comes out the worsted party.

Though in the great majority of cases the white man is the aggressor, on occasions the Negro, to resent what he conceives to be insult and injury, bathes himself in blood. This was the case in Brownsville, Texas. Here a number of Negro soldiers of the 25th Infantry Battalion left barracks at night, and went through the town shooting right and left, in revenge for alleged slights put upon them by the inhabitants. In consequence the regiment was disbanded, causing much ill-feeling among the Negroes.

It may be truthfully said that, in very few cases of homicide when the victim is a Negro, and a white man is the culprit, is adequate punishment, according to British or British Colonial ideas, inflicted by the Courts. If the contrary is the case, the white man killed, and the Negro arrested, it must be a stronger jail and a more determined Sheriff than most in the South, if the Courts have any opportunity to decide the case, for the mob take the matter into their own hands and the accused is lynched without form of trial.

If I am to make the position of the races in the South clear, if what I say is to have anything of value or warning for my South African readers, I feel I must go into this phase of the question, mob murder, without glossing over any of its revolting details. I would also premise that, horrible and nauseating as are the cases I recite, I so far consider the susceptibilities of my readers that I only quote a few. Many more could be cited.

There are no exact or official statistics showing the actual number of cases of lynching which have occurred in the United States, and before the year 1830 we have no record at all. From 1830 to 1840, according to records kept by the " Liberator," an anti-slavery paper, it appears the law was generally allowed to take its course. From 1850-60 there appears a greater tendency for the people to take the law into their own hands. Out of forty-six Negroes put to death for murder, twenty were legally executed, and twenty-six summarily executed by the mob. Of these twenty-six, nine were burned at the stake. For the crime of rape upon white women, three Negroes were legally executed and twelve lynched, of whom four were burned to death.

For the years 1871-73 there were seventy-five lynchings. In the next decade the numbers rose rapidly. In 1882 one hundred and fourteen persons were lynched, in 1883 one hundred and thirty-four, and in 1884 no less than two hundred and eleven. From this point the " Chicago Tribune " takes up the tale of infamy, and from 1885 until the present day has kept a record which is probably approximately correct. From this and other calculations we may, I think, conclude that there have been nearly 4000 cases of lynching in the United States.

In the sixteen years from 1884-1900 there were 2516 cases recorded; of these 2465 were men and 51 women, 2080 occurred in the South and 436 in the North. It will be noted that the victims are not only men but women, and incredible as it will seem to some, and quite contrary to the accepted ideas, twenty-three of the female victims were white women. The alleged crimes of these white females are thus scheduled :—

9 for murder or complicity therein.
1 ,, being disreputable.
1 because of mob indignation.
1 ,, ,, race prejudice.
1 for miscegenation.
1 ,, arson.
2 ,, theft.
7 ,, unknown crimes.

It does not appear that any burning desire for race integrity was responsible for this particular group of lynching atrocities.

Fortunately it seems pretty certain that of late years the number of cases is not increasing, indeed from the statistics of the "Chicago Tribune" it would appear they are becoming less frequent, but even so, the list is a saddening one. I give the numbers as published for twenty-seven consecutive years : these are apart from deaths in race conflicts :—

	White.	Negro.		White.	Negro.		White.	Negro.
1885	106	78	1895	59	112	1905	5	61
1886	67	71	1896	51	80	1906	8	64
1887	42	80	1897	44	122	1907	3	60
1888	47	95	1898	25	102	1908	7	93
1889	81	95	1899	23	84	1909	14	73
1890	37	90	1900	8	107	1910	9	65
1891	71	121	1901	28	84	1911	8	63
1892	100	155	1902	10	86			
1893	46	154	1903	18	86			
1894	56	134	1904	4	83			

I wish I could truthfully say that, concurrently with the slight decrease in numbers, the atrocities accompanying the deaths were diminishing in cruelty. Recent revolting cases, and the consensus of informed opinion, lead me to the conclusion that the contrary is the case, and the fierce savagery that is so often the most painful feature of these orgies of blood is not diminishing in intensity. Cutler says: "If the cases of burning alive form a list that is at all complete, there is ground for believing that, as the practice of lynching continues, the punishments inflicted tend to increase in severity, and the victims are tortured more and more until death comes to their relief".

The figures given by the "Chicago Tribune" indicate the race of the sufferers. It will come as a surprise to many of my readers, as it did to me, to find so many white men on the list. The number of whites has, however, greatly decreased of late years, very much more so than in the case of Negroes. In 1885 there were no less than 106 cases of lynching white men; these had fallen to 3 in 1907 but the number rose again slightly in the subsequent years. The climax as regards the Negro seems to have been reached in 1893, but a comparison of the years 1885-8 with 1908-11 does not show any great cause for congratulation that these lawless acts against Negroes are in process of dying out.

In the figures given, probably all reported cases are included, but I am told by those who know the South, that all do not appear in the public press. The country is large and nights are dark, and Sheriffs are not over-anxious to push themselves forward when at best they will only earn intense unpopularity, and at worst may get a bullet lodged in a vital spot.

I find among ordinarily well-informed people, who do not know the United States, and who have not made a special study of the subject, an impression that lynching is confined to the South, and that the reason or justification for it is the brutal and lecherous assaults on white women by Negroes. It is a fact, however, that this particular and abominable crime is not even alleged to be the cause in the majority of cases : those in which it is claimed to be the reason for lynching do not amount to more than about 25 per cent of the total number. And this particular crime has not come in with lynching; it was not unknown among the Negroes in slavery days. Cutler in his "History of Lynching" says : "Strictly speaking this crime has not come into existence since the Civil War as is stated by some. It is not a new crime to the Negro. It has merely increased and become more common along with the general increase in criminality manifest in the Negro since emancipation."

As one who has lived for the greater part of his life in the closest touch with an African people, and shares the feeling of horror with which an attempt at the violation of a white woman by a member of this race is felt—felt to the innermost fibres of being—I can sympathize with the detestation felt, and the exasperation raised, by this crime in the South.

I can even imagine myself, under the goad of some such diabolical instances of violation as have actually happened in the South, temporarily losing my reason, and killing the perpetrator at sight. There are rights of manhood and of race, and there are feelings so deep and strong, that to restrain and delay the leaping natural impulse is impossible.

Such cases, however, do not happen in the lives of most men, even in the South. This justification, if justification it is, cannot be allowed to have force in the vast majority of cases of lynching in the South. The pleas are often paltry in the extreme, and indicate a loss of self-control that is unworthy of reasoning humanity. Sadly too often a cruel deliberate vindictiveness is the note, which is out of all proportion to the offence, and which expresses itself in deeds that shame the cruellest tortures inflicted by the aboriginal Red Indian, or the Spanish Inquisition. And this in the 20th century—to-day.

It would be grossly unfair to charge all the mob licence and ferocity to the South. It is stated that in sixteen years there were 2080 recorded cases in the South, and 436 in the North. The proportion of Negroes in the North during this time, as compared with those in the South, would certainly not be more than 1 to 8, probably less than this figure. This would indicate that, taking this as the basis of computation, the Negro is in greater danger of mob violence in the cultured North than in the backward South. It is also stated, and probably with truth, that the greater efficiency of the police in the North prevents many riots and attempts at lynching from culminating in the tragic finale. No less than twenty attempted lynchings were frustrated by the activity of the constabulary within the limits of the city of New York in one year.

Nor can the North plead that they are innocent of the premeditated and revolting cruelties by which the victim is too often put to death in the South. It lies as a stigma on the Quaker State that at Coatesville, a few miles from the city founded by William Penn, quite recently a wounded Negro was dragged from hospital by an infuriated mob, bound to his stretcher, and thrust into the fire. When in his agony he burst his bonds, he was thrown back again, and died in unutterable torture.

Still, when all possible extenuating circumstances are granted, this crime remains a black blot on the South. I know it is felt deeply and keenly by many Southern men and women, who would give their most precious possessions if they could wipe out this disgrace which blackens the character of their people.

When one reads of the offences for which men and women are done to death by mobs of their own people, it seems incredible that for such apparently trivial causes such dreadful punishment should be exacted. It seems to me to throw a lurid light on the hearts of many in the South, which must be filled with corrosive race hatred, to be guilty of such diabolical acts even when moved by the electric influence of a crowd of like passions. I give a few of the offences alleged : gambling, conspiracy, voodooism, cutting levées, drunkenness, strike rioting, poisoning cattle, writing insulting letters, and for these the utmost penalty was paid.

To many the idea of lynching is associated with a hempen rope, a short shrift, and a comparatively painless death. Such must revise their conceptions. I give a few instances.

From the report of the case of George White (coloured) who was lynched for the murder of Helen Bishop, a white woman in Delaware, only four hours from New York, the following may be cited : "After the man was dead by burning, throngs of women surrounded the smouldering embers. Some hurled on more wood to keep the fire going so as to reduce to dust the remnants of the body of the Negro. White boys and girls snatched pieces of fuel from the fire as souvenirs of the mob's violence." To show the intensity of feeling roused, and how it is aggravated, even by some whose position and calling are associated with peace and forgiveness, I quote : " Between the date of the above murder and the lynching, the Rev. Robert A. Ellwood, pastor of the Mount Olivet Presbyterian Church, preached a Sunday morning sermon which is thus reported : ' He advocated moderation and then drew an agonizing picture of the murder of Miss Bishop. He counselled patience, and then denounced the Supreme Court, declaring that by refusing to depart from the regular procedure to try White, it was setting an example in patience for the people. He drew a fore-cast of precisely what.happened, and sternly laid the blame at the feet of the Judges of the Court, and added a final appeal to the passions of his audience by dramatic-ally waving over his head blood-stained leaves from the thicket in which Helen Bishop had been killed, and which had been specially obtained for the purpose by one of his elders. The people went from the church livid with passion, and early this morning the deed was done.'"

At Paris, Texas, the Negro, Henry Smith, was lynched for an outrage on a young girl which resulted in her death. The circumstances were horrible. He was taken by a mob, and before burning was tortured, red-hot irons being thrust into his eyes, down his throat, and on his abdomen. Photographs of the scene were taken and published. It is alleged that gramophone records were taken of his screams. The crowd numbered thousands, and included many women and children. It is thus reported in a local paper: "A mob of angry men and women numbering thousands wreaked the most frightful vengeance on the body of the Negro, Henry Smith. They took the prisoner from the guards bringing him here, dragged him with a rope round his neck to the scene of the crime, subjected him to every conceivable torture, and then burnt the pitiable wretch at the stake. When the news came last night that he had been caught the people seemed crazy with joy, and thirsted for his life. By trains and wagons, on horses and afoot, the people piled into the city."

Jefferson parish, New Orleans, was the scene of a lynching, and the preparations are thus described: "An iron stake was driven into the ground to which he will be tied. Fat, fuel, and resinous material to surround this. Long irons like branding irons are in readiness, and when red-hot the man will be tortured with them while the fire below him burns. A rude gallows tree above the pyre has been built from which the murderer will be suspended over the fire by his arms."

Commenting on the lynching of one Sam Hose, a Negro, the "Washington Star" says: "The stories of the Inquisition, of the African cannibals, of the Roman Emperors, of the fanatical Aztecs, of all the savage and barbarous peoples who have left records for blood lust in the pages of history, warrant the expectation that even this abomination may soon be exceeded by another, more sickening in its methods, more revolting in the spectacle of presumably civilized men and women in the torture of a fellow-being ".

This case and the others so far mentioned were in revenge for the outrage of a woman of their own race, and this, as stirring the deepest feelings in our nature, may be held as condonation by some. No such excuse can be offered for the following.

A Negro man in Mississippi became involved in a quarrel with a white man who was on the point of shooting him when the Negro fired and fatally wounded him. He fled into the woods along with his wife. Bloodhounds were put on the trail, and after a long chase they were captured. According to an eye-witness they were tied to trees and forced to hold out their hands while one finger after another was severed. Their ears were then cut off, and both fingers and ears were distributed as souvenirs. A large corkscrew was next bored into their arms, legs, and body, the spiral tearing out large pieces of quivering flesh. Neither man nor woman begged for mercy nor uttered a cry. They were finally roasted alive.

Reported in the "New York Times" of 8 February, 1903: "A coloured man, Luther Herbert, and his wife were burnt at the stake at Memphis, Tennessee, for murdering a white man. Before the mob separated seven Negroes had been done to death. The sixteen-year-old son of the coloured couple was forced to attend and witness the burning."

It was not my experience to see either a race shooting or a lynching. I met, however, a young Englishman who had been an eye-witness to a Negro hunt, and who described it to me with visible signs of emotion. He saw the Negro, little more than a boy, racing panic-stricken, the mob pursuing him and firing as they ran. He appeared to be wounded and took refuge in a drain. Shots were fired into the drain, and he was dragged forth bleeding, and hurried to his death, which my informant did not see. He was so sickened and horror-struck at the tragic nature of what he beheld that he hurried away from the scene. As long as he lived he said the burning memory of it would remain.

When suspected persons are rushed along to their death without inquiry or form of trial, by an infuriated mob seeing blood and panting for revenge, it is not likely that the victim is invariably the guilty person. There are many sections of the country in which race relations are tolerable, and whites and blacks live in amity. It is probable that before blood is shed, there is generally a period of strained relations between the races, and then a small matter may cause an outburst. The tense inflammable race feeling only needs a whiff of suspicion to make it leap into flame, and there is little disposition to inquire too closely into the actual guilt of the suspected one. In any case, say the baser sort, it is a lesson to the nigger.

Frederick Law Olmsted was in Knoxville, Tennessee, just after the burning of a Negro. A citizen to whom he spoke admitted there was no proof of the guilt of the Negro beyond his own confession. Olmsted suggested he might have been mad. "What if he was," replied the citizen, "the thousands of Negroes who were rounded up to see him burnt were not, and they had been taught a lesson." Judging from conversations of my own I fear this spirit is present at many such scenes.

An incident which gave some insight into the common Southern feeling with regard to lynching came into my experience. I was staying a few days at a coloured institution, run by a coloured man and his wife with financial assistance from the North. A musical entertainment was given, and somewhat to my surprise, several white men, living and working in the immediate neighbourhood, attended. Among them was the son of a highly respected citizen from the county town. In conversation this young fellow spoke of his father's long friendship with the father of my host, whom he described as an excellent character. To prove the estimation in which his father held this coloured man, he said that on one occasion a lynching took place in the neighbourhood, and the white people were intensely excited and exasperated. Rumour went that the coloured man had expressed disapproval of the action of the mob, who were preparing to visit their disapprobation upon him, when my informant's father intervened saying, "he knew this nigger and he was a good one," and the allegation was a damned lie. A committee was formed to make further inquiry, and the question was directly put to the coloured man. The answer was: "Bring me the man who heard me say it". This somewhat inconclusive answer seemed to settle the matter, probably by this time the anger of the mob had cooled down. This was very interesting to me. My informant did not appear to think for a moment that a nigger had the slightest right to resent, or even question, the illegal killing of one of his race, and apparently both his father and himself would have been prepared to support the due punishment of any Negro who so offended. The sole question was whether the offence had been committed, and the defence was that the Negro was a good one, and not likely to commit such a breach of the good manners expected from such a one! Singular!

Although between three or four thousand lynchings are admitted to have taken place in the United States and although one happens in this very year of our Lord every few days in some section of the country, I never heard of any one instance in which adequate punishment was meted out to the perpetrators. Inquests are sometimes held, sometimes even mock trials. In many cases those actively participating are known and openly boast of it, but they are not arrested. Public opinion would resent the execution of any white man for doing what is often regarded as a public service.

The verdicts of some juries reflect the popular opinion, and some may be cited. One runs thus: "The deceased came to his death by swinging in the air". Another: "We do not know who killed deceased, but we congratulate the parties on their work ". Again : " The deceased came to his death by taking too great a bit of hemp rope " ; and more seriously : " The men who participated in the burning were among the best citizens of the country, and nothing but a desire to protect those who were nearest and dearest would have moved them to undertake such measures ".

We have seen that the ostensible reason given for lynching is the prevalence of what is called in the South "the usual crime," when as a matter of fact only about twenty-five per cent of these mob murders are even alleged to punish the crime of rape. But I do not wish to speak lightly of this atrocious offence, nor attempt to defend on any ground those who are guilty of it. I believe it is a real danger in the South, and that the dread of it takes the happiness out of the lives of some sensitive white women, and makes the white man feel uneasy if his women folk are left alone and unguarded. I remember visiting the home of a clergyman situated by itself in the country. My friend came from the North, but had long resided in the South, and all the time had been engaged in religious and educational work among the Negroes. I noticed that the windows of his house were barred, and the verandahs were especially protected. I asked the reason, and was told that such precautions were necessary, the danger was a real one, and the dread of it ever present. He never left his wife alone.

In the South as in South Africa, the crime has become more frequent since the races mixed together in everyday life on the same plane, and since the black man was freed from control. In the Southern States the control was the hard hand of the slave master, in South Africa the control was exercised by the chief and tribal system. The release has in both cases led to licence. It has been argued that the crime is committed in retaliation for the cruelties inflicted by whites—is, in fact, race revenge. W. P. Livingstone says : " The crime is primarily one of race

12

reprisals, because of the miseries and wrongs they have suffered. In the case of criminal assault, they know that such a form of retaliation touches the whites to the quick." This theory supposes malice aforethought, a brooding over race injuries and reasoned plans for vengeance. It does not accord with my conception of the character of the Negro, and I do not agree with this explanation.

I think Alfred Holt Stone is nearer the mark. In a paper read before the American Economic Association he says relations in the Yazoo delta of the Mississippi are amicable, and attributes this to the fact that the whites are a class apart, large employers of labour, and there is no white labouring class, particularly of field labourers. He gives the following case: A young mulatto came to work for him who had been sentenced for assault on a white girl. I gather he came as one of a chain gang of convicts hired from the State Government. Stone asked him about the crime, which at first he was unwilling to discuss, but then said: "You don't understand, things are so different here. I was hired to an old man over there by the year. He had only 40 acres, and he and his folks did all their own work, cooking, washing, and everything. His daughter worked right alongside me in the field every day for three or four months. Finally a day came when no one else was around, hell got into me, and I tried to rape her. But you folks over here can't understand, things are so different. Over here a nigger is a nigger, and a white man is a white man, and it's the same with the woman." Stone goes on to say that there was no fault on the part of the white girl —no hint of collusion. At the same time, in his section, i.e. the Yazoo delta, Negro rapes on Negro women were not uncommon.

I would like to cite a case given by Dr. W. D. Weatherford in his book "Negro Life in the South," which throws a light on the possibility of blackmailing. I do not think such cases are common: still it shows the power put into the hands of unprincipled white persons:

"William McArthur has been for many years the coloured janitor of a white church in a former Slave State. He owns a farm and city house, has a bank account, and could loan money more easily than most of the church members he serves. His reputation for character is as good as theirs. When therefore a disreputable white woman attempted to blackmail him by threatening to charge him with assault on a child, he naturally went to the church officers for advice. They believed in him as they did in each other, but put him on a midnight train for California. To his Northern pastor it was incredible that a man of his reputation should have to flee like a thief. The answer was: this community is likely to lynch first and investigate afterwards. So McArthur went—he could afford to—saying with pathetic humour, I always wanted to travel West anyhow. After six months he felt safe to come back and take up his work. Not long after the community did lynch three Negroes on an Easter morning. The grand jury, investigating afterwards, found that two of them were certainly innocent. Only bayonets saved the Negro quarter from burning. Then McArthur came to his pastor to know where, under the Stars and Stripes, a self-respecting and respected black man could buy his own vine and fig tree and go and sit down under them in the ordinary security of Christian civilization. Now McArthur's character is fixed in adversity, while it seams his brow and weights his steps, does not make a social rebel of him, but his boy, when last I saw him, was behind the bars. Now I charge that America did not give McArthur's boy a square deal. Of course he has a responsible soul, will, and conscience enough to make some impression on his own moral destiny. Let him bear his full share of the blame, but let us weigh this; he had felt the helplessness of the property owning Negro before the blackmailer, had seen his father a fugitive at midnight, his life hanging upon an idle word: had heard just men confess their inability to protect one in whom they had all confidence:

12 *

had vainly longed for a fatherland which could guarantee somewhere a peaceful death to one who had lived in honour : had smelled the burning flesh of innocent men of his own race. Besides all this, his own weakness had been trafficked in by a venal police power. Such things are not calculated to make a young Negro into a model citizen. You tell me that, after all, the cord and torch are rare, that statistically one is more likely to die from falling off a step ladder at home than a Negro is to be lynched. I reply that when one has come under the shadow of such a tragedy he can never forget it. It stamps his imagination for all time and sears his soul against the social order in which it is tolerated."

A Commission of Inquiry was appointed by the Union Government of South Africa to inquire into this crime, and they found that there were many contributory causes, some of which might be debited to the black man, and others for which the whites were to blame. No one outstanding reason could be given. Propinquity, and the close intermixing in the relations of life of low-class whites and natives predisposed to it, and this, as we have seen, is also responsible in part in the United States. The Commission found that indiscreet action by some white women was in part responsible, particularly in households in which native males were the domestic servants. I will show later that the Southern white man cannot be acquitted of race depravity. No such charge can be brought against the Southern white woman. Professor A. B. Hart says : " The male half of the South have all their life been exposed to a peculiarly facile temptation. Heaven has somehow shielded the white woman of the South from the noxious influence of a servile race. In slavery times and now there is not a fairer flower that blooms than the white Southern girl."

Those who commit this crime are usually those belonging to the more degraded and nomadic class. The educated Negroes claim that, as a class, they are innocent, and Hampton and Tuskegee, Fisk and Howard point out that their graduates are entirely free from this stigma. Although white women from the North have taught in the South since emancipation they have not been molested, though often living in communities almost entirely black.

The unutterably vile physical and moral conditions in which some Negroes live, especially in the towns, and their vicious nature and hopeless lives, seem in part responsible. Better homes, a cleaner environment, religious and moral teaching, would probably reduce the evil. And it must be insisted upon, continence on the part of the white man, who is only too prone to debauch the coloured woman.

Meantime this open sore suppurates, exasperating the white man and giving him occasion for mob violence and cruelty. These reprisals, however savage, will not eliminate it. The opinions of thoughtful men who have studied the question on the spot bear this out.

Professor W. C. Wilcox, the statistician, in a close analysis of a series of lawless acts in Georgia says: "But the point of view I would urge is that the illegal execution of Negroes, even when torture is added, has an inciting rather than a deterring influence upon a large number of potential criminals". The Governor of Georgia in a message says: "Lynch law does not stop murder or arson or robbery or rape". Thus the "Atlanta Constitution" rather despairingly says: "The punishment of criminals who are overtaken, no matter how swift or bloody, seems to have no effect whatever upon the criminal class of the Negroes. They seem to go as cheerfully about their crimes as if they were candidates for a martyr's crown; they murder, ravish, and rob with the zeal and fervour of religious fanatics."

If the South would take a greater interest in the Negro, in his material and moral welfare, give him better and more suitable education and greater opportunity, cleanse the plague spots in their cities, they would do far more to exorcise this evil than by taking illegal and savage vengeance on guilty and guiltless alike.

In such mob vengeance the sin against the Negro is great, but the sin against the whites is greater. For every black criminal slain by mob violence, a thousand white criminals are made. Purge the South of this offence and the path is straightened to better race relations.

I cannot do better than quote Edgar Gardner Murphy who says : " The mob which abandons the processes of self-control weakens the personal self-control which slays and conquers crime, and increases by its ferocities the very animalism it has attempted to destroy. Its instruction in horror touches the minds of tens of thousands, its barbarities burn to-day the guilty and to-morrow burn the innocent."

CHAPTER XX.

BLOOD ADMIXTURE—THE SIN OF THE WHITE MAN.

THE Negro in the United States is sometimes so little a Negro that he would pass unchallenged as a white man in any all-white community. I have seen children who are classed as Negroes with blue eyes, freckled faces, and red hair. I have seen people who, when they travelled in the coloured car, have been told by the conductor to go into the white car, "where they belong," and who had to explain that they were Negroes.

A man visited a Southern town and mixed socially with the inhabitants. He became quite popular in local society. One day a lady saw him and denounced him as a Negro. A Committee was formed, and they ran him out of the town, threatening the direst vengeance if he dared to come back. He went to his home in South Carolina, and gathering documentary evidence he returned, accompanied by friends and relatives, to prove that he was unquestionably a white man, belonging to one of the most reputable families of his native State. The Committee again investigated the case, and the man was received as white by and into the society which had ejected him as a Negro!

Probably from two and a half to three million Negroes have visible signs of white blood. The race gains every drop of white blood that is poured into its veins. The Negro who said, "Not a drop of our blood is lost to us, the white man takes care of that; if you haven't got but one-sixteenth part of black blood you are a Negro all right," stated but the fact.

That the prejudice against those having any drop of African blood, as well as the all-black Negro, is present

183

in the North as well as in the South can be amply demonstrated. The Rev. John Snyder gave a case in the "Forum" thus: "There was in a certain school in Pittsburg a very beautiful and intelligent young lady. In scholarship and deportment she stood for a year at the head of the school. At the end of that time some one told the principal that his favourite had a few undiscoverable and unsuspected drops of African blood. She was turned out of doors as ignominiously as if she was guilty of inchastity, or was affected with some infectious disease."

It may be that in the North a few of the near whites whom I have described go over into the white camp, and are lost to the Negro race, but they must be few indeed. I was told by a well-known author of African descent that more went over than was generally believed. I asked how many he had known in his own experience, and he replied probably twelve or fifteen. Such a number makes, of course, no practical difference even in the North. In the South I never heard of such a thing, nor do I think it ever happens. The gulf between the races is so deep and wide, the risk of being found out is so great, and the punishment if discovered so severe, that however much the near white may desire it, he remains in the black camp—a Negro. In his native area he would of course never attempt it; his ancestry is known, and he must remain in the place to which he was born. It seems strange that such do not remove to a distance from their birthplace, and then attempt to enter a society for which, in appearance, culture, manners, and ideals, they are more suited than many already in its ranks. The plain truth is they dare not. If a person such as I have described did so cross the line his life would not be worth living, it would be a long-drawn-out dread. At any time an old acquaintance, black or white, might recognize and betray him. If then he had become intimate with the white society of the place, and especially had he married a white woman, a cruel death would probably be his fate.

Little wonder that they remain on the black side, although they may have as little of the African in their nature as they have in their appearance.

The sins of the fathers are indeed being visited upon the children. It is this element in the race problem that makes it so difficult, that creates such acrid bitter feeling, and for it the white man is responsible. The Southern white woman is free from complicity. I said the white man, for although the South bears the full blame, I am told by unprejudiced and competent authorities that the Northern white man cannot be altogether exculpated. During the four years of civil war, fought on Southern soil, with Negro refugees crowding into the camps, the Northern soldiery were not always continent. So much must be said in justice to the South, but since those days the full weight of responsibility and blame must rest upon the South.

Mitigation of sentence may be pleaded, and I want to give due weight to all that can be possibly urged of explanation and defence. The passion for race integrity does not burn with that fierce glow in the breasts of black as it does in white bosoms. Both the coloured woman and the white man are placed in circumstances full of facile temptation. Complaisance and weakness meet opportunity and power. There is too seldom a bulwark of high moral principle against the power and temptations of status and wealth. Public opinion among their own does not adequately safeguard the weaker race. Edgar Gardner Murphy says: "The possibility of race fusion is not now repugnant to the instinct of the average Negro as it is to the instinct of the average white man, and this fact, the fact that the instinct of the black man is usually ready to abandon the individuality of his race, puts the white population upon its guard, and leads it to perceive a sinister significance in some of the most harmless occasions of racial contact".

There is much evidence to indicate that temporary illicit unions are a source of pride to some of the weaker race and sex, and that a yearning for recognition and contact with the race that stands to them for the highest they can conceive, leads many to yield.

Wm. Archer recognizes this when he says: "The ultimate forces at war in the South are the instinctive, half-conscious desire of the black race to engraft itself on the white stock, and the no less instinctive horror of the white stock at such a surrender of its race integrity. The horror is all the more acute, morbid if you will, because the white race is conscious of its own frailty, and knows it is in a sense fighting against perfidious Nature." And again: "The essence is simply this—the youth and manhood of the white South is subjected to an altogether unfair and unwholesome ordeal by the constant pressure of a multitude of physically well-developed women, among whom, at the lower levels, there is no strong tradition of chastity, and to whom the penalties of incontinence are slight". But he justly goes on to say: "In a country where such terrible humiliations await those in whom there is the slightest trace of black blood, it is surely manifest, that the people who impose these humiliations and scout the idea of legal marriage, ought to visit with the severest penalties any relation (necessary illicit) between a white man and a coloured woman, any augmentation by the white man of that half-breed caste on whom the colour disabilities press with such peculiar cruelty".

It is said by one writer, speaking of race amalgamation: "The intense, the yearning desire of large bodies of Negroes is for social recognition among the whites, more especially for intermarriage with their haughty, old-time despisers. Who does not know this, simply does not understand the dominant facts of Southern life."

I quote this last statement to indicate a very prevalent opinion held in the South, an opinion which explains much of the race antagonism, and which has a basis of truth, on which, however, I think the writer cited has laid undue emphasis.

Still the fact remains that opportunity and temptation are ever present, and the tragic fact is that the white man yields, and the race that demands race integrity is chiefly guilty of race betrayal.

Ray Stannard Baker gives the case of one who is representative of far too many: "In one town I visited I heard a white man expressing with great bitterness his feeling against the Negro, arguing that the Negro must be kept down, else it would lead to the mongrelization of the white race. The next morning, as chance would have it, another white man pointed out to me a neat cottage, the home of the white man who talked with me the previous evening. And I saw this man's coloured children in the yard."

A naïve letter appeared in "The Times Democrat" of New Orleans, dated 21 June, 1907, expressing in unconventional style what is the opinion of many: "Will you kindly publish the following without attaching my signature or divulging it in any way? I have several brothers who are old-maidish enough to have nervous prostration if they should see my name attached to such an unmaidenly, immodest letter, but I do my thinking without any assistance from them, and hope for the sake of peace in my family they will not recognize me in print. I am a resident in a large town in the Yazoo-Mississippi delta, where miscegenation is common, where if a man isolate himself from feminine society, the first and only conclusion reached is, he has a woman of his own in saddle of a duskier shade. The conclusion is without exception true. If some daring woman, not afraid of being dubbed a Carrie Nation, were to canvass the delta counties of Mississippi, taking the census, she would find so many cases of miscegenation and their resultant mongrel families, that she would bow her head in shame for the flower of Southern chivalry gone to seed."

Marriage between the races is forbidden in all the Southern States, and also in many of the Northern ones, but although attempts have been made to pass legislation making concubinage and casual connexion penal offences, they have not been successful, and the only tribunal is public opinion. For a community priding itself on race purity, for one revelling in deeds of blood to punish offenders of a weaker race, for one in which the children of their own loins born to the mother's kin are doomed for ever to a position of degrading inferiority, public opinion has little of the true ring.

"The Times Democrat" of 15 February, 1906, points this out : " It is a public scandal that there should be no law against miscegenation on the Statute book of Louisiana, and that it should be left to mobs to break up couples who offend. The failure to pass a law of this kind is attributed to the white degenerates, men who denounce social equality yet practise it, men who are more dangerous to their own race than the most inflammatory Negro orator or social equality preacher, and who have succeeded by some sort of legislative trickery in pigeon-holeing or killing the Bill intended to protect Louisiana from a possible danger. Such men should be exposed before the people of the State in their true colours."

And again in the Court at Meridiana, Miss., District Attorney J. H. Currie thus spoke : " The accursed shadow of miscegenation hangs over the South to-day like a pall of hell. We talk much of the Negro question and of all its possible ramifications and consequences, but the trouble is not far afield. Our own people, our white men with their black concubines, are destroying the integrity of the Negro race, and raising up a menace to the white race, lowering the standard of both races and preparing the way for riot, criminal assaults, and finally a death-struggle for race supremacy. The trouble is at our own door. We have tolerated this crime long enough, and if this country is to be run by policy and not by law then it is time to rise up and denounce this sin of the earth."

As I write a case is reported from the town of Wagner, Ok., that throws a lurid light on these baser race relations. A number of young white men had invaded the

Negro section of the town and apparently had a hilarious time. Two of them separated and went into a Negro house, and as they left a woman came out, sprang upon one, and stabbed him to the heart. A mob got together, broke into the jail where the woman was incarcerated, and lynched her. The local references make it clear what the object of the men was. The deceased man had been married only a few months.

Some years ago in South Africa, I had a talk with a born Southerner who was visiting Natal at a time when the oft-recurring question of the employment of male natives as domestic servants was being discussed, and when, as usual, many advocated on various grounds their displacement by native women and girls. He admitted the evils of our present system, but very gravely pointed out what was happening in his own country, where Negro women worked in the households. He was a fervidly patriotic Southerner of old family, and jealous for the reputation of his own people, but sorrowfully said that to the demoralization of these women, often by the men of the household, much of the evil was due. He deplored it, and frankly said that too often the men took advantage of their status and position to press attentions that otherwise might have been rejected. I found these views were shared by many in the South, and it made me feel that, before attempting to alter our present system, we should see that conditions for the protection and safety of female native domestics, and for the preservation of racial integrity, were much better than they are at present in South Africa.

Whether the evil is in process of diminution or not is a matter on which I found much difference of opinion. It is impossible for a visitor to get accurate particulars of such an unsavoury subject, which is kept secret by those immediately concerned, and often unknown in its details to others living on the spot. The varying opinions I heard were based on local experience, which, judging from what happens elsewhere, is not everywhere alike even in the same country and under similar local conditions. In one place the influence of a number of high living men and women, and the establishment of a sensitive public opinion, will keep the locality clean. In another, baser influences may predominate, and the evil may grow. In accordance with these varying experiences one heard, on the one hand, that miscegenation was increasing, on the other that it was less prevalent than in past times.

No one Southerner knows the facts as they are throughout the South, the country is too large and conditions too various; many do not know or only guess in a general way, at what is happening near their homes.

The consensus of opinion is, however, that whether miscegenation is actually increasing or not it is far too prevalent everywhere in the South, and that public opinion does not condemn it as it ought. It is stated by Southern men that the offence is often condoned by white society, and those known to be guilty are accepted by and marry white women.

W. P. Calhoun says: "Go into any town, city, or community of the South, and you are confronted by mulatto children of all degrees of colour. These children often bear the surnames of their male parents. The Negro woman living in this State is not lowered in the estimation of her race, but is envied and considered a fortunate being. This state of things is known to old and young. The white man is condemned by his race and loses that position in society he ought to have. It is against the chances of his marrying, and yet by one of those unwritten laws of society for which there is no accounting, to a certain extent the matter is winked at, and the white man, though known to be guilty, passes as respectable, and in numbers of cases finally marries some pure and virtuous girl of his own race. These same white men should be more seriously condemned for their conduct to the Negro who is so much inferior to them."

To preach sex morality is everywhere a thankless task; to preach it in an atmosphere charged with racial prejudice is doubly difficult, though infinitely more essential. Northern men and women have suffered for spreading the doctrine of social equality, but what can their influence be as compared with the actual practice of Southern men themselves, when they prove to Negro women that they are desired and may enter into the closest of all relations with the race calling itself superior.

With the South I believe in race separation, but if that separation is to break down before the lusts of the stronger, and result in the demoralization of the weaker, in bringing into life those who, while sharing their blood, shall be doomed for ever to stand below them, and if it is to foster such scenes of bloodshed as I have described, then better destroy the barriers of race.

Whatever may be the opinion about the Jim Crow car, the denial to places of public entertainment, and separation of the races in school and church, it is essential that if the South is to escape the condemnation of the civilized world, it must see to it that the Negro receives equal justice in the courts, that lynching be made impossible, and that the standard of honour be so raised that the chastity of the Negro woman is safeguarded as that of her white sister.

CHAPTER XXI.

THE BASIS OF RACE HOSTILITY.

FEAR is the mother of hatred. I have shown in a previous chapter that the white man in the South is saturated with race hostility to the Negro, and that though the Negro responds in kind, his animosity is not nearly so virulent, nor does it take on such violent forms of expression.

If the average white man in the South were asked his reason for this feeling he would probably answer that this emotion, and its expression in repressive and hostile acts, is to prevent any possibility of race equality. He fears that if he does not make it evident that he will not tolerate any action which indicates equality, that equality will be demanded, and he would probably sub-divide the claims into social, political, and industrial equality.

If social equality is granted it is equivalent in his eyes to intermixture of the races, and the loss of what he professes above all to cling to—his race integrity. I have shown in the last chapter that, however vehemently he may voice his doctrine, his acts are in strange contrast to it.

Race admixture has gone a long way, and for this the stronger race is responsible. Does nursing race hostility prevent it? Is it likely that with the advance of the Negro in wealth, education, and social status such admixture will become more prevalent? The answer lies with the white man.

Prone before him lies the weaker race, all that they value is in the hands of the white man. It does not appear that in the past race degradation has prevented race amalgamation.

Long ago G. W. Cable wrote: "Is it not wonderful? A hundred years we have been fearing to do entirely right, lest something wrong should come of it, fearing to give the black man an equal chance with us in the race for life, lest we might have to grapple with the vast vague Afrite of amalgamation, and in all these hundred years with the enemies of slavery getting from us such names as Negro worshippers, Negrophiles, and Miscegenationists, and while we were holding ourselves rigidly separate from the lower race in obedience to a natal instinct which excommunicated them socially and civilly, just in proportion to the rigour, fierceness, and injustice with which this excommunication has fallen on the darker race—the amalgamation has taken place."

Concurrently with the rise of the Negro a hope will enter into his life and will engender race pride, a feeling of race solidarity, and a desire to be sufficient to himself, but if all he can hope for, if all he values in life, is in the possession of the stronger race, the pride that suffices will never be evolved.

Edgar Gardner Murphy says: "The true and permanent way to lead the Negro race to keep wisely to itself is to make it sufficient within itself. The race which is for ever forced to go outside itself to touch the broadest and richest life of the generation, will never be consciously and finally anchored in the doctrine of race integrity. The true basis of race integrity is not in race degeneration but in race sufficiency."

There is no evidence that with justice at the polls the Negro race would dominate the political situation. His freedom would indeed free the South from political thraldom. E. G. Murphy again says: "Every possibility of Negro domination vanishes to a more shadowy and more distant point with every year. Among all the absurdities of conjecture and among all the misgivings of theoretic horror, there is just now no phantom so spectral in its substance or so pitiably trivial in its proportions as this peril of Negro domination. The

13

soldier of old who bound his captive to his wrist, bound more than his wretched captive. If we are so morbidly afraid of the spectral possibilities of the Negro's freedom that we must keep him for ever in prison, then let us remember that on both sides the prison door there is a man in duress; he who keeps a jail is hardly freer than his prisoner. This is the domination we have to fear."

In a later chapter I deal fully with industrial competition. Whatever may be the case in South Africa with its overwhelming virile black population, and with all Africa and its teeming millions behind, it is clear to me that the question in the South is not the industrial survival of the white man, but the possibility of a field of work, with hope in the future, for the black man. Encouragement and help for him along this line will not supersede the white man but give increased opportunity to both. If the white man is but true to himself he need never fear that his children will be ousted by the black in the South.

As I show later there is a danger of conflict in the industrial field and I do not wish to ignore it; this should be foreseen and provided against, and it can certainly be minimized along the lines I suggest in a later chapter. There is ample room in the South for both. The real danger, and what the white man should fear, is his race demoralization from contact with the members of a race steeped in misery and vice. He should dread the sapping of his energies likely to happen if he can shirk the discipline of hard work, and place the burden on another. He should fear the effect on his children of autocratic power over those who may be treated unjustly without fear of retaliation. Contact with a race which may be inferior but which has a race pride, and which disdains to stoop to baseness is innocuous. Contact with one deprived of hope, with debased standards insinuating them into his life, may lead to the moral degeneration of the stronger.

This both South Africa and the South should fear.

CHAPTER XXII.

THE TWO SCHOOLS.

UNTIL late years it could hardly be said that there was any public opinion among the Negro people with regard to their position in the land. As a mass they accepted without demur what the white man offered, and what he taught. It has, however, now become apparent that those who think and feel are divided into two camps, and each of these is commanding a larger measure of attention and support from the people. Both these camps aim at the uplifting of the race, but they lay stress on different aspects of the question, and their practical efforts to attain their ends are widely different.

The one has its centres of influence in the North, the other in the South. Associated with both are many white men and women, and among the most prominent leaders of both are men of mixed blood.

I have often referred to those belonging to the militant section of the Negroes, and have given their opinions on many matters, and these I would first describe. They belong to the school having its headquarters in the North, which it is stated was made possible by the pioneer work of W. A. Trotter, and expounded in the pages of the "Guardian". At the present day the movement is led by Dr. W. E. B. Du Bois, who was formerly a professor in Atlanta University (coloured), and who is now living in New York, and entirely devoted to the work of organizing an association for the advancement of the coloured people, and issuing on their behalf a monthly paper called "The Crisis".

To make the distinction clear I ought here to say that

the other school is that which preaches the doctrine of personal self-development and social service, which I have shown to be so admirably taught and practised at Hampton and Tuskegee. Many white philanthropists are associated with these and similar efforts, but the most conspicuous and well-known of the exponents of this school and doctrine is Dr. Booker T. Washington.

Before opinions and methods crystallized into what may now fairly be termed two schools there were men and women who held to the doctrine now being preached from New York, and there were those who were putting into practice what is now being done on a larger scale at Hampton and Tuskegee.

In those days both were content to work for betterment along their chosen lines without clashing; it seems now, however, as if on one side, that of the militant school, there is a marked disposition to criticize and even belittle the policy of the other, and to ascribe a certain tendency to increased severity in the South to the mistaken ideas and alleged lack of principle in their policy.

I had opportunities of talking with Dr. du Bois and some of his Northern friends. I had ample opportunity of thrashing out the question with many of his supporters in the South. I have carefully read many of the publications issued under the auspices of the organization which advocates his policy, and have kept in touch with the views of the party on current racial topics.

Their watchword is Thorough or No Compromise. They take their stand on the Federal law of the United States, which explicitly forbids any distinction in political affairs or public social life, and which declares that all men are free and equal, and shall have equal opportunities and privileges. They fasten upon all distinctions made between white and black, and denounce them with acumen and with bitterness. Constant opportunities are presented in the actual operations of social differentiation to give openings for sarcasm and ridicule, and they fully

avail themselves of such.   The pages of the magazines
and pamphlets they issue give full particulars of all cases
of injustice and discrimination against the coloured race,
and give them with the fullest emphasis.   Any attempts
at compromise, even reasonable compromise on matters
of principle, they treat with scorn, and lash the weak-
kneed with stinging bitterness.   They demand the utter
extinction of the colour bar, and claim that every man
and woman shall be judged, and take their position in
the land, on their character and attainments, irrespective
of race or colour.   I believe I am rightly interpreting
their creed when I say that this shall not be limited in
any way, and that they favour—they certainly do not
denounce—miscegenation.

However they may feel in their heart of hearts, a lofty
optimism is the ruling note of their writings, speeches,
and conversation ; they not only declare that right and
justice must prevail, but they say the coloured man
throughout the Union has at last awakened, and has the
will and the power to enforce his rights, and will not be
denied.

Whenever and wherever I met the disciples of this
school I knew what to expect, a list of grievances, in-
justices, and insults, and I got to expect exaggeration.
As my personal experience widened with my travels and
observation, I was able to cite what I had seen, sometimes in extenuation, sometimes in explanation, but this
was seldom favourably received.   It seemed to me, that
rather than accept palliatives, even when tending to
establish permanently better relations, they would reject
them, and unless any change went to the root of the
matter, would prefer to hear that the bonds were
tightened rather than relaxed, thus giving them additional cause for complaint.

I have before me a copy of a letter couched in the
most courteous terms, written by a white sympathizer,
and remonstrating at the tone of certain articles which
criticize recent racial occurrences, and counselling that a

more moderate tone be adopted. The reply, which may be said to represent officially the opinions and temper of this school, is full of stinging bitterness, with caustic and biting references to such careful and cushioned friends, who will not follow them all the way.

There is a conspicuous absence of anything like a constructive side to their policy. In scathing terms they refer to the industrial movement among the Negroes, and deride the efforts to make a carpenter out of that which they contend is not yet a man. First they say let the Negro be made a man with a man's rights, and then set to work to make him what else you will. Records are certainly given in their publications of success in practical life achieved by Negroes, but with the principal aim, as it seems to me, to prove him the equal of the white man in any walk of life. This party or school do not, however, seem to have made any organized attempt practically to assist the Negro to improve his material condition by education or otherwise.

There is ample scope among the Negroes for warning and reproof; the cause of many of their troubles lies on their own heads, but unless for their submissiveness, and this receives severe castigation, there is little of blame for all the shortcomings of the Negro people.

Their practical work takes the shape of legal proceedings against those who have made illegal discrimination, and they have moved the courts in many instances, and have many times succeeded in establishing their cases. Travelling agents have been sent through the Northern and Western States, and many meetings held in furtherance of their ideas. I have not heard of such attempts in the real South. I can imagine that, unless the language used and ideas promulgated were very much modified, it would be an exceedingly dangerous mission, and probably they do not at present seek martyrdom.

I heard white men and women who were engaged in educational, social, and religious work among the Negroes in the South speak warmly against this movement. It struck them as somewhat cowardly to fulminate against abuses in the comparative safety of the North, and create bitter disaffection among those in the South who might have to suffer grievous wrong as the result of imbibing such teaching.

How far they are gaining adherents among the mass of the Negro population, especially in the South, is, I think, indeterminate. Their publications indicate ever-increasing circulation, and an increasing membership in the North. The impression I got was that it was essentially a Mulatto movement. The leaders I met were mostly men of mixed blood, and whatever may be the composition of the rank and file, it may be taken as true that those who inaugurated the movement, and those who give it force and direction, are in the main whites and part whites. This is what I should have expected.

Very soon after landing in America I made the acquaintance of some of those who hold these tenets, and who take a leading part in spreading them. Coming as my first introduction to the Afro-American race question on the spot, it was exciting, even inspiring. I heard of insult and injustice growing more and more in both North and South, until the Negro, his long-suffering dormant soul at last awakened, was going to rise in the might of his right, and at whatever sacrifice, demand and force equal treatment. I was told that I should find in the course of my inquiries that the Negro was in deadly earnest, determined to combine, and to make that combination effective. He had found out that silent submission to injustice only provoked it, and that the record of the last decade proved it. The bonds had been tightened, the discrimination had invaded one sphere of activity after another, and at last the too patient black man had learned his lesson, and no longer would he turn the other cheek, but resist, and if necessary strike back.

I was not prepared for such a root and branch doctrine, but I felt it was a phase of the question that I must investigate. The first opportunity came quickly. I was informed that the last injustice of the white South was to separate in the cities the sections in which white and black might respectively live. In many Southern cities segregation ordinances had been introduced with this object, the nearest of which was Baltimore, and here, as elsewhere, intense indignation had been aroused among the Negroes. They and their white friends were going to protest to the uttermost, and one of the indignation meetings was to be held in Baltimore in a few days. I imagined this occasion would throw a light on the attitude of the Negro people, and I made up my mind to attend.

I may say here that this movement towards segregation was what my friends described. I was informed by both Negroes and whites living in the cities referred to, that some years ago a coloured person could buy a block anywhere if he had the purchase price. Gradually white neighbours objected, and in some cases prevented a sale, in others they bid a higher price. Until lately there had been no organized attempt to do this. Now however public feeling was aroused, and pressure was brought to bear on Negroes, estate agents, and the legislature. Hence this projected ordinance. It was pointed out that it was largely based on economic reasons, it being held that the presence of Negro residents caused a depreciation in the value of property. On the other hand I found that the rent charged to Negroes was higher than that paid by white occupiers for the same accommodation, and also that it was not uncommon for white men to acquire and monopolize for their own advantage all the valuable business sites in an area in which Negroes are the only residents. I may say also that the active spirits who lead this militant movement have by strenuous opposition succeeded in delaying the movement in many cities.

What chiefly interested me, however, was to discover, if possible, how far the mass of the Negroes were actuated by this new spirit of revolt, how far they were prepared to make sacrifices to stem aggression, and I hoped that this gathering of protestors would furnish some indication of the extent to which they were roused.

On my arrival in Baltimore notice of the meeting was sent to me, and I found it was to be held at eight o'clock in the evening in a very large and handsome Negro church on a thoroughfare I easily found. I arrived at the spot some minutes before the hour, and seeing no one near the church, strolled about until the time of starting, when the door was opened and a few people were inside the building, probably fifty or sixty in all, mostly women and children. A benevolent-looking old coloured gentleman came forward and showed me into a front pew. Very slowly the numbers increased, and one or two Negroes, apparently ministers, fussed about the platform. In my notes written the same evening I say : " The little movements behind the scenes, the coming forward of the benevolent one to count the chairs on the platform, the chirping content of all with the delay, all struck me as very childish and irresponsible ". At last, forty-five minutes late, the proceedings began with the church three parts filled. Local men took only the minor parts, two occupied the chair, one giving place to the other after an interval, but neither took an active part. A Negro minister opened with prayer.

Three excellent speeches were delivered, two by whites, and one by a near white, dealing with the disabilities and the prospects of the race, the necessity for organization, and particularly with the injustice of the proposed segregation ordinance. The attitude of the audience, the Baltimore Negroes who were to suffer the injustice, was my chief concern, and I watched them closely. As no local speaker dealt with the subject I had only the semi-articulate ejaculations and remarks, and the attitude, attention, and applause of the audience to guide me. I have attended and taken part in many indignation meetings, and it has been my duty as an elected legislator to gauge public feeling. At some of these gatherings the veriest amateur could feel the hot temper of those present : it vented itself unmistakably, at others the feeling was lukewarm and needed much whipping up. But never have I been present at such a mild exhibition as the one I am recording. There was ejaculation and applause, plenty of it, generally at the humorous hits, which were highly appreciated, otherwise the applause was often wrongly placed. Before the principal speakers had finished the large building was quite full. The atmosphere of the crowd was certainly not one of indignant protest, there rather breathed a warm social feeling of human beings met together for pleasant communion. There were a few who riveted their attention on the speakers, and who appeared appropriately moved, but the majority gazed on their friends, whispered and nudged, and were certainly not moved to desperate earnestness by the threatened violation of their rights. The business of the meeting was not over till 11.15 p.m., and then with a movement of relief the gathering resolved into a social conversazione, the people moved about, chatted, joked, and when I left at 11.30 p.m. they showed no signs of dispersing.

I quote from my fresh impressions, noted down immediately I left the meeting: "I was much interested. The whole tone was irresponsibility, the late start, the childish coming and going, the tentative applause often given at the wrong time, were to me indicative of a people glad to come together on any pretext, intensely social, but lacking in purpose and resolution." When I thought of the swarms of hard-faced, white Americans in the streets and hotels, who were doing things, and determined to do things in their own way, and when the time came to stand no nonsense, I felt indeed sorry for this people, so easy and ineffective. What can they do? And I felt that these black people were out of place, simple copyists; this big church is the Evangelical with a little flamboyant colour, the whole proceedings, prayer, tone of voice, dresses, attitude, all copied. I felt they were a people defrauded, poor and simple compared to our Zulus, who have at least retained their language and customs and something of the manliness of the savage. Are they also to go this way and become Niggers, or if you like them, darkies ?

I think I have given a fair statement of the doctrines, attitude, and aspirations of this school of Negro thought. I hope I have not in any particular been unjust to them. I have a great respect for their earnestness, and the strenuous, often self-sacrificing work of their leaders. I have the deepest sympathy for the Negro in his legitimate grievances, and detestation for the unjust manner in which he is treated, but what I write will be of little value if 1 do not record exactly what I saw and the exact impressions I received.

The spirit and trend of the other or constructive school is best seen in the great training institutions of Hampton and Tuskegee. As I have said, I visited both these places, and also many smaller institutions founded on their model in many parts of the South. My visit to Tuskegee coincided with a Congress on the Negro called by Dr. Booker T. Washington. Those attending were for the most part of African race. I induced many to speak privately, yet without reserve, of the disabilities of their people in the South, and learned much from them. But the public speeches and addresses were in a different key. They dealt with what had been achieved, and breathed encouragement, and urged to further effort. Experiences were exchanged, and the best methods of setting the Negro on the path of spiritual, moral, and material progress were discussed. The atmosphere of Tuskegee is not favourable to pessimism ; it fosters hope, a hope that does not seem misplaced when one sees sixteen hundred bright alert youths of both sexes being so admirably trained to carry the gospel of practical work and social betterment to their people. The life-history of the principal is itself an inspiration. From the lowest depths of poverty and ignorance, in spite of difficulties which seemed insurmountable, he has risen to his present position of leadership, and built up, in the midst of the hostile South, an institution that commands the admiration of

all, even of those who judge it by the standards of
Europe and the North. Here it stands, a concrete example of the doctrine of the constructive school.

The leaders and apostles of this school see in the South
a people ignorant, illiterate, indolent, without foresight or
much natural aptitude to enable them to make a place for
themselves in the society in which their lot is cast. They
see their people neglect the opportunities to advance
which are open to them, and instead of living independent
and manly lives, they are too often the victims of the
stronger race, or live as parasites in the towns. These
leaders feel that the task of uplifting this people is
one of such magnitude, that to be successful they must
concentrate every thought and effort upon it. They
clearly see that until the Negro can be clean, moral, self-
respecting, free from debt, living in wholesome surroundings and bringing up his family in the nurture and
admonition of the Lord, he will remain a byword and a
scoffing, contemptuously pushed aside, or exploited by
the stronger race.

Consistently, therefore, is preached the saving doctrine
of clean homes free from debt, and to make such homes,
in which the coming generation may have wholesome
surroundings, is one of their main objects. To earn
honestly a better livelihood, to practise self-restraint and
judgment in spending their earnings, is insisted upon.

The doctrine is not one of personal self-seeking or
aggrandisement. While there is a strong individualistic
note, the duty of each to the race is ever raised on high,
and individual development goes hand in hand with social
service. With a clear view of the dangers of city life to
the race, it is urged that the people shall conserve and
foster their natural aptitude for country life, fasten their
roots in the soil, and acquire land ; and help and opportunity have been given to them to become thus independent.

The Negro is ever too prone to bewail his fate and
place the blame for his misfortunes on others ; the luxury

of self-compassion is one he is too ready to indulge, and his nature, infested by this parasite, becomes soured and cannot nourish the sturdy plant of self-help. It is from a shrewd knowledge of this failing, and not because they are satisfied with his politico-social position in the South, that they discourage repining at disabilities, and rather point to the heights which may be scaled by industry, knowledge, and self-restraint.

This is an inspiring and constructive policy which can be understood by the lowliest, and which bears in it the germ, not only of material, but of spiritual progress, and to which the Negro is certainly responding with an enthusiasm which is a bright hope for the future.

At the Tuskegee Conference on the Negro to which I have referred I gave an address on race relations in South Africa, and while advocating for our Bantu people education suited to their needs, pointed out the possibilities of race jealousy and conflict. Dr. Washington congratulated me on my effort, and when I attempted to discuss the possibilities of race conflict in the South due to jealousy of the increasing efficiency of the Negro, he declined to follow. His people, he said, like any other, would get the place and the social recognition they deserved: let them prove themselves worthy of respect and they would obtain it. A high note, and one which in the circumstances of the South showed a practical wisdom and sagacity I could not deny.

His attitude may best be expressed in his own words: "My own observation has convinced me that in those States where the leaders of the Negro have been encouraged to turn their attention to politics, the masses of the people have not made the same progress that they have in those States where the leaders, because of racial prejudice or for other reasons, have been compelled to seek their own salvation in education and building up, in moral and material directions, the more lowly members of their own people. I do not wish to make comparisons, but I think I may safely say that in no other part of the United States have the masses of the Negroes been more completely deprived of political privileges than in the State of Mississippi, and yet there is at the same time scarcely any part of the country in which the masses of the people have built more schools and churches, or where they have gained more solid foothold on the soil and in the industries of the State."

But the prophet and his doctrine are denied and denounced by some among his own people.   His detractors take a high stand.   Man does not live by bread alone, they say, and if his spirit is starved that his body may be clothed, he does not live.   The policy of Hampton and Tuskegee is looked upon coldly, and sometimes even condemned as worldly and material, and lacking the true nourishment of the bread of life.   The first essential to raise a people, they say, is to efface the stigma of inferiority, to give them the freedom that will enable them to walk erect, men in the sight of men.   While injustice stalks through the land it is fatuous and cowardly to appear to ignore it; and to place material ends before a race who should be fighting for justice, is to condone unworthily.

Such critics point out that since Dr. Booker Washington first arrested public attention by his celebrated speech at Atlanta, when he foreshadowed the possibility of racial co-operation and peace, race conditions have, on the contrary, become increasingly acute, and they point to many circumstances which indicate this.

Thus William Archer, in speaking of the years which have elapsed since this famous declaration, says: "Since Mr. Washington uttered this aspiration the years have brought its fulfilment no nearer.   Both Negro education and white education have advanced in the interim, the respectable and well-to-do class of Negro has considerably increased, but the feeling between the races is worse rather than better.   The old time kindliness of feeling between the ex-owner and ex-slave is rapidly becoming a mere tradition.   No common memories or sentiments hold together the new generations of the two races, they are growing up in unmitigated animosity. In the North too, while the dislike of the individual has greatly increased, the theoretic fondness for the Negro has very perceptibly cooled."

Prof. Kelly Miller, in his essay on Race Adjustment, deals with this charge and says very justly : " Dr. Booker Washington's critics assert that his leadership has been barren of good results to the Negro race, unmindful of the magnitude of the contract he has promised the American people that he would solve the race problem. Under his regnancy it is claimed that the last vestige of political power has been swept away ; civil privileges have been restricted ; educational opportunities, in some States at least, have been curtailed ; the industrial situation, the keystone of the policy, has become more ominous and uncertain, while the feeling between the races is constantly growing more acute and threatening. In answer to this it is averred that no human power could stay the wave of race hatred now sweeping over the country, but that the Tuskegeeans' pacific policy will serve to relieve the severity of the blow. All the leaders before him essayed the task in vain and gave up in despair."

It must not be thought that these two schools divide the Negro race. It is only after all a small minority who think or even feel. These few on both sides are attempting to leaven the mass with their doctrine, but it is only the fringe they reach, the vast majority are content to slide through life.

Both will, however, have an increasing influence on the people, both are deeply in earnest, and are bound to make an ever-widening impression. And under present conditions there is room for both. While race discrimination, culminating in lynching, continues, it is well in the interests of white as well as black that there should be a vigilant eye kept on all the possible sources of injustice, and that protest should be made. The history of the last few years shows that there is, among a section of the whites, a constant disposition to encroach upon, and still further limit, the liberties and opportunities of the Negro, and vigorous protest, and at times a fight to a finish, are inevitable and unavoidable. Common manliness demands it.

When this is frankly admitted, it still leaves us free to criticize the present methods of this militant school, and it may be pointed out in the friendliest spirit that the bitter tone adopted in some of the publications issued by them is only likely to embitter in turn. I met many friends of the Negro in the South who were not only fair-weather friends, but were among those whose everyday lives were made more difficult by reason of their well-known friendship, who deplored this, and pointed out how much more arduous their task was made by the unbalanced, exaggerated, and acrid writings of this section.

Too often, however, this class of friend is not only not considered by the extremists but is openly derided.

And the same derision is often poured upon those of the constructive school. Yet while I feel there is a place and a duty for the protestors and fighters, how much bigger and more hopeful is the field of work of the constructors. When one surveys the millions of backward Negroes living from hand to mouth, who unless roused will find themselves mere flotsam and jetsam on the complicated civilized conditions that are on them, and when one considers the opportunities for an ample and satisfactory life if only they will seize them, it is difficult to see that anything is of any importance except the rousing, before it is too late.

I have admitted the importance of watchfulness and protest against injustice, but how unimportant it seems when one realizes what a great uplifting and constructive work lies to the hand of those who are fired with the enthusiasm of Dr. Washington. I can quite understand that those who fully grasp this have no time for fulminating against grievances; they cannot spare a moment from the building of the great edifice whose towers and

turrets they see in their visions, and cannot be diverted
to answer the criticism of the other party.

I feel I am with them.   The possibilities for good in
their constructive work are immense, the time during
which it may become fully effective is limited ; let them
press forward and do all the rescue work they can before
the time of opportunity passes.

When I first landed in the United States I felt much
sympathy with the protestors, at many tales of injustice I
felt hot, and still burn with indignation.   Gradually it
came to me that the ignorance and futility of the race
were responsible in part for these, and the great work
was to make them fit to live and work in their present
difficult and complicated environment.

And this is the task of Dr. Washington and those who
work with him.   No lover of humanity but must wish
them God-speed in the task of raising a race.

CHAPTER XXIII.

THE NORTH—A VOTER WITHOUT A LIVELIHOOD.

LONG before the Civil War the enslaved Negro looked to
the North as the land of freedom and opportunity, and
many thousands, through the help of white friends and
their organizations, escaped thither and there made their
homes. This tendency continued, and up to a certain
point became accelerated. In one decade the Negro
population of Philadelphia increased 56 per cent, that of
New York 66 per cent, and that of Chicago 111 per cent.
This was largely due to immigration from the South ; the
effective natural increase was small indeed : in New York
in one year, 1908, there were 2212 deaths and only
1973 births.

After emancipation the Negroes regarded the North,
and especially the Republican party, as their friends, and
have until late years touchingly stuck to this tradition, notwithstanding many rebuffs and disappointments. This is
told in feeling terms by a Negro who has made his home
in New York and who tells of the simple test by which
he learned he had reached the city of freedom. Born in
South Carolina, as he attained manhood he desired
larger self-expression, broader human relations ; he desired, as he again and again expressed it, "to be free".
So leaving the cotton fields he started one day to walk to
New York. After a number of days he entered a city,
and uncertain of his geography decided that this was his
journey's end. "I'll be free there," he thought, and
opening the door of a brightly lit restaurant started to
walk in. The white men at the table looked up in
astonishment, and the proprietor, laying his hand on the

young man's shoulder, invited him, in strong Southern
accent, to get into the kitchen. "I reckon I'm not North
yet," the Negro said, smiling a bright boyish smile.

Interested in his visitor's appearance the proprietor
took him into another room, and talked with him far
into the night, urging the advantage of staying in the
South. But the youth shook his head and next morning
trudged on. At length he reached a rushing city, tumult-
uous with humanity. He tasted the freedom of passing
unnoticed and acting as a white man. The inference from
this story is that he had found freedom, freedom to do as
he willed without any discrimination. But it is doubtful
whether, if he entered New York to-day, he would consider he had found freedom.

This post-war exodus to the North was to the
Northern cities, comparatively few settled in the country
or followed country pursuits. They took whatever callings were open to them, and few being skilled, they had
perforce to accept menial or manual labour, and compete
with the immigrant.

Long before emancipation and for some time after it,
the freedmen in the North occupied many positions of
trust, and apparently had much the same chance to earn
a living as had the white man. In the "Philadelphia
Negro," a valuable monograph edited by Dr. W. E. B.
Du Bois, it is stated : "In 1810 the Negro formed one-
tenth of the population of the City. It is probable that
between 1790 and 1820 a very large proportion, and
perhaps most of the artisans of Philadelphia, were
Negroes. About this time the whole of the catering was
in their hands, and they were autocratic in this line,
setting the fashion and serving the best families and
clubs. The names of Boyle Augustin, Prosser Dorsey,
Jones and Minton were well known. Of these Dorsey
was the most unique character ; with little education but
great refinement of manner, he became a factor of real
weight in the community. Both artisans and caterers
went under to foreign competition."

14 *

In making a comparison of the past and present in the North it would be a mistake to consider that, because the North entered into a sanguinary and costly war, straining their resources to the uttermost, the result of which was the emancipation of the slave, that therefore the general public of the North regarded the Negro as a man and a brother, and were prepared to grant absolute political and industrial, much less social equality. Many facts can be cited to show that this was not the case. Still there was a great wave of sympathetic feeling, and abolition and the principles and doctrines associated with it were a great power in the land.

As a South African I felt it would be of the greatest interest to try to discover, after nearly half a century, the present feeling and tendencies in the North.

Here, of course, I had to be guided by those of wider experience, and first I will give the opinions of some of these. I was told by several well-to-do and educated mulattoes resident in Northern cities, that there was more freedom for them in past years than there is now. They had now to watch their footsteps ; they might venture and receive courtesy, they never knew when they might meet insulting rebuffs.

Speaking of the present as compared with the past the editor of the " Philadelphia Negro " says : " It is a paradox of the times that young men and women from some of the best Negro families in the city have actually had to go South to get work if they wished to be aught but chambermaids and bootblacks ".

I remember an eminent mulatto speaking in London on this subject just before I embarked for America, and saying in effect that whereas some years ago all accommodations and conveniencies in the North were open to him, just as to a white man, to-day he had to be careful where he went.

I found the general consensus of opinion confirmatory of this tendency. Some Northern Negroes with whom I conversed attributed it to more frequent communication with the South, saying that Southern men and women came North and spoke out on the Negro, and their sentiments and prejudices had too often been accepted by their Northern acquaintances. This is probably a factor. The increase of Negroes in the cities, and a more intimate personal knowledge of the characteristics of the race has been another. The ideal of the Northern city man is hustle and efficiency, he cannot tolerate slackness, procrastination, dawdling, and indolence. His time is too precious to be wasted on those who fail to make good, and the character and traits of the average Negro are antipathetic. He cannot exploit him as he can the hard-working and often thrifty immigrant, and he has no use for him, and contemptuously pushes him aside.

There are still the spiritual descendants of the abolitionists, but even among many friendly to the Negro, and often among those engaged in philanthropic work, there is a note of discrimination that has, I am told, grown perceptibly. They no longer accept the doctrine of equality without qualification, and few, for instance, are prepared now to support the policy and action taken by the Federal Government in enfranchising the Negro at the close of the Civil War.

This change is reflected in the attitude of the average citizen, and especially the employer and working man, in the gradual closing of many branches of labour to the Negro, in which, as I have shown, he had an opportunity, and sometimes almost a monopoly, in past years.

Many authorities could be cited to show this change of opinion, and I find none who claim that the position of the Negro in the North is becoming more satisfactory. Dr. William N. D. Berry, pastor of a coloured congregation in Springfield, Mass., is thus reported: "Eighty-six per cent of the coloured labour of our city is confined to servile employment by pure race prejudice, which has closed the door of industrial employment against them. The situation in Springfield is fairly typical of the condition in this respect of the black man throughout the North." President Eliot of Harvard University says: " The uneducated Northern white is less tolerant of the Negro than the Southern whites. More trades and occupations are actually open to Negroes in Southern than in Northern States." Mr. Dooley, who so often hits the bull's-eye in his Irish-American humour, says: " He'll ayther have to go North and be a subjeck race or South and be an objeck lesson. 'Tis a harrd time he'll have of it anyhow. I'm not so much troubled about the Naygur when he lives among his oppressors as I am when he falls into the hands of his liberators. When he is in the South he can make up his mind to be lynched soon or late, and give his attention to his other pleasures, in composin' ragtime music on a banjo, and wurrkin' for the man that used to own him and now only owes him his wages. But it's the devil's own hardship to be pursood by a mob of abolitionists till he's dhriven to seek police protection."

W. P. Livingstone arrives at the same conclusion: " In New York twenty years ago he had the practical monopoly of many employments he is no longer permitted to enter. Wherever there has been an increase of the coloured community the avenues in which they make a living have been steadily closed. It is true they are often inferior in skill and capacity, but this is not the reason, because educated Negroes find still greater difficulty in obtaining positions. It is the colour that forms an insuperable bar to appointment."

In her valuable and critical, yet deeply sympathetic book, " Half a Man," Miss Mary Ovington has the following which I think bears out my general conclusion: " A prominent New York coloured man once said to me : ' I cannot conceive what it would mean not to be a Negro. The white people think and feel so little, their life lacks an absorbing interest'. This is the characteristic fact of the life of the well-to-do Negro in New York. He is not permitted to go through the streets in easy comfort of body and mind. Some personal rebuff, some harsh word in newspaper and magazine, quickens his pulse and rouses him from the lethargy that often overtakes his white neighbour. Looking into the past of slavery, watching the coming generation, the most careless heart is forced into serious questioning. A comfortable income and the intelligence to enjoy the culture of a great city do not bring to the Negro any smug self-satisfaction, only a greater responsibility towards the problem that moves through the world with his dark face."

Both on the occasion of this visit to the United States and on a previous leisurely journey across the continent from California to the Atlantic I visited places of public resort in the Northern cities to find out for myself the attitude and bearing of white towards black. The public conveyances were free to all. If Negroes were travelling in company they were often hilarious, and sometimes unduly so, and though I never heard a rebuke from whites, I felt sometimes the atmosphere was charged with disapproval. Solitary Negroes travelling often took seats, especially in a crowded conveyance, with hesitation, sometimes with humility.

I often entered the middle-class restaurants which are such a feature of American city life, but I cannot recall seeing a face that distinctly belonged to a coloured person. My observations were confirmed by residents, though opinion differed as to what would happen if an unmistakable Negro entered and demanded refreshment. Much would depend on the temperament and opinion of the proprietor and his clients. In any case the experiment would demand more moral and physical courage than is possessed by the average man.

Unquestionably the status of the Negro in the North is one of dubiety. He may be passed in silence, he may receive contumely, assuredly he is never welcomed.

Although there are no segregation ordinances prohibiting white and black from living in the same areas in the Northern cities, as a rule the Negroes occupy certain defined areas. I visited some of these sections, which were invariably in a low part of the town, and the state of the road and pathways indicated but scant attention on the part of the municipal authorities. There seemed but little attempt at order and cleanliness on the part of the residents; dirty houses, unclean yards or alleys, crowding ragged children, disorderly women, and hulking, loafing men were numerous. This is, of course, partly an effect and partly a cause.

Criminals among the city Negroes form a higher percentage than in any other class of the community; this is proved by statistics and admitted by the Negroes and their friends, though naturally the latter debit it to poverty and unclean environment. The percentage of criminals varies of course in different cities and districts, and statistics must be accepted with caution, still they certainly confirm the generally accepted statement that the Negro in the North is peculiarly addicted to crime.

In the district of Columbia the Negroes are under one-third of the total population. Washington City has 86,702 Negroes out of a total population of 278,718, yet they furnish seventy-four per cent of the criminals, and out of 125 persons committed for serious crime in 1904 no less than ninety-four were Negroes.

Taking the whole of the Northern States together, from Nebraska to Maine, the proportion of the Negroes is but 0·99 per cent, but the percentage of crime committed by them is 10·74 per cent.

The learned editor of the " Philadelphia Negro " admits this predisposition to crime and laments it. It is from the pages of this study that I give the following table.

Criminality of various races in Chicago :—

	Percentage to total population.	Percentage of criminals.
Irish	6·4	10·3
Germans	14·6	11·1
Norwegians	2·0	1·3
Swedes	3·9	2·5
Russians.	0·7	0·8
Bohemians	2·3	1·2
Poles	2·2	1·7
Italians	0·5	1·2
Negroes	1·3	9·8

Summary of above :—

	Percentage to total population.	Percentage of criminals.
Principal foreign nations .	32·6	30·1
Negroes	1·3	9·8
All others	66·1	60·1

In the whole North, according to Professor W. C. Wilcox, there were twelve white criminals to each 10,000 of the population, but the proportion of Negroes was sixty-nine. It would also appear that this tendency is not decreasing although I have not the latest figures. Professor Wilcox states that while in 1880 there were seventy-seven Negro criminals in each 10,000 this had risen in 1890 to 100. He says the primary causes are immorality and defective family life, while an important one is the increasing industrial competition with the whites, which makes life harder for the Negro, under which he succumbs to crime.

It is not alleged that in the Northern Courts (and we are dealing with the North now) the Negro does not receive even-handed justice, though of course he probably suffers by reason of his poverty and ignorance. It is also said, and truthfully, that he is often committed to prison when the richer white man is able to pay a fine. In the figures given, however, these figures are eliminated.

One exceedingly unsatisfactory feature of Negro life in the cities, and this applies to the South as well as to the North, is the preponderance of women, which in nine of the larger cities ranges from 116 to 143 women for each 100 men. An analysis has been made of the occupations of 23,448 Negro women in the city of Washington, D.C., which shows :—

21,018 in domestic and personal service.

1617 ,, dressmaking.

519 ,, professional (teachers).

294 ,, all others.

The men are chiefly employed in low paid and menial callings. Out of 8000 in Kansas City over 5000 were returned as labourers and over 1100 as porters. None were in clerical or commercial employment, and only 30 were returned as teachers, the balance were employed as janitors, teamsters, waiters, and in other similar callings which demanded little skill, and led to little advancement. It is true there are a few professional men, doctors, lawyers, and dentists, but they are few as compared with the labouring and unskilled. In Texas there was one Negro doctor to 9000 Negroes and one lawyer to 40,000. In South Carolina one doctor to 22,000 and one lawyer to 29,000. In Atlanta City, Ala., one doctor to 24,000 and one lawyer to 52,000. I have no reason to think the proportions are greater in the North.

Under these circumstances it is not surprising that marital conditions are extremely unsatisfactory, and sexual immorality prevalent. Some of the figures given are appalling and seem to point to a general state of promiscuity.

Professor Kelly Miller, himself a Negro, and a strenuous defender of his race, goes so far as to say : " The criminal and moral status of the Negro race is threatening its physical continuance. After we have made all possible allowance for historic causes and pled all possible exculpatory excuses, the plain, unpleasant, unvarnished fact remains — the American Negro must conquer his vices or be destroyed by them."

A. H. Shannon, M.A., B.D., in his book on "The Racial Question" says : " I am satisfied that every instance

of degradation in any European city at the beginning of
last century may be more than matched in horror by
examples of degradation to be found among the Negroes
in our American cities ".

I give the following table of illegitimacy for the City
of Washington, D.C., premising that improvement in re-
gistration accounts in some measure for the increase in
later years, as this would conceivably tend to raise the
Negro figures and not appreciably affect the white.   Still,
when making all possible allowance, it is a sad contrast.

Year.	White per cent.	Coloured per cent.	Year.	White per cent.	Coloured per cent.
1879	2·32	17·60	1888	3·49	22·18
1880	2·43	19·02	1889	3·59	23·45
1881	2·33	19·42	1890	3·34	26·50
1882	2·09	19·73	1891	2·90	25·12
1883	3·14	20·95	1892	2·53	26·40
1884	3·60	19·02	1893	2·82	27·00
1885	3·00	22·88	1894	2·56	26·46
1886	3·28	22·86			
1887	3·34	21·27			

Under such a state of things clean home life is almost
impossible, and it is tremendously to the credit of some
that they do preserve it.   But the majority of the children
brought up in the cities are doomed to a vicious if not a
criminal life.   I have no figures at hand to denote the
juvenile criminality of the Northern cities, but in Atlanta,
Ga., in 1906 the following numbers of Negro children of
tender years were before the Court on various charges :—

Years of age	6	7	8	9	10	11	12
Number charged	1	7	33	69	107	142	219

It is appalling !

The vital statistics of Negroes in the larger Northern
cities, and the same is true in large measure of those in
the South, are extremely unsatisfactory.   After analysing
the Census returns Professor Kelly Miller reaches the
following conclusions :—

(1) The Negro death-rate is nearly double that of the whites in all the large cities. (2) This rate is mainly due to excess of infant mortality. (3) Consumption and allied pulmonary complaints carry off proportionately three Negroes to one white person. (4) Negro death-rate seems to be slightly decreasing. (5) The mortality of the city Negro seems to be about double that of his country brother.

It would appear that the statement about infant mortality is not exaggerated, in all the cities it is extremely high. In New York in 1908 the rate among Negroes was 290 per 1000!

It is only fair to say that there are many who, while admitting the criminality, immorality, and disease among the city Negroes of the North, point out that this is due to their shocking environment, and particularly point out that those Negroes living in clean and sanitary areas are no more predisposed to disease than the whites in the same sections. This may be the case, but these are isolated instances on which it is impossible to base general conclusions.

It is, however, undeniably true to say that up to the present the Afro-Americans have as a race shown little power to resist pernicious city conditions and little ability to rise to the industrial opportunities they offer. It is also correct to say that general race conditions in Northern urban areas are extremely unsatisfactory, and what is more, they do not show signs of any considerable measure of improvement.

Professor Kelly Miller says: "The status of the city Negro seems to furnish a contradiction to the prevalent belief that education will solve the race problems. Experience seems to show that the problems grow in difficulty as general intelligence increases. In the city of Washington, and in a corresponding degree the same may be said of other cities, the educational facilities for coloured children are practically as good as any offered the most favoured class of children anywhere on the face

of the earth.   These schools have been crowded for a
quarter of a century and have now more than fifteen
thousand in attendance, and yet the race problem at the
national capital is not solved."

In 1896 J. P. Hoffmann, a professional statistician,
published a book entitled, " Race Traits and Tendencies of
the American Negro ".   In a very detailed manner inquiry is made into the physical condition of the Negro,
and comparison is made with what he was in slavery
days.   The conclusion of this statistical study is that the
Negro is not holding his own against the white.   The
figures and facts are almost entirely taken from the Negro
in city life, and mostly from the cities of the North.
The pessimistic conclusions of the author are not, I think,
true of the whole race in the United States, certainly not
true of the rural Negro, though they are probably correct
if only stated of the race in the cities of the North.
The significant thing in this inquiry is that for the admitted demoralization and low vitality Hoffmann blames
race characteristics and distinctly says : " It is not in the
conditions of life, but in the race traits and tendencies
that we find the cause of excessive mortality ".   This is,
of course, a direct contradiction to those I have cited who
blame the vile environment and poverty of the Negro for
his demoralization.   I think myself both are factors and
act and react on each other.

If, however, this poverty-stricken environment is to be
improved the city Negro must earn more, and herein lies
the difficulty.   He is prone to indolence, easily satisfied,
and easily depressed at the best; at his worst, he would
rather steal than work, and rather live on the proceeds
of prostitution than either.   But let him be ever so industrious, ever so willing to put his neck under the yoke,
he must fight the bar of colour ; he is judged, not by his
own character and achievements, but by the low
character attributed to his race.

He is living under modern conditions in which those
who would succeed must co-operate with those having

like aims, to watch and defend their interests. The white working man has done this in all the skilled and in many unskilled callings. But usually the Negro is ruled out.

If he happens, as is unusual, to be in such numbers that he must be regarded, if he is a potential strike breaker, then the self-interest of the white worker demands his recognition. As he is generally a unit and unable to influence the situation he is not counted.

It is difficult to see how his status can be improved. In the well-paid trades an apprenticeship or its equivalent is necessary, and if the Negro is unwelcome as a capable journeyman, he is less likely to be taken on either as an apprentice or as an improver, especially under Trades Union conditions, when his work would not be economically remunerative to the employer. Trades Unions are often prepared to order a strike if non-Union men are employed, and yet often enough these Unions will not allow a fully competent Negro within their ranks simply on account of his colour. It appeared to me that the statement of Edgar Gardner Murphy is true of the Northern cities in which I made inquiry. He says: " The large and imperious developments of Trade Unionism in the North are already eliminating the Negro as an industrial factor. Nothing could be more searchingly relentless than the slow, silent, pitiless operation of the social and economic forces that are destroying the Negro, body and soul, in the Northern cities. None know it so well as the Negroes themselves. The race prejudice, which Professor Shaler of Harvard University has recently told us is as intense in the North as anywhere in the world, first forbids the Negro the membership of the Labour Unions, and then forbids to the employer the services of the non-Union labourer. If the employer turn wholly to the non-Union men he finds that, rather than work beside the Negro they throw down their tools and walk to the door. And so the dreary tale proceeds."

The Negro may vote in the North. The white man

there has not seen fit, nor found it necessary to introduce grandfather clauses, nor to demand an intelligent understanding of the Constitution of the United States, and thus shut out the Negro. He is on the register. But before any section of the voters can make their influence felt and get assured recognition of their wants, they must co-operate, vote intelligently, and bring pressure to bear on their representatives. Easily cajoled by astute politicians, easily bribed by them, the Negro, lacking in numbers and combination, throws away this opportunity of betterment. His friends speak sadly of his turpitude. Miss Mary Ovington says: "With the great majority of coloured voters the choice of a municipal candidate is based on the argument of a two dollar bill, or the promise of a job, combined with the sentiment, declining every year, for the Republican party, the party that once helped the Negro and may help him again. The public standing of the mayoralty candidate, his ability to choose wise heads of departments, the building of new subways, the ownership of public utilities, these are unimportant issues. The matter of immediate moment is what the vote is going to mean to the black man himself."

To sum up the position in the North, it would appear that while the coloured man may ride in the public conveyances, get the poor man's justice before the Courts, and exercise the vote, he is always subject to contumely and restrictions. He may not have to face the open active bitterness of the South, but he must reckon on an increasing contemptuous prejudice. He is being worsted in industrial competition, and only retains the right to work in ill-paid callings undesired by the whites, and consequently has to live in surroundings that tend to drag him down.

He has the vote—but without a livelihood.

CHAPTER XXIV.

THE SOUTH—A LIVELIHOOD WITHOUT A VOTE.

MY object in the present chapter is not to make a close study of the economic position of the Negro in the South, with details of his earnings, necessary expenditure, possible savings, and the channels in which he may profitably utilize them—all this I will deal with later. I want here to make a comparison of his general economic position and opportunities in the South with those in the North, which I have pictured in the last chapter.

I have elsewhere expressed the surprise I felt on finding so much of the manual labour of the South done by white men. Coming with a long South African experience, from a country in which all manual toil is done by black men, it was a novelty to see white men in large numbers engaged in work we are accustomed to call "Kaffirs' work".

Being familiar with the tenacity with which the South African white skilled artisan clings to his monopoly of highly paid labour, and the demand he makes that colour and not competence shall be the test of a skilled man, it was another surprise to find, comparatively speaking, so little of this feeling in the South.

It became clear to me afterwards that I had not realized the comparative numerical inferiority of the Negro in America as compared with our natives, which compels the white man in the South to undertake some of the necessary manual labour; nor had I understood the tradition of slavery times, when slave artisans did the building and the blacksmithing for the plantations and for the plantation towns.   For I found that not only did white men undertake manual labour, and black men work at skilled trades, but in many cases they work side by side, as in loading and discharging cargo, and in laying bricks on the same building.

There may have been times when employment was hard to get in the South, but certainly at the time of my visit, neither white nor black, if willing to work, need be idle.   Unemployment as we understand the term in Britain was non-existent.   I was told by Negro and by white man alike over and over again, and in all sections of the country, that there was work for all.   One Negro in Georgia said, no one need go hungry in this country. Another, every man in Alabama can have at least one meat meal a day.   Another, all can get work, and if a labouring man sticks to his work he can save money, but they don't all stick.

All the students learning trades at the various industrial establishments I visited assured me that they could get work at journeyman's wages when they left, some said they would work for white employers, some for Negroes, and some said relatives would employ them, or they would start business on their own account.

A working blacksmith I talked with gave me to understand that at times the white employer preferred the Negro to men of his own colour.   In his trade, in that section, there were no effective Trade Unions.   He could easily get work in any part of the South at $75 a month or even more.   He said he remembered waiting along with a white man on a white employer who had a vacancy, and though the employer did not choose there and then—with a meaning smile—he got word next day to take up the job.   "Perhaps," he said, "the master thought the coloured man would give less trouble than the white man."

It is true that in agricultural and other unskilled labour wages are low, but the necessaries of life are cheap, and the climate does not demand the heavy expenditure

15

in warm clothing and fuel that is necessary in Britain and the North.

It is equally true that the unskilled married man, when his family is young, may find himself with nothing left when their expenses are met, indeed in this case it is common to run into debt. But I found that young people in their teens could obtain work at wages which were high as compared with those paid to adults, and in many cases in which the head of the house earned only a meagre wage, the total amount brought into the family was large, quite sufficient to secure considerable savings, if the family was united and thrifty. One youth I spoke to told me he got work when only twelve years of age in a store in a small country town at $15 a month, and later got $20 a month. Another had two brothers, 14 and 15 years of age, who got a dollar a day each, working in a fertilizer factory. Another told me he knew many youths in their early teens receiving from $2½ to $4 a week. The girls in such a family can always obtain situations as domestic helps at say $2½ a week and their keep.

I do not wish it to be inferred that all avenues are equally open to black as well as white in the South. I notice that Alfred Holt Stone, in contrasting the economic opportunities of the Negro in the South with his limitations in the North, says: "He is permitted to work in the South at any occupation under the sun, because he is still the labourer to which we are most accustomed, and as yet the white man does not want his job". The reservation in the last sentence is significant, but apart from this my observations did not lead me to the conclusion that, ample as his opportunities in the South are, all occupations under the sun are his to choose. I question much whether an educated Negro would be welcome as an ordinary store assistant or clerk, or whether he could find employment as draughtsman or accountant in an office, or other similar employment; still it is true that as compared with the North his choice of occupation is much greater, and more well-paid callings demanding skill are open to him.

The industrial situation to-day is that all kinds of labour is in demand; the skilled artisan can get a high wage, far above his subsistence outlay in the case of a single man, and ample for the needs of his family if married, even if they are all non-earners. The semi-skilled single man has also a considerable margin, the semi-skilled married man with a young family can come out, and those with an earning family are in a comfortable position. The manual labourer, if single, can, if he choose, save money, the married man with a young family will often be pinched, but as the family grows up will regain a fairly comfortable position. I am assured that this has been the situation for some years past and I found it to be the position to-day, but I do not wish it to be inferred that it is to be so in the indefinite future, and that no anxiety need be felt as to the industrial outlook of the Negro.

In re-reading William Laird Clowes' book, "Black America," written over twenty years ago, I was struck by his forecast as to the probable trend of industrial race life. He says: "The white man cannot compete as labourer or even artisan on equal terms with the black. He needs higher pay and better food. In black centres therefore the poor white man finds himself daily more out of his element." I felt that if this was true the years that had passed would show some practical proof of this tendency. Later on I will give the results of my own observations, and cite the testimony of more recent observers. I will anticipate the verdict so far by saying here that this prediction of Mr. Clowes has not so far been confirmed, nor does it appear likely to be sustained in the future.

Any competent observer must see in the South, as in South Africa, a gathering storm, which means ultimately not only industrial war, but industrial plus racial conflict. In South Africa it has not yet come, nor in the South has it yet arrived, although with us it is a constant theme

15 *

of discussion, and many white workers speak as if we were already in the throes. This is not so, we are not yet even on the edge, it may be delayed or minimized, but it is difficult to see any force or combination of forces that will permanently prevent it. Opinions differ widely as to the eventual outcome, though such opinions are often held dogmatically as if the issue was clearly apparent. One man says the white man will always retain the highly paid work, and the native will always remain a manual labourer and servant; that he has no capacity for anything higher. Another sees in the increasing adaptability and education of the native the death-knell to white industrial supremacy.

I frankly confess I do not know, the only thing I can clearly see is conflict. On the one side will be better education, political power, labour organization, higher wages, and comparatively small numbers; handicapped by the sinister fact that the members of this race are relieved of much strenuous labour that makes for efficiency. On the other, great numbers with little co-operation or organization, at present at all events, but willing to work for low wages, with a natural fitness to the climate and surroundings, with gradually improving efficiency, and with the training that manual labour gives.

It is not the man who thinks below the surface who would venture to dogmatically predict the issue. But there will be an industrial and racial drama played out in South Africa, and so in the South.

Already many in America feel the change coming and predict still greater changes. Dr. Booker T. Washington says the next twenty years are going to be, in many respects, the most serious in the history of the race. Within that period will be largely determined whether the Negro is going to be able to retain the hold which he has now upon the industries of the South, or whether his place will be filled by white people from a distance. Alfred Holt Stone says: "To-day the most portentous figure on the economic horizon of the Negro is his white

competitor ".   Professor Kelly Miller writes thus : " The
number of Negroes following mechanical pursuits is quite
considerable in the South, but fades away to vanishing
point as we proceed North.   Even in the South the Negro
mechanic is fast giving way to the conquering European
workman.   If we may read the shadow that coming
events cast before them, it seems clear that within half
a century Negro workmen along the lines of higher
mechanical skill will be as rare in Atlanta and Richmond
as they are in Boston and Philadelphia."

W. P. Livingstone, in " The Race Conflict," thus expresses his opinion : " Indications exist that the white
working man is now beginning to crowd out the coloured
working man, while any attempt to substitute coloured
for white labour is always keenly resented and usually
results in failure ".   And again the same authority says :
" The general conclusion one draws from a general survey
of the situation is that the Negro as an economic unit
is being quietly but resolutely boycotted by the white
population, and is gradually ceasing to have any industrial
relation to it.   He is steadily being forced into a separate
industrial existence.   The position is full of menace and
danger.   The struggle is one for existence, for life itself,
and life is of more value than civil and political rights."

P. A. Bruce, in " The Rise of the New South," published in 1905, says : " The development of the South
along industrial lines is going to make life harder for the
black man.   The day will come in the South, just as it
came long ago in the North, when for lack of skill, lack
of sobriety, and lack of persistency, the Negro will find
it more difficult to stand up as a rival to the white working man.   Already it is the ultimate fate of the Negro
that is in the balance, not the ultimate fate of the Southern
States.   The darkest day for the Southern whites is
passed, the darkest days for the Southern blacks have
only just begun."   Ray Stannard Baker, on page 85 of
" Following the Colour Line," quotes a remarkable and
brutally frank letter from a white workman, the gist of

which is : "I only want niggers to do the dirty and un-pleasant work ; if they get trained and try to do my work, I kill them".

If I read the conclusions of this last-named writer aright, he does not take quite the same view as the other authors I have cited, but seems to think the industrial awakening of the South will give increased opportunity and scope for the Negro. I confess I find it difficult to follow him to this conclusion.

The Southern States have been, and still are to a large extent, in a backward industrial condition. Their natural resources are enormous, land is plentiful and cheap, and the manual labourers, as well as the skilled artisans necessary to such a state of society, have been in demand. Life has been comparatively easy, food plentiful, and competition has not been keen. Notwith-standing social disadvantages and drawbacks, it is im-possible that any part of the United States can long re-main in this state. The last decade has shown long strides towards modern industrial conditions. With these will probably come a great demand for manual labour, but a demand for greater adaptability ; competi-tion will be keener, the whole industrial fabric will speed up. Experience in the North seems to show that under such conditions the Negro gets left behind. Suited in many respects to a society of which unscientific agri-culture is the mainstay, he has not yet proved himself capable of taking a satisfactory place in the more complex industrialism of modern times. It is significant that in the greatest manufacturing industry of the South, the cotton mill, the Negro has been entirely barred. Is this going to be the case as others are established ?

Closely knit and completely organized Trades Unions are not yet conspicuous in the South, but the movement has begun. The industrial future of the Negro will depend to a considerable degree on whether or not he will be admitted to white Unions, or conversely, will have the ability to co-operate and organize on his own account. The tendencies in this direction are not at present uniform or clear. I did not hear of any purely Negro trade organizations entirely distinct from white Unions. In some callings however, such as miners and iron workers, which are concentrated in small areas, and in which large numbers of both white and black are employed, the white Labour Unions have been forced to recognize their black fellow-workers. Previous to recognition the employers had taken advantage of the Negro as a strike breaker, and when attempts had been made by white and black to co-operate, they had raised the cry of Nigger equality, and thus gained an industrial victory by raising a social bogey. The stratagem was, however, so obvious that the white workers encouraged the Negroes to form separate Unions but linked with their own under joint leadership, thus making it impossible in the future to set race against race. Such corporate action for common ends should tend to attenuate race feeling. I am unable to say from my own experience what the results in this direction have been, but a close study of local conditions in the iron and coal area, say at Birmingham, Ala., should give interesting data.

Notwithstanding this experience in the coal and iron districts I do not think it likely that, until industrial forces have been more closely marshalled, the white Unionists will welcome Negro members or even tolerate allied Negro Unions. Race feeling must be reckoned with. In trades scattered over a wide area, or those in which Negro workers are few, the tendency will probably be to ignore them, or refuse membership to them when they make application. This is the case at present in many trades. Other Labour Unions specifically, by their rules, deny membership to Negroes. The following list of Unions, which is probably not complete, refuse under their rules to admit the Negro : engineers, firemen, telegraphers, carmen, switchmen, electric workers, boilermakers, and wire weavers.

As more technical and complex training is required with the incoming of modern methods and machinery, such as the substitution of electric power for steam, so the Negro becomes less in his element, and it is difficult to see how under present conditions in the South he is to get the necessary knowledge and skill. This handicap will be a factor in keeping him to manual labour, or at best to the old time trades, and prevent him joining the army of recruits to the modern callings. Broadly speaking, the outlook in this direction does not seem too hopeful.

If this was all, and the future of the Negro depended on his keeping pace with the industrial developments that are bound to come, I should be inclined to share the somewhat pessimistic ideas of some of the writers I have quoted. But it is not all. The present situation gives the Negro a present opportunity. There is work for him, and bread for him, and more, he can by industry, thrift, and foresight gain a surplus. He may not be able to find a place and compete in the complex industrial organization that is being gradually woven, but those who are engaged in it must have food and raw material. The man providing these, the worker on the land, will have an honourable and remunerative place in any industrial system. In this field, as I have hinted and will demonstrate, the Negro is to an encouraging extent making good. Here is a future for him. His leaders are urging him to strenuous, intelligent, and sustained effort in order to secure this place, and he is responding.

Edgar Gardner Murphy says: " The South has sometimes abridged the Negro's right to vote, but the South has not yet abridged his right in any direction of human interest, or of honest effort to earn his bread. And the right to earn his bread is at present of much more importance to him than the right to vote."

In the South a livelihood—without a vote.

CHAPTER XXV.

CITY AND COUNTRY.

THIS will be but a short chapter. In drawing the pictures I have done of conditions in the North and those in the South, it has been, in the main, a comparison of the condition and prospects of the Negro in city life and in the country. But the point needs emphasizing, especially for my South African friends. Whatever may be the genius of certain West African peoples of more or less mixed blood for living in densely crowded cities and evolving a city civilization, it is not the life natural to the Negro of the South, nor to the Bantu people of South Africa.

Our native people of South Africa are a race whose whole tradition is that of a pastoral and agricultural life, who, if uninfluenced by the white man, and freed from the economic pressure due to his presence, would ask nothing better than a life on the land. Forced by circumstances to leave their homes and go to centres of industrialism to earn a livelihood, they yet yearn with a great yearning for the old life and return to it as soon as possible. It is unhappily too true that the pleasures of city life are ensnaring some of the young people, and they find the life led by their fathers tame and insipid, and in some cases never return to it. I feel that this tendency, if allowed to develop, will lead to the demoralization of both races, and will engender race conflict, and I have written and spoken in favour of a policy that will mean the strengthening, and not the weakening, of the love of the Bantu for the life on the land.

Even if it means the postponement of industrial

233

development it will mean a saner, more wholesome life for both races, and will be much more likely to result in the happiness, safe development, and true prosperity of both. I foresee that if the South African native people of both sexes and all ages are tempted to live permanently in our cities and densely populated centres, they will fail to make a satisfactory place for themselves. They are not fitted to withstand the temptations which will beset them, their place will be the lowest with little chance of rising, and in addition, their presence and competition will rouse the jealousy and hostility of the white man. We may safely predict their demoralization, and in their fall they will drag down the white man, and at the same time both races will be increasingly embittered by contact and competition.

The hope of the Bantu and the safety of the white man lie in giving the former a healthy, hopeful life in wholesome surroundings, with opportunity for development therein. In the interests of posterity, we should see to it that the Bantu people have sufficient land on which they may live their natural life. If from land hunger, greed of gain, apathy, or all combined we neglect this, our children will have heavy toll to pay. Long ago I saw this, and the longer I live in South Africa the clearer it seems to me.

One of the most interesting points I desired to elucidate on coming to America was how far a people akin to our Bantu had prospered or otherwise in the complex life of cities, and how far, like our own people, they desired and seemed suited for country life. In this particular branch of my inquiry, as indeed throughout it all, I had to remember that I was not considering a purely African people but one having probably twenty-five per cent of the blood of the race who built the cities, and whose genius originated and controlled all the complex activities of American civilization. I found that though the proportion was small, there were many thousands of coloured people who had "made good" in all the large cities North and South. I visited many of these and found clean orderly homes, often in surroundings which made one marvel that they had not succumbed to the baseness which everywhere surrounded them. But the proportion was small after all, and although I have only my general impressions, based upon many visits to these homes, to rely upon, my conclusion was that the majority of those who had thus established themselves were of mixed race.

The rest seemed hopeless, there seemed no realization of their degradation, and no desire to rise out of it. They fell prone before the temptations that surrounded them, and too often wallowed in vice and crime. Healthy child life was impossible, the home was the street. Even the best of them could not rise to the opportunities the city gives to other races, the majority barely held their own at their miserably low level. They were a constant menace and source of demoralization to the whites by whom they were surrounded. Infinitely better for both races, at whatever cost of money, or of ease to the whites, if they could be entirely removed. The city is a veritable sewer and death-trap for the Negro; the gain to the race in numbers, character, and efficiency, achieved in more wholesome surroundings, is lost amid infinite misery and degradation in the cities.

The prophets and seers of the race can preach no doctrine more urgently needed than resistance to the uttermost of the lure of the city.

The present life of the average Negro in the wide spaces of the South is not ideal. It lacks much to make it whole, and to fill all the demands of his nature. But all the necessaries for a wholesome simple life are present, and within him, if he likes to call upon them, are powers to make it fuller and finer. Neither man nor Nature can prevent his steady advancement if he so wills. Indeed Nature, with genial skies, abundant rainfall, and a soil that will readily respond to intelligent labour, smiles with

promise. Every advance makes further progress easier.
And in following the plough, the Negro does no violence
to his nature and natural gifts. The bewilderment and
helplessness he displays in centres of population, and
which condemns him to the contempt of the stronger
race, is here replaced by a familiarity with his surroundings which, joined to industry and thrift, will earn for
him their respect.

The success already achieved by many of his race in
this field is full of promise, and will be a beacon light to
those who are still struggling. The wisest leaders of his
race, and the wisest of his white friends, are constantly
urging him to this. I speak perhaps dogmatically, but
I can prove my words—on the land is the salvation of
the Negro.

CHAPTER XXVI.

LIVING EXAMPLES.

SCATTERED throughout the South are individual Negroes who have built up homes, often from nothing, which demonstrate what is possible when the will to do is present.

For several days I stayed at such a home and found the experience one of the most illuminating I had during the course of my journey. To reach the place I had to drive some 16 miles from a small country town which was the rail terminus. The weather had been wet, and the journey reminded me of many I had taken in South Africa. After the first mile or two the road was extremely bad, in places knee-deep in heavy mud, and full of dangerous holes. We had to cross several streams (branches as they call them in the South) running swift and deep, and at one or two a number of wagons and buggies were collected waiting for the water to go down. At some little risk we crossed, and finally got to the home of my host.

I found an excellent double-storied house, standing in a large yard planted with Bermuda grass, with many rose trees, and notably a magnificent Marshal Neil with hundreds of fragrant flowers growing over the wide verandah. There were outbuildings, stables, cowsheds, and barns, all built of wood, and though untidy as compared with an English standard, infinitely better in construction, and far cleaner than many belonging to white farmers I had seen in the South.

I found splendid mules, good cattle and pigs, and

innumerable fowls and turkeys, and far around the house was cultivated ground. Standing in the yard were about twenty-five bales of cotton which I learned subsequently was held back from sale, because my host was unwilling to sell at present prices, and was keeping back for an advance. Water was laid on to the house; it was fitted with the telephone, and in a garage was a motor-car. I found my host was not at home. The late rains had prevented work at a watermill he owned, and he was away there taking advantage of the present fine weather to make up lost time.

His wife, a very pleasant and exceedingly well-spoken mulatto woman, meanwhile showed me my bed-room. It was upstairs and was, I think, the largest apartment I had hitherto slept in during my present American visit. There were five windows commanding extensive views, a stove, easy-chairs, and a most comfortable and scrupulously clean double bed.

My supper was served in an ample dining-room, and everything on the table, milk, cream, eggs, butter, fruit, preserves and most excellent corn bread, was of the best. Here I may say that both my host and hostess at first, and for some time afterwards, declined to eat with me; it was not the custom, but towards the end of my stay they were prevailed upon to take their places at the table.

It was getting dusk when the master of the house arrived from the mill, dusty and tired, and no wonder, for he had left the house between one and two in the morning, and had been working continuously ever since. He was a mulatto, probably fifty-five years of age, intelligent and well spoken, direct and lucid, one who inspired you with the confidence that his statements were correct, and his conclusions arrived at after due consideration. He did not hesitate to express his views, and to correct you if he thought you were in the wrong. When talking of his own personal experiences, he was natural and modest; the long talks we had on the character and prospects of his race were truthful and open, but not, as will be seen, very hopeful. After his supper, and over a wood fire, for the nights were still a little chilly, we had a talk, which, with those he favoured me with on other occasions, gave me an insight into actual conditions and personal experience for which I feel most grateful.

He began his working life as a labourer, working on a farm for a wage of ten dollars a month and his food. Till he married he never bought a suit of clothes, his apparel was of cotton grown by his parents or himself, and spun and woven and made into garments by his mother. As a labourer he stinted and saved till he accumulated $100, and from that time he had never worked for a master.

With the $100 he leased some land, bought a working horse for $50, and began ploughing on his own account. He then bought land and gradually added to it, obtained cattle, and with the manure improved the land he bought. Bit by bit he worked up, until now he was owner of the place I was in with all that appertained to it, and 2400 acres of freehold land without incumbrance.

The land was not naturally rich, but manuring and cultivation had so improved it, that much of it now yielded a bale of cotton to the acre, and it was getting still better. He rented out one part of his estate, and had sixteen coloured tenants working on shares, and two white men also rented portions. Having so much land, his neighbours, other than tenants, were at a distance, his estate was a self-centred community. He got on well with his white neighbours, and had personally no complaint against them; their relations were amicable.

I asked about his tenants, and more particularly whether any of them were acquiring property, and becoming financially independent. He answered emphatically, but I thought rather sorrowfully, "No Sir, not one. They are," he said, "all thriftless, and are in debt and will remain in debt." They are most of them good workers, they grow good crops, quite as good as most of the white men in the section; it is not indolence that prevents them rising, but extravagance, unthrift, and desiring a good time in the present. They cannot resist the temptation to spend, and even here, away from the railway, the travelling agent puts the temptation before them, and they incur debt to obtain luxuries. They will buy tailor-made suits costing $16 to $20 or even more, shoes costing $5 and then plough in them, buggies, sewing-machines, organs, and gramophones they must have if their neighbour has such. Beguiled into buying on the instalment system, they often fail to meet the instalments when due, and then borrow elsewhere at high rates of interest to keep them up, and thus become further involved.

One of his tenants, a hard worker, with a wife and two children, who had been on the land for several years, had an average crop of from twelve to sixteen bales of cotton, and last year raised in addition 230 bushels of corn, and yet at the present moment was in debt between $400 and $500.

When a new tenant applied for land he almost invariably wanted a loan to begin with, generally to settle up his indebtedness elsewhere. Just lately one came and asked for $100 to pay off a white man, professing this man was his only creditor. Immediately this amount was settled other claims were put in, and $200 more had to be provided.

It was quite a common thing for the tenants to sell all the corn they raised, knowing full well they would need it later, and then travel to town and make occasion for a holiday and buy at higher prices.

My host employed farm labourers, they got from $12 to $15 a month and their board and lodging, their food being the same as the farmer eats. Yet he never engaged one without having to advance $10 or $15, and before the labourer has been at work a week he invariably borrows more, often to purchase some trashy luxury.

The same thing, he said, happens in the towns. Extravagance and thriftlessness are conspicuous there. The

Negro can get work in the towns easily enough, but my informant told me he had noticed that in many callings he is giving place to white men.   Since he remembered, the coloured man had been supplanted in many branches of work which had been exclusively his own. When he visited the county town he found that even the barbers and shoeblacks are sometimes white, though àt one time all were Negroes.

Skilled Negro artisans can also get plenty of work; there is, he said, a good demand for them, and they work alongside white men, but he does not think they are increasing in numbers as he would like.

There are professional men of Negro race.   The doctors, who are most numerous, are not, he thinks, making much headway.   So many of our people, he said, work for whites that they feel if anything is wrong they must send for a white doctor.   Being often in debt they are not their own masters, and cannot choose whom they would.

In commerce and mercantile life he thought there was not much advance.   Our people, he said, do not support their own : there is no union among them.   They go and spend their cash at the white store and then come to the black store when they want credit.   Much might be done if the Negroes stuck together, but they won't, and I have no hope that they will do so in the future.

He was despondent about the attitude of whites and blacks generally ; things were worse, he said, than twenty years ago : the white man was harder on the black, he crowds him more, is not so kindly, but takes advantage and exploits him.   By his weakness the black man plays into his hands.

He himself was on the register ; if he chose he could cast his vote, but he did not take the trouble.   It was no use, the white man would not let it count for anything of use to the black.   A few others he knew were on the voters' roll, the white man put them there in order to be able to say they were not excluded, but like him, they did not go to the poll, and for the same reason.

16

Speaking of race antagonism, he said he had just received a letter from a married daughter living in Arkansas, near the scene of the present great Mississippi flood.
The Negroes there are tenants or workers for the large
white landowners, and the latter are afraid if the Negroes
left the estate on account of the rising river, they would
get scattered, and they would never recover them, so
they forced them to remain on the estates, and in consequence over one hundred were drowned. His daughter
told him that one planter or landowner met in town some
of those who had left the land, and he shot three at sight.
Asked what would be done to him, he answered probably
nothing, but in any case, if there was an inquiry, he
would plead self-defence, and he would walk out.

I asked whether education would help matters and
he said yes, it would. Like so many uneducated men of
character, ability, and efficiency, he seemed to have an
almost pathetic belief in the value of what he had never
received, and the lack of which he had personally experienced. He said both white and black were ignorant
and prejudiced. Many whites would not bother to send
their children to school, though fair schools were provided for them, and the position of Negro education was,
he thought, worse than it was years ago. The State appropriation for his section was miserably small. Tuskegee
and similar institutions were doing good, but it was
nothing among the shiftless, careless people scattered
over the land.

I took walks in the neighbourhood and visited the
fields and the cabins. The latter were of a rather better
class than usual, but all might very easily have been
made much better. Passing one in the early morning,
I heard an organ wailing out hymn tunes, the fence was
all broken down, the yard and wood pile wanted attention. The vegetable gardens were small and poor, and
although rose-bushes grew wildly and wantonly in many
of the yards, it was due to climate and not to culture. I
passed one cabin with the yard littered with broken

buggies: wheels, bodies, shafts, and axles were lying about in confusion. I guessed these must have been the broken remains of eight or ten vehicles, and yet there was no appearance of a workshop. Later I asked my host about it, and he said the occupier of the cabin had bought them one after another, some new, some second-hand, and as one got broken had somehow obtained another, mostly on credit. He reckoned there were the remains of a dozen buggies in the yard, and no attempt was made to utilize the parts or repair the broken ones.

While I attached great value to the opinion of my friend, both in local and general matters, I could not help thinking that he was too pessimistic, especially for one whose career in the practical affairs of life had been a signal success. I may say I had similar conversations with several other coloured men living in the same neighbourhood, a building contractor of long experience, a blacksmith, a mattressmaker, several teachers, male and female, and others, and though they did not strike quite such a pessimistic note as my host, they generally corroborated his facts and conclusions. My readers will find that I do not accept this view in its entirety, but balance it by observations and experience gathered elsewhere. Still it is of value to get the unbiassed, matured opinion of such a man as my friend.

My hostess showed me one day her stock of canned fruits, preserves, and hams and bacon. I could attest the quality from actual experience, and the quantity and get-up would have been a pardonable source of pride to an English farmer's wife. Pears, apples, peaches, and grapes grow easily and in abundance, and as there is little local demand she preserves them. Early potatoes and peas they expect to eat on Easter Sunday, and the first strawberries about the same time. This is followed by a second crop. Corn she said can be grown by all; if bought it cost about a dollar a bushel at present. All vegetables can easily be grown. Onions of very large size and mammoth pumpkins will keep through the

16 *

winter. Sweet potatoes are a big crop, and sugar-cane will ripen in the season, and from it they make their molasses. Eggs are plentiful at this time, and the price is twelve cents a dozen, at the highest they reach twenty-five cents. Chickens are cheap in proportion. They could not market all this small produce at high prices, but they could live extremely cheaply and well. No one, she said, need go hungry, and no one with land properly utilized need buy any article of food ; they could live well all the year round on what the land produced. On the table in abundance might be fowls, eggs, pork, bacon, vegetables of all kinds, corn and all its grand products, molasses, milk, butter, and fruit in plenty.

My friends had sent into the world sons and daughters, some scattered far, others living near. The latter seemed to be following in the footsteps of their parents, their houses were good, and their surroundings clean and pleasant. One or two were engaged in teaching their race the way their father had trod in life and work.

I am thus stating the case of an individual because it shows what is possible to a man of Negro race in the South land, and also because here I had an opportunity in quiet over a fire and pipe to get the opinions of a shrewd observer on the conditions and prospects of his race.

It will be illustrative of his feelings if I tell, as told to me, the story of a visit to the North, some incidents in which had touched my friend deeply. He decided, with his wife, to pay a visit to the World's Fair at St. Louis. Holidays did not come frequently into their life, they could afford it easily, and they wanted to experience something of the bigger world. When they boarded the train the local white conductor, who knew them well, offered to put them into a sleeper, otherwise they had to sit up all night. This kindly offer was evidently much appreciated by them, but they declined it, fearing such a breach of Southern custom. They had been told by a travelled daughter to go to a coloured hotel in St. Louis, but the white hackman there who asked their patronage, said it was not a fit place for them, and recommended a white boarding-house, and took them there. In perturbation of mind they entered a very nice house with white folks sitting about. Fearing greatly, they were moving to depart, when the proprietress came forward, and probably understanding, asked if they were French as she was. They replied, of French descent but born in America. A bedroom and a bath attached was given to them, and they spoke with a depth of feeling that touched me of the kindness shown to them. They said they were treated just like the other boarders, and when they went out to the Fair for the day, a lunch was prepared for them, their every want was anticipated. The only drawback was the ever-present dread that some one from Alabama might recognize and denounce them. They left this place of happy memory and went North to the great lakes, where they spent a day or two at a holiday resort. They came back to St. Louis, but not to the French boarding-house, but to the one their daughter had recommended. The contrast was nauseous, dirt, discomfort, disorder, bad food, unclean beds, no light, no water. The price was the same, but it was evident that the marked and unpleasant contrast was felt to be a reproach to their colour. The other was as evidently a memory to be cherished. It was not the World's Fair, not Chicago nor the great lakes that was of prime importance: these were hardly mentioned; it was the kindly consideration of the railroad conductor, and their reception and treatment at the French boarding-house that made the holiday the happy event it had evidently been to both of them.

Throughout the South may be found men of Negro race who have similarly " made good ". And not individuals alone, there are communities of freeholders who are permeated by the same spirit of self-help, and who, out of individual success, have built up a corporate life rich in effort for the common good. There are counties in the South, with a preponderating Negro population, in which the bulk of the coloured farmers own the land they till, free of all incumbrance. In one instance at least these freeholders form ninety per cent of the total number of coloured cultivators.

In some instances these communities owe their existence to some self-helpful yet self-sacrificing individual, often to the presence of one who has been trained at Hampton or Tuskegee, and is giving of that he has been taught. In comparison with the millions who live for the day, and are bond slaves to the future, they may not be many, but the ringing notes of purposeful work are being heard and heeded by more and more, and I cannot doubt, but that following on the attainment of the material, will come a desire for a higher and deeper culture.

CHAPTER XXVII.

THE GREAT OPPORTUNITY.

I ONCE heard an eloquent and distinguished Negro leader, whose blood and characteristics were predominantly white, deliver a moving speech on the prime importance of cherishing those of the race who were gifted with exceptional talent or genius, and seeing to it that they got every advantage, and were not neglected nor discouraged. The speech was addressed to a large audience of Negroes. I was the only white man present. I looked for an intelligent response, but felt the message fell on stony ground. While understanding, I dissented. Looking at the people it seemed to me the theme should be discipline and duty for the mass, and the practical way to secure the one and instil a sense of the other, was to show them the way to hope and independence, to urge them to take the opportunity they have, and make the necessary effort and sacrifice to build up healthy homes on the land.

Professor W. C. Wilcox says: "Where such a lower people has disappeared, the causes of their death have been mainly disease, vice, and profound discouragement. It seems to me clear that each one of these causes is affecting the Negro race far more deeply and unfavourably at the present time than it was at the date of their emancipation. I have not found one expression in the South of dissent from the opinion that the joyous buoyancy of the race is passing away, that they feel upon them a burden of responsibility to which they are unequal, that the lower classes of the Negroes are resentful, and the better classes are not certain or sanguine of the outcome. If this judgment be true, I can only say it is the most fatal scourge of national decay and death."

Is there justification for this sense of discouragement? Is there no hope for the race?

Dr. Booker T. Washington added to the piled up debt his people owe to him by undertaking a journey through the South and East of Europe, and there investigating the actual conditions of life of the proletariat, and especially the life and opportunities of the peasantry. His published optimistic conclusions in the book describing his experiences, "The man furthest down," should put hope into the hearts of the Southern Negro. He found life for him in the Southern States far more tolerable, and opportunity far greater, than for the peasantry of the old European countries he visited. Later on I venture to make similar comparisons in regard to many of the great things of life, with classes and communities with which I am familiar, and I emphatically say, that when the fullest weight is given to the many reasons for discouragement, there is a bright hope for the Negro in the future, if he is man enough to seize it.

The great question of the immediate future seems to me to be: Has the race the insight to see the great opportunity and the concentrated force of purpose to seize it? For there is a great opportunity open to the mass of the Negro people, such as is offered to few of the backward races of the world.

To prove this I must bring forward in marshalled order some facts and figures which I have been leading up to in previous chapters.

In travelling over the South land the impression the visitor gets is one of ample space for development. Even in the older States not one-third of the total area could be called improved, and more than one-half is uncleared and uncultivated. A much greater proportion of the land than in South Africa can be put under the plough, and the rainfall is abundant and well distributed. It is true that much of the land has been distressingly abused and gone out of cultivation, but by modern methods of manuring, rotation of crops, and green soiling, it can be gradually built up again, possibly even beyond its original fertility. The climate and soil are suitable for a great variety of crops, both those of the temperate and those of the sub-tropical zones. Timber for fuel and ordinary building is everywhere plentiful, and the country is well watered by many streams. When I compared it with the sun-stricken karroo of the Cape Colony, without fuel, water, or shelter, and the arid wastes of large extent in the interior of Australia lacking in all these, it seemed to me a land to which Nature has given, as compared with many others, all that man requires to build up prosperous and happy homes.

The terrible, often life and soul destroying isolation of these other lands need not be endured, and the economic loss due to lack of communication with the outer world need not be experienced. The water-ways are noble, and railways intersect the land. Judging by the standard of the producing British Colonies land is cheap; judged by its possibilities it is very cheap. I made inquiries in all sections as to price, possibilities, and market rates for produce. I found that ordinary farm land, without improvements, could be bought at from $5 to $25 an acre according to fertility and proximity to rail. There are sections suited to special cultures which are correspondingly low in price. In the tide water areas, land suitable for growing early vegetables, which bring high prices in the Northern cities, may be bought at prices which allow of handsome profits in this branch of agriculture. Flat pine lands were pointed out to me which would yield a profit of $35 an acre on lumber and turpentine, and which when cut over and well cultivated are very fertile. This land could be bought at from $10 to $35 an acre according to facilities for transport.

As I have already dwelt on this question of land values in a previous chapter, I will not now go into more detail. I have made it clear, I think, that there is cheap land in abundance to be bought, and there is no bar to the Negro buying it. Is he in a position to do so? I made many inquiries and give the results below. Southerners familiar with their own section may probably find these figures do not fit in. I had to take the country as a whole, and I think they are fairly correct. I placed them before many experienced men, both white and black, and they were approved by the majority as being a fair reflection of conditions in the South as a whole.

I first take the lowest class of worker, the wage-earner on the land. The agricultural labourer, who is generally a single man, gets from $12 to $15 a month with food and lodging. He has only clothes to buy, and there is no reason why he should not save from $100 to $120 yearly. In four or five years he could certainly save a sum of $500, probably more. With this could be bought outright 25 acres at $10 the acre, a working mule at say $125, and the balance for plough, implements, and food till the crop was realized. I am well aware that this would be cutting it fine, and judgment and economy would have to be exercised, but I know it can be done. The probable result would be a gratifying reward for the exertion and self-denial. It is possible to get from such an area 20 bales of cotton each weighing 500 lb. which at 12 cents per lb., and with seed worth $10 to the acre, means $800 gross. From this must be deducted fertilizer at $5 the acre, say $125, and extra labour in the picking season, say $75, sundries another $100, or a net return of $500. I am aware that a bale to the acre, even on such well-fertilized land as this would be, is beyond the average at present grown, but even if only 10 bales were obtained there is a comfortable balance to the good. Once the first struggle is over, the position of such a man should gradually improve. His land would be getting heart, and he could accelerate the improvement by increasing his livestock. Fair cows can be bought from $20

to $30, and really good ones from $40 to $50. Ordinary
work horses may be bought from $80 to $120, and good
trained mules from $125 to $200. Pigs and poultry are
cheap.

Now for the opportunities of other classes along the
same lines. Labourers other than farm hands often
earn more than the figures we have been dealing with.
Railway labourers, platelayers, etc., may receive from
$1¼ to $3 a day. Teamsters from 75 cents to $1½, dock-
side labourers can earn much more, though here the
work is not continuous. The remuneration of unskilled
work varies of course considerably, but the main point
is that there is no unemployment, and certainly at the
wages I have mentioned the single man can save if he
will. I inquired about the cost of board and lodging for
men of this class, and again got answers that varied, but
I think it is quite possible, if a man likes to rent a room
and provide for himself, he can live, not only sufficiently,
but well, on $2½ to $3 a week. This means the possibility
of saving, but it is only possible to the man who can deny
himself the pleasures of the moment for the greater end
in the future. It is probable that, notwithstanding the
higher money wages of the town labourer, he cannot save
much more than his brother in the country, but that, for
the single man, is sufficient to enable him, after a few
years' saving, to make an independent start on the land.

When we come to the case of the single man who
is a skilled artisan there can be no question but that he
has a big margin for saving. His wages vary in different
sections, but $3 a day may be taken as an average rate,
and $4 is not uncommon. He may earn by the hour
from 35 to 45 cents; in one section I visited it was
driven up to 65 cents for a time. In some country districts
wages are paid by the month, and $75 was mentioned as
an average wage. Here living expenses would be correspondingly low. Even taking this lower remuneration, and
deducting $20 a month for board and lodging, and $10 a
month for clothes, the artisan would have a balance of

$45 to the good in the month or no less than $500 in the year.

I am satisfied that industry and thrift will enable the competent, industrious single Negro artisan to save this sum in an average year. One hundred pounds sterling saved every year; how many millions in Britain never even dream of it, or if they did, their dreams would never be realized. Yet here it is quite possible to these Negro artisans of the South.

In five years the savings of such a man, invested at a moderate and safe rate of interest, should amount to $3000. This means that if he liked to take to agriculture he could at once purchase and stock a small improved farm, or a larger unimproved one, and raise enough in a very few years to return the purchase price. Such a man need never be in debt. He could buy his requirements and sell his produce on the very best terms, as well as any white man, and yearly improve his holding and add to his possessions.

All this it may be said appears to be possible for the single man in regular employment, but what of the married man. I have already pointed out that the unskilled married Negro labourer with a young family has a very hard time to make ends meet whether in town or country. And so the unskilled married labourer has in every country. In the South such a man has an advantage in the comparatively high wages often earned by young people, and if the family pull together there is no reason why, here again, an independence on the land may not be achieved with the help of the young people. A family of six, father, mother, with say two boys and two girls in their teens, although all unskilled, might expect to earn a total income of $20 a week. Father and eldest son say $1 a day each, the second son $4 a week, and the two girls say $2½ each a week with board. On combined earnings such as these a sum might soon be saved sufficient to buy a farm on such terms as I have mentioned, and once on the land every member of the

family is valuable.   A single man on the land must concentrate on the paying crop, which here in the South is
cotton, but with a family it only requires common sense
and industry to arrange a division of labour by which
not only could the cotton crop be grown, but the greater
part of the food required by the family also.

I know it will be said of this proposition, as I have
heard it said of other schemes that involve hard work to
ensure success, that no allowance has been made for re-
creation and amusement, nor for doctors' bills, accident,
death, or a dozen other contingencies.   Quite right, we
all have to face these things, and it is impossible to say
what these contingencies may be.   But with regard to
relaxation and amusement, I would say I offer hope in
life and work which will make it of little account.   The
underfed, stunted, anæmic city dweller, whose life consists
in performing one monotonous mechanical task all the
hours of daylight, and without hope of doing anything
else for the term of his natural life, craves the artificial
light, the glare and romance of picture palace or music
hall.   But the man who feels that every spade struck into
his soil, and every load of fertilizer applied, is to bring
him its natural return, and who sees in field and barn
and on his table the fruits of his labour, who knows that
each year's toil brings him nearer independence, has no
time or money to waste on such gaudy misrepresentations
of life.   He has work in the present, and hope for the
future, and what better gifts come to any of us?

I have spoken thus far as if this great opportunity
was to be taken by each individual without the co-operation and help of his fellows, and have shown that it is
possible to the individual.   But the benefits of co-operation and mutual help are being taught to and learned by
the Negro in the South.   It is written large in the
teachings of Hampton and Tuskegee, and may be seen in
actual work in many sections of the rural South.   It
will be said that the Negro is at a disadvantage in buying
his land, implements, and necessaries, and in marketing

his produce. So he is to a certain extent : all isolated small producers are, all over the world. But if he combines with his fellows there is no reason why he should not be as favourably circumstanced as the best.

If twenty young Negroes met together and decided to work and save to this end, and while retaining their individuality, co-operated together to invest and buy and sell, all that was possible to them as individuals becomes certain as co-operators, and the stimulus of mutual help and the strength that comes of united effort is theirs.

Even without such direct economic co-operation, communities of Negro farmers as they became larger would become self-contained. There would be room and work for the Negro carpenter and blacksmith, for the Negro storekeeper, for the Negro teacher and preacher, for the Negro physician and business man. Nor need it be said that the life of such communities must be narrow, and that human nature needs a broader, richer life, linked with the culture of the past, and reaching forward to a higher culture in the future. There has been too much of this kind of talk proferred to the unbalanced Negro mind in the past, and I cannot see that it has tended to set him firmly on the true path to a broader, richer life. I would be the last to depreciate the value of a true culture in life, and I would agree with those who say that the highest thing in life is to learn to live. But the path is long and steep, and what the Negro wants at present, and before everything else, is a clean home life, a hope in his work, and freedom from the harassing dread of race antagonism. The two first named he may have if he seizes the great opportunity. Banded together in rural communities, he may be largely free from race antagonism. The white man will still make the laws to which the Negro must submit, but the daily dread of exploitation and injustice he may leave behind, and live with his own folk, free to mould his life as he will.

Nor need that life be circumscribed to things material. Thousands of his own race are being trained to help him in his practical efforts and to add to them knowledge of deeper things, intellectual, moral, and spiritual. Friends, both white and black, would rejoice to help those who seriously set out to help themselves in all that made for a higher life based on material well-being.

There is no desire on the part of such friends to condemn all to the life of a peasant, immersed in water and soil, but rather to give to the race opportunity through hopeful work to the best of which it is capable. But they rightly want to put first things first, and rightly realize that for such a people, weak in purpose, and prone to flutter after shadows, the rural home is the true beginning.

Cherish the gifted of the race say some. Lift the mass say I, and in doing so is the true opportunity for the gifted, for the trained educated leaders; not in following will-o'-the-wisps and wailing that they are shut " Behind the veil," but in leading a people into God's sunlight, and making hopeless lives full of hope.

The Negro has many friends in the North who have given, and are giving, largely of brain and heart and substance to help him. I can think of no more practical way to help him at the present time, than to buy up large areas of unimproved land, establish communication, and subdivide and sell in suitable farms to those willing to make the effort and sacrifice to obtain them. It would need judgment and local knowledge and supervision, but it need not mean any pecuniary loss. It would not mean giving or pauperizing, but helping with capital and business experience. At Hampton, Tuskegee, and elsewhere money from this philanthropic source has been wisely expended in training men and women of Negro race capable of leading in this movement. It now requires that the Negro masses should have the opportunity of taking full benefit of those who have been so liberally provided with the training necessary to enable them to help their own people.

And the South should help. Far too many in the

South lean upon the Negro to their own undoing. The existing modifications of the old plantation system, under which white landowners rent their lands on the share crop system to Negro tenants is bad for all. It makes good farming and permanent improvement impossible, and drives out all hope from the hearts of the tenants. It frees the landowners from their proper responsibility, and encourages them to wring the uttermost out of those who in turn ravish the soil, without regard to the future.

If the rural South is to be socially and industrially healthy there must be a chance in life for those who till the soil, both white and black. The first need of the South is homes, and the white South will be blind indeed if they place obstacles in the way of the black man making his home on the soil. No one suffers more than the white Southerner, man and woman alike, from the immoral and criminal Negro population of the towns and cities, and they would be the greatest gainers if these cesspools could be cleansed.

I do not hope that the great opportunity will draw from the cities the present Negro population. They, like the submerged tenth of the great cities of Europe, have been so deeply inoculated with the virus, that they can never be reclaimed. The preaching of the gospel of rural regeneration, and the experiences of those who have accepted it may, however, stem the present drift. It has, indeed, already lessened the flow in that direction.

It is likely that as the opportunity is seized by more and more, one effect will be to increase the rewards of labour, both to those who remain in the cities, and to those who are tenants and labourers on the land. The employers of such labour in the South, like many in South Africa, take the mistaken view that this will be an economic disaster.

With us in South Africa there is an increasing minority of employers who, from insight and experience, take a wiser view, and who recognize that higher wages paid for manual labour does not necessarily mean in-

creased cost of production. They have begun to ask
how it is that countries in which the wages of farm labour
are far higher than with us in South Africa, can yet
export to our market all kinds of farm produce and beat
our own in quality and price. They are beginning to
find that even a native farm servant who values his job
because he is satisfied with the conditions, is a more
satisfactory, and even cheaper labourer, than one who
is unwillingly working out an accumulated debt at perhaps half the current wage. It is a hard lesson to learn ;
the other course of paying the minimum seems obviously
so much more in the interest of the employer that it is
little wonder that the doctrine has fallen, for the most
part, on deaf ears. But the South must learn it too, and
the only way is through experience, and if Negro labour
becomes scarcer and higher in price the first step towards
economic efficiency has been taken. It will not only
make the employer increasingly anxious to get the best
results from his labour, but as it has done with us in
some measure, it will prompt him to use labour-saving
machinery. Though situated in the land in which agricultural machinery has been brought to its highest perfection, and in which it is used far more than in any
other country, the South is woefully behind in this
respect. Once machinery is used, intelligent labour is
required to take full advantage of it, and proportionately
higher wages can and must be paid to the more skilled
operator. If the Negro can do it he will have the chance :
if he cannot or will not, he will gradually be supplanted
by those who can and will. Meantime, if through the
Negro acquiring freehold land and becoming an independent farmer, the large landowner finds he must give
more consideration to his tenants, and the employer that
he must give higher wages to his hands, the South as a
whole will gain immensely—economically, socially, and
morally.

Scared by the greater hold the Negro is getting on
the land, a movement has been started among the whites

17

to prevent him acquiring in areas that are at present mainly in the hands of the whites, and legislation is demanded to attain this end, and thus legally secure segregation or separation in the rural areas, such as is being attempted in the cities.   In South Africa this doctrine of the separation of the races is held by a majority of the Europeans to be the true policy, and the principle has been accepted by the Legislature.   In 1913 a Land Bill providing for territorial separation was passed through Parliament, and a Commission was appointed under the Act.   It is now engaged in provisionally demarcating the areas which it is intended shall eventually be white and black respectively, and meantime the leasing and sale of land between the races is prohibited.

With this policy in South Africa I am in accord.   I think the principle is one which, if wisely carried out, will be for the ultimate benefit of both races.   I only approve, however, if the requirements of the native people are conceived in a generous spirit, that the present and future needs of the people are properly provided for, and the white man is willing to make the sacrifices which such a policy entails upon him.

I am not, however, in favour of such a legal territorial separation in the South land.   Land and people, history and custom, are different there to what obtains in South Africa.   Any such legislation would be bitterly resented by the Negro people, who would regard it as an attempt to deprive them of their last hope.   It would be exceedingly difficult to put it into operation, would cause much hardship, and rouse the strongest race animosities.   The wise course is to place no obstacles in the way of the Negroes acquiring land, indeed to help them to do so, particularly when, as the wisest of the race desire, they shall acquire it in communities, and thus practically segregate themselves.

If such segregation led to the formation of Negro communities entirely apart from the life of the State and the current of civilized life around them, with the prospect of personal and communal deterioration, I would be against it. But I can see no reason why it should be so. The best of the race would join the movement, the educated and trained would be available to keep the community life at a high standard, while the highest voluntary assistance and advice of the philanthropic whites would be willingly given. And I have little doubt but that, as the South began to realize that here was a movement making for racial amelioration, and the weakening of racial animosities, State assistance would be given, and given with increasing generosity. Whatever the temporary drawbacks and difficulties, the white South will take a very short-sighted view of the situation if it puts any bars in the way of the Negro getting on the land on terms which will enable him to advance and become economically independent.

The marital and family life of the Negro is at present deplorable ; all the friends of the race feel it keenly, and its effects do not stop at the Negro ; in this better life the tendencies would make for a strengthening and purifying of family life, for unity and co-operation where now they tend to disintegration.

The friends of the race, and the friends of the whole South, should impress on the Negro that now he has a chance, but that the chance is one, if not taken now, will pass never to be repeated. Individuals and races have their opportunity which if neglected never comes again. If the Negro race cannot see and seize this one, the increasing competition of urban life, the ever-augmenting complexity of our civilization, will find him unprepared, and the outlook for him is dark indeed. He will remain a helot, not bound by the material shackles that bound his limbs in slavery times, but as much a slave as though those fetters remained.

17 *

CHAPTER XXVIII.

COMPARISONS.

THE American Negro knows no other land. The majority have no knowledge of history. After listening to the tales of woe they recited to me, I sometimes told them of the past and actual condition of other peoples who have passed or are passing through trial and tribulation—I felt that if they could make comparisons they would find they were not, as so many of them suppose, the only race which had been unjustly treated.

I have shown in previous chapters that I do not disregard or lightly regard some of the disabilities placed upon, and the injustice suffered by, the Negro people in America. But over and over again as I listened and saw I made comparisons.

The most natural one was the people of similar race in the Union of South Africa. When I was told of the educational disadvantages of the Negroes in the South, I contrasted it with what is offered to our natives. Instead of the numerous public State schools for Negro education which, though poor and ill-equipped, are everywhere available, there are not in the Union of South Africa any Government schools for native education at all. Grants in aid are given to missionary bodies which provide schools and comply with the Government requirements, but the appropriations in the South are munificent as compared with those in South Africa. The Orange Free State with a native population of about 360,000 contributes the miserly sum of £4,000 annually, or say $20,000 in all, towards native education, and in the other provinces the appropriations are not on a much higher scale. As for higher education there is not a single State institution either for higher literary, vocational, or other training, in the Union of South Africa. Only one voluntary institution in the whole Union—that of Lovedale, supported by the Presbyterians of Scotland —is in any way comparable with the many in the South.

When this state of things is compared with the Universities, Normal Colleges, Medical and Dental Colleges and industrial institutions provided by the States, and by philanthropic bodies for the higher intellectual and vocational training of the Negro, it makes a South African wonder at the complaints of the Southern Negro at his lack of educational facilities.

Even when compared with those provided for many white children in South Africa these stand out as being liberal. I remember well when in my own province of Natal, the European residents in the country districts had to provide for the education of their children themselves; there was no State aid. The children were generally taught by their parents, or contiguous families clubbed together and engaged a tutor or governess. It is only within the last four years that there has been in Natal a College affiliated to the South African University; before that time the highest education a youth of European descent could get, in the colony of his birth, was that given in two schools with a higher grade than that of the primary school.

When I saw in the South Negroes engaged in varied skilled work, and often working alongside white artisans, and when I found that the wages of both were approximately the same, I could not help contrasting it with the position in the Transvaal and Natal, where such a thing would be impossible. No employer in either of these States dare ask a white artisan to work alongside a native, however good a workman or however respectable the latter might be. In the Transvaal a native or coloured man is prevented by law from doing any work on the mines excepting manual labour; all the highly paid and skilled callings are, by law, kept exclusively for whites. Again I could not help drawing comparisons.

In three out of the four Provinces forming the Union of South Africa, no black man has the right to vote, no matter how highly educated or civilized he may be, and it is extremely unlikely that this privilege will be granted to any natives as far as we can see ahead in either the Transvaal, Natal, or the Orange Free State. The Negro in the South has a far better chance of making his voice heard in the Legislature than has the black man of South Africa in his native land.

The separation of the races in all social matters is as distinct in South Africa as in the Southern States. There are separate railway cars, separation is also the rule in all other public conveyances, and no black man enters hotel, theatre, public library or art gallery.

In South Africa the children of black and white are separated in the Schools, indeed in Natal there are distinct schools for natives, Indians, Natal half-castes, Mauritians, and natives of St. Helena, and it is quite understood that there would be serious trouble if the light coloured were asked to attend a school provided for full blacks.

These distinctions are accepted by the native and he not only does not ask for their removal, but would probably prefer to keep distinct and not mix with whites. It was when I heard the position of the American Negro so frequently described as unique, that I recalled and contrasted it with what was happening to an African people in a land they rightly called their own.

It happens that I am not only familiar with the life conditions of the Bantu people of South Africa, but I know something of the life of the labouring class of Britain both as it is to-day, and as it was when I was a youth before leaving my English home for South Africa. Forty years ago I knew conditions in the manufacturing districts of South Lancashire and West Yorkshire from actual personal experience. I remember well a man

working as a porter in a large warehouse, whose wages
were 14s. a week, who on this had to keep a wife and
three children and walk four miles to and from his work.
This is less than three and a half dollars a week! I heard
of no such miserably paid labour to full-grown men in
the South. The position of the agricultural labourer in
those days—the days before Joseph Arch—was economically worse than that of the Southern Negro on the land.
Wages in many counties did not average more than 12s.
a week, less than three dollars, and the cost of the necessaries of life was higher than in the South. Socially, the
agricultural labourer of those days in England was almost as much in a class apart as the Negro is to-day in the
South. It is true he might travel first-class on the railway if he paid first-class fare, but this was not, nor was it
ever likely to be, a matter of supreme importance to him.
It did matter that his food was insufficient to keep up
his strength; it did matter that his work was so hard and
incessant that he became prematurely aged; it did matter
that his children could not be properly fed, indeed often
went hungry; it did matter that in his old age he had no
alternative but the workhouse. His opportunities for
education were grotesquely meagre as compared with
the Negro of to-day. A denominational school, with a
curriculum arranged so as to keep him in his place, and
no possible chance of the High School and University
training which the Negro may have. The political
liberty practically denied to the Negro was equally
denied to him, and his interests were ignored or over-
ridden by the master class just as those of the Negro are
ignored by the white man.

In all the material things of life the Negro, as I saw
him in the South, is far better off than the unskilled
labourer of England as I remember him forty years ago.
And is the English labourer much better off to-day? In
millions of cases he is not. While the average wage of
the agricultural labourer in Ireland is 9s. 11d. per week,
and the average over large areas in England not much

higher, while the conditions of unskilled labour in the cities are as depicted by Mr. Charles Booth, the Negro may have the cool satisfaction of knowing there are lower economic depths than the black man has plumbed. The starved white man is now allowed, by those who deny him a living, to exercise his judgment in deciding who shall starve him, and he is not liable to be lynched, but when a man and those belonging to him are being slowly ground to death by economic forces, it is understandable that he might be willing to allow someone else to go through the farce of voting, and be willing even to run the risk of a lynching, if he could be sure of three meals a day like the Negro of the Southern States.

And the Negro has a hope and opportunity denied to the agricultural labourer and the unskilled and casual worker of the cities of Britain. No rural labourer in Britain has the chance of getting his own land, becoming independent, and gradually moving upward, which I have shown is possible to all of the Negro race. If the Briton remains on the land he does so as the worker for another; if he leaves for the city it is to compete with millions.

CHAPTER XXIX.

OPINIONS OF OTHERS AND THEIR APPLICATION.

YEARS ago, as to-day, thoughtful Americans, viewing the distraction of the South due to the race problem, and seeing little hope of amelioration, much less a solution of the question, fearing indeed that it would become increasingly difficult with the passing years, looked round for some National policy which would solve it once and for all.

Despairing of any such within the United States, they cast their eyes abroad, and naturally first looked to the Continent from which the Negro came. At a time when the exploration of Africa had only revealed to Europeans one or two thin tracks into the interior, and even the coast was imperfectly known, it seemed to them that there must be ample space in which to settle the 4,000,000 Africans who were in America at the close of the Civil War. Even later than this writers may be cited who saw in deportation to Africa the only solution of the question. Eminent men were quoted as being favourable to this scheme: Thomas Jefferson, De Tocqueville, and Abraham Lincoln were called in evidence. But time passed, and what might then have been conceivably possible, became a lost opportunity. The Negro increased in the land, and Africa became partitioned out among the European powers, and the door was for ever closed.

Then came the advocates of complete segregation within the Union, those who proposed gathering together the Negro race and placing them in the South-West in separate States, which were to be wholly black, but yet within the Union.   The rapid settling by whites of all the newer territories soon placed this among the once possible, but now impracticable schemes.   To-day it seems beyond the wit of man to devise any proposal that shall solve the question by removal, the two races must work out their destiny on American soil together.

Four Englishmen have studied the question on the spot and written on it: Sir H. H. Johnston, W. P. Livingstone, W. Archer, and W. L. Clowes. The two first-named had knowledge of African peoples under other conditions. Sir H. H. Johnston's experience of the native races of Africa, their affinities and languages, is probably unique. W. P. Livingstone has an intimate acquaintance with the race position in Jamaica.   So far as I know both W. Archer and W. L. Clowes had no special knowledge of backward peoples.   W. L. Clowes' book, "Black America," was written over twenty years ago, and his conclusion was that only by emigration of the Negro race back to Africa would peace be obtained.   Much more recently W. Archer, in "Afro-America," sees four possibilities: (1) worry along till probably the Negro dies out, (2) education of both races, and living together in mutual toleration without clashing, (3) miscegenation, and (4) deportation or segregation.   Each of these is discussed by him, but the only one he thinks practicable is the fourth, and this he limits by saying deportation overseas is now impossible, and finally favours the segregation of the Negro by forming a black state or states within the Union.   Sir H. H. Johnston either did not see, or was not impressed by, the tragedy of the races, and did not suggest any definite policy of betterment.   W. P. Livingstone's writings are to me very suggestive.   Before visiting the United States he had written an instructive book on the colour question in the West Indies, entitled "Black Jamaica".   In this volume the note was one of sympathy with the Negro, and a qualified hope was expressed that he would finally attain to a higher status. On the whole the book was optimistic in tone.   While not blind to the shortcomings of the race, he believed that in Jamaica the Negro would develop and not deteriorate, and that conditions there were favourable to such advancement. After reading this book, I was much interested in reading his experiences and conclusions after travelling through the Southern States, as contained in his later publication entitled "The Race Conflict". The difference in tone between the two books I find marked and significant. His conclusion with regard to the present position in the United States is that, "if nothing is done to alleviate existing conditions one can foresee the inevitable end as clearly as if it were visible to the eye. The struggle will go on increasing in intensity as the Negroes advance in material capacity and material resource; the passions of both races, now fitfully venting themselves in lawless action, will rise beyond control, and a catastrophe will ensue which will startle the world." He discusses the various suggestions made for solution and discards them all. With regard to race fusion, which has by some been seriously advocated, he says: "The only effect which the suggestion has on the whites is to rouse their fiercest passions, and to make the proposal seriously would be to doom the Negro to destruction. Those who discuss it cannot know what they are talking about."

He then makes suggestions of his own which seem to me to be based on his knowledge of British methods of dealing with backward races, which would be less likely to occur to one accustomed only to the formula of the United States Constitution, and the methods adopted and possible under it. He would frankly recognize race differences and the present race inferiority on the side of the Negro, and be willing to surrender the nominal position of equality conferred by the 13th, 14th, and 15th Amendments of the Constitution. He would regard the Negroes as the wards of the Government and provide a Bureau for their protection and advancement. He also suggests a council of investigation to study the race and their relations to the community. Social as well as political equality should be denied, but absolute justice should be given. He realizes the stupendous difficulty of the problem, but thinks that by openly facing it and dealing with it in the way suggested, peace may be secured, and the white man—freed from the dread, explicit or implied, of Negro equality—would assist to bring it about.

This suggestion was specially significant to me, and I think will be so to my South African readers, and deserves some consideration.

The position in the South is that, with a coloured population only equalling 29 per cent of the total, after fifty years of legal freedom and legal equality of opportunity, with considerable opportunity for education, and little bar to industrial opportunity, the position is so acute that a disinterested observer, sympathetic to the Negro race, sees only catastrophe ahead, unless the legal status of the Negro is reconsidered, and instead of leaving him to fight his race battle alone the Federal Government takes him under its guardianship. In short, he would revert approximately to what is the present method of government of natives in South Africa.

We must remember that the Negro in America has been in intimate contact with the white race for nearly three hundred years, speaks the language of the country, and in customs, religion, and aims has, perforce, adopted those of the white man.

There are those in South Africa who would take the contrary course to that advocated in Mr. Livingstone's book, and who, in a country in which the black population outnumbers the white by five to one, and with the whole of black Africa behind them, would encourage them by industrial pressure and other means to distribute themselves among the white population, and by example and precept accelerate the disposition to drop their language, customs, and race identity, and to form an integral part of the population.

The conclusions in the book we are discussing should serve as a warning to those leaders of the native people in South Africa, who profess to think that, with education and equality of opportunity, racial peace will be assured.   It should also serve to make those think, who, for the sake of economic advancement, would not hesitate to bring the native people into surroundings in which they would be brought into industrial competition with the whites, and which would inevitably tend to race conflict and race hatred.

Such contact in America has neither led to the true advance of the black, nor the advance of the white, nor to racial peace.   The wisest friends of the American Negro, both white and black, after all these years of contact, would welcome a separation of the races such as is still possible to us in South Africa, and would make heavy sacrifices to ensure it.   We still have black States.   We still have Basutoland, Bechuanaland, Swaziland, the Transkei, the large reserves in Zululand and the locations in Natal and the Transvaal, and yet short-sighted ones would break them up, and force the landless inhabitants to become vagabonds or industrial serfs, scattered throughout the length and breadth of the land.

To such the experience of the South should act as a warning.   We have our difficulties and dangers ; there are some inherent in the present position, but a reckless breaking-up will raise others infinitely more dangerous, while a wise conservatism may give us time for study and experiment.

My theory of the native policy for South Africa is in striking harmony with what is suggested in W. P. Livingstone's book as the right policy in the South.

I frankly recognize the differences in the races and believe that we must accept this in our practice.

I advocate territorial separation, the conservation of what is good in native life and custom, and the gradual teaching of what they can assimilate from our civilization, and to this teaching and uplifting work I would encourage the leaders of the native people to devote themselves, and show them that the true field for their training and ability is to help their own people.

I deprecate hasty legislation and changes in administration, and would govern them largely by personal sympathetic rule.

At the same time in their own affairs I would grant them a measure of self-government under wise white counsel, but not to the extent of never allowing them to learn by their own mistakes.

Education suited to their needs should be given and moral instruction should accompany it, and religious belief and observance should be encouraged.

Especially would I give them better means of livelihood and a clean home life, by instruction in agriculture and the handicrafts that follow it, and a hope in life in their greater economic opportunities.

All this should not be at the whim and changeability of Parliamentary representatives chosen by the white people to serve their own interests, but as the studied and considered policy, thought out and laid down by a competent, permanent council of Europeans, whose life's work it should be. Native opinion should be heard by means of native councils, this opinion should be considered and co-ordinated by the permanent European council, and voiced in Parliament by a limited number of members specially elected to represent the natives.

Too late it may be for the South, but I feel that if some of her best men, who are at present filled with doubts as to the future, and with their tragic experience ever before them, could counsel us, they would say that on such lines, and not in the way that was forced upon them by the conquering North, lies our hope for the future in South Africa.

CHAPTER XXX.

THE FUTURE.

If I take a more hopeful view of the future than is generally expressed, it is not because I do not fully realize the serious, almost menacing position of the present. I know the white man in the South is filled with race prejudice, often amounting to race hatred. I know this actually does break out in frequent race riots and murderings, culminating in burnings and indescribable torturings. I know the black man is often hopeless and sometimes filled with bitterness at the white man, and at the lot the white man prescribes to him. I know the majority of the Negroes are shiftless, often immoral, and not seldom criminal. I know that in the cities the Negro race is at the bottom, and that there shows little sign of rising. I know that while the white man shouts for race integrity, he is covertly belying this by his acts, and taking advantage of his wealth and position to debauch the coloured woman, and raise up a race of bastards with bitterness in their blood. I know that injustice in the Courts, and individual injustice and exploitation are common, and that the Federal law, giving freedom and equality to all, is set at naught by State law and custom. I know that in the North race prejudice has grown stronger of late years, and that the Negro, in proportion to the rest of the population, is poorer and in worse condition than at any previous time. I know that in the South there is no diminution of race prejudice, and although the attitude of the average white man has somewhat changed, it cannot be said that the mass are any more inclined to tolerate the Negro now than they have been in the past.

All this is true, and it seems to justify fully the pessimistic verdict of the great majority of those who have investigated and written on this subject. And yet there are substantial grounds for hope.

I returned to New York from my Southern travels, my head seething with the problem of the Negro, his disabilities, his weaknesses, his opportunities. I am usually a sound sleeper, but one night my subject drove sleep far away, and I arose, and with the heavy still air full of the clanging and hooting of tramcars, automobiles, and elevated railway cars, I put down pithily the conclusions at which I had then arrived. I reproduce them here as they came hot from my brain immediately after my experiences.

It should be put frankly that while one may not be superior to the other, the races have special powers and special limitations, and are essentially different.

The idea that the Negro has only to get similar education to do as the white man has done in all his varied activities is absurd, though this opinion is strongly held by those of mixed descent.

The Negro has had half a century of the very best help, the best brains, the kindest hearts and the heaviest purses of the North and he has shown :—

A value as a worker in gangs in heavy work, as in tar asphalting, and the like, and in mines and foundries ; this is the big black man.

A value as tiller of the soil, especially as a progressive peasant proprietor.

An incapacity for commerce and finance.

Weakness in foresight and thrift.

An unfitness for city life ; he has never shown any of the Jew's capacity to benefit by the labour and necessities of others. He is unselfish.

Some power of organization which shows itself in Church life and in Friendly Societies.

A power of assimilating a spirit, and getting knowledge under guidance, and of being disciplined and true
to uniform, as at Hampton and Tuskegee.

Wise guidance and foresight should give him his opportunity of building up country homes in communities.
For this life he is fitted.

Black men and white men pepper-casted through a
section, leads to exploitation and white irritation, and no
adequate advantage is gained because, in my opinion,
under such circumstances the black man is not encouraged
by example.

Negro communities are certainly in some danger of
becoming little Haytis if unassisted, but here Hampton
and Tuskegee can and will help by giving their graduates
as guides.

Communities should be co-operative and would act as
bulwarks against the white aggressor and exploiter.

Such separation would lead to gradual dissolution of
the plantation share system, and this would be a good
thing for both white and black to help to put king cotton
in his right place.

The South is essentially a country for rural homes for
white and black, for intensive farming with the fullest aid
of science and labour-saving appliances, for that mixed
and progressive farming in which all the family may
have a share.

If these lines are right, then the educated and trained
of the race have a great field before them, and the South
should encourage and subsidize Hampton, Tuskegee, and
the other centres which are providing teachers and leaders.

If the Negro cannot take this chance now offering he
probably remains a serf.

If as some of his friends wail, subtle influences are
working against him and fifty years of freedom are not
enough and he can't do any better, then the statement of the
average man that he must not and will not count in the
community is about correct.

If I am right, and the Negro is not going to compete

seriously with the white man, and Negro domination is a myth, the white man should free himself from race dread and be more generous, and not listen to the politician who cries "Nigger"—but help; still keep the races separate, but give the Negroes a chance of which they can avail themselves.

Heavy as is the loading against the Negro the factors that make for hope in my opinion outweigh it. First every Negro can get work, and it is possible for them not only to subsist but to save.

They can buy land and become economically and socially independent.

The best South is wakening up and is going to help them in their struggle.

It is probably due to the fact that, while I was in the country, the South was organizing for social study, social service, and social sacrifice as never before, that makes me think, unlike my predecessors, that there is hope for the Negro, and that possibly the worst point in race relations has been reached. Thoughtful and wise Southerners there have always been, who have been centres of local enlightenment, and who have kept race relations tolerable around them. This is the day of organization and co-operation, and these scattered ones are now coming together for mutual help and strength. The Southern University men are carrying on investigations in order that action may be soundly based, philanthropic organizations are meeting together and uniting their strength. At the great meetings of the Southern Sociological Congress at Nashville, Tennessee, at which I was present, it was announced that white and black students of their respective Colleges were to unite in Social study and work, and that the girls of the High School were to co-operate with the coloured girl students of the Negro College. When I told this to Southerners at a distance they could hardly believe it, but it is true that the best of the thoughtful South is seriously putting forth its best to help the Negro to a better and cleaner life.

So far there has been no movement of a political nature in the South to call attention to and remove some of the disabilities under which the Negro suffers, nor do I think it likely that any concerted political action in this direction will be taken. The leaven of the new attitude will work, and will, I think, gradually soften the present harsh conditions.

As a preliminary the South must get rid of its present dread of political and industrial Negro domination, and the mistake of thinking that racial admixture is prevented by preventing the Negro from rising. It surely should not be difficult to see that the Negro is never going to dominate, either in politics or in industry. From the first few hours I was in the South I felt, and I am as sure now as I was then, that the white man will ever rule and lead in the South. As for race integrity, it is entirely in the power of the white man. Let him but act as he talks, and race integrity is secured. And every step which leads the Negro to respect himself, and makes for race consciousness and race pride, is an additional safeguard.

These fears removed, it is surely possible for the South to take steps that, while keeping the races separate, will make for an understanding and practice that will remove the present friction and tension, and tend to mutual tolerance. The steps necessary to this end do not involve any surrender of those principles so strongly held in the South, and with which we in South Africa agree, viz., that the races are different, that a measure of separation is best for both, and that race admixture will not be tolerated.

The principal sins of the white South against the Negro and which must be purged before racial peace can come to the land are: (1) Miscegenation, (2) Lynching, (3) Injustice in the Courts, (4) Unfair discrimination in travelling, etc.

The first and greatest of these is illicit miscegenation, and the greatest safeguard against it is a true and not

18 *

a spurious desire for race integrity. The theory is universally granted, the contrary practice too often condoned. A sterner expression of public opinion on the one hand, aided to some degree by higher and better education, should make for the elimination of this fertile source of race contempt and race hatred. Could the Negro only see that the stronger race disdained to take advantage of the easy opportunity to lower themselves and their too facile victims, it would be proof of the earnestness of their desire for race purity for both, and go far to attenuate race despair. Is it too much to hope that a crusade against this race sin should be undertaken by the best of both sexes in the South?

The second great sin is one in which public opinion should be aided by the law. A greater respect for law is one of the crying needs among all sections in the United States. This will surely come with the movement now being inaugurated both North and South, for a stronger, purer civic and public life. A few drastic examples of the leaders of these criminal mobs, who torture to death their fellow-citizens, would go far to make them hesitate to break the law again. It would perhaps be a counsel of perfection to urge a root and branch reform in the method of appointing the judiciary and legal executive, but a strengthening of the local police, especially in rural districts, might often nip possible lynchings in the bud. It is hardly conceivable that in the twentieth century, with a public spirit making for general civic betterment aroused throughout the land, that this system of private vengeance should be long allowed to continue. With this would go another fertile source of race hostility.

The third evil, the difficulty of the black man getting even-handed justice in the Courts, does not involve any relinquishment of the race doctrines held in the South. It is only common justice that is asked. If the South demands that those who administer justice shall be high-minded and just judges, the grave indictment that must now be made against the Courts in the South would disappear.

Distinctions made in travelling are legal by State law, and as I have shown, I think a separation of the races is here desirable, but the law distinctly provides for equal conveniences and cleanliness for the same rate. I think the Negro often exaggerates the differences, but a scrupulous care that the law be enforced, would again remove a cause of offence.

Practical reforms such as these are possible, and if made would help the situation greatly, and the South need not, in putting such into effect, relax by one jot or tittle its claims to protect itself against race admixture and social equality.

Of all the more drastic remedies suggested in the many books I have read on the subject, that of W. P. Livingstone, which I outlined in the last chapter, is the one which appeals to me most strongly. This probably because it is the British and British Colonial system with which I am familiar, and because I see in the strengthening and wise adjustment of this policy of separation, guardianship, and wise control, the greatest hope for the races in South Africa. Had this policy been adopted in the United States at the time of emancipation, when it was practicable, some at least of the present tension might have been avoided. I cannot think, however, it is wise or politic to attempt it after fifty years. It is in the first place foreign to American ideas and institutions, and would probably be rejected by both races. The leaders of the Negro people would undoubtedly regard it as a retrograde step. Nominally at all events they have equal rights, nominally secured to them by the Constitution of the United States. However far it might make the position clear, and however much the mass of the people might benefit by Government guardianship, they would regard it as a degradation. And we must never forget that we are not dealing with a homogeneous people like the Bantu of

South Africa. Among the Negroes are many who are practically white, and to place them under tutelage would destroy the present hope that in time they might attain to actual and not merely nominal freedom. Economically the Negroes are inextricably mixed up with the whites, and any effective control exercised by a Federal Bureau would conflict with present economic conditions, which would be strongly resented by the individualistic white man. Jealousy of State rights would also be roused, and it is not to be unduly pessimistic to foresee conflict between individual States and the Central Government.

The day is past for this remedy, and unless we can see in the working of present forces an amelioration of present conditions, the outlook appears hopeless. Neither by colonization, nor segregation, the hope of the earlier inquirers; nor fusion, nor by Negro submersion nor annihilation, can we hope for solution. Only if we see hope by working on present and possible conditions is there any light in the future.

My hope for the South therefore lies first in the great opportunity for the Negro to acquire land, live in self-contained but advancing communities thereon, and thus remove the dangers of race conflict coming through race contact; and second, in the belief that the best South has awakened to the danger of a demoralized and hopeless Negro people in their midst, and are going to work for better conditions of life. Also that with better educational facilities the Southern people as a whole will become more law-abiding, and have a juster sense of their responsibilities, and that miscegenation, lynching, and injustice will gradually become less frequent. Respect begets respect, and if the Negro people show a changed spirit by following the advice of their wisest leaders, they will gain the respect of the white South, and once the tendency has changed in direction, results will follow in all directions in which the races touch. And in no way could the Negro better command that respect than by beginning seriously and soberly to take advantage of the great racial opportunity, and fit himself for the task of making the highest and best use of it. The present situation and its issue lies not so much, as heretofore, in the hands of the white, as in the hands of the Negro himself. The great question seems to me to be: Can he rise to his opportunity?

Even should he do so to the extent his most ardent well-wishers would desire, I freely recognize that this is no final solution of the race problem in the South. There is no final solution possible, and the Negro will remain a problem for generations to come. But tendencies may change, and the present trend towards increased hostility be gradually altered to one moving in the direction of greater hope for the Negro, and greater help from the white race. Concurrently with this may come a less contemptuous and hostile attitude on the part of the whites, a greater belief in and respect for law and justice. While socially the races may remain separate, each following its own course of development, they may unite for common and national ends, the strong no longer dragged down by the weak, nor the weak oppressed by the strong.

It is such a trial as comes to but few races, but a wise appreciation of the difficulties, and a strenuous effort to overcome them, may make for the highest development of both groups.

To the white South may be told the words of an English writer which, though written of somewhat different conditions, are still applicable: "The running of a tropical Colony is of all tests the most searching as to the development of a nation that attempts it; to see helpless people and not oppress them, to see great wealth and not confiscate it, to have absolute power and not abuse it, to raise the natives and not sink yourself—these are the supreme tests of a nation's spirit".

And for the Negro—to toil towards development in spite of contumely and injustice, to respect yourself when others despise you, to fight temptation towards sloth and pleasure, and subordinate self for the good of the race,

CHAPTER XXXI.

FOR SOUTH AFRICA.

I KNOW that my South African readers, who for the most part will be practical men of affairs, will ask what definite and specific lessons of value to us in South Africa I learned from my visit to the Southern States. I will put my conclusions under this head as tersely as possible :—

(1) That the gift of self-government to a people unfitted for it may not be a boon but a bane, and we cannot in South Africa solve the native question by simply giving the franchise to the Native, and telling him to protect himself. It has been tried in America as I have shown, and failed.

(2) That if the vote is denied, the responsibility for protecting and developing the backward race lies on the stronger; a heavier responsibility than they would face if they gave the franchise. The American people did not shoulder this responsibility, hence much of the trouble of to-day.

(3) It is said and truly, that, as the Negro advances in education and copies the white man's mode of living, race hostility increases ; when he is in a different sphere and accepts it he is tolerated. When he impinges on the life of the white man he is disliked. This is evidenced in the United States, both North and South.

(4) One of the most difficult phases of the question is the matter of the educated black man. To educate, and then debar and crush, is cruelty indeed. Whatever policy we adopt in South Africa must include hope and a sphere for the educated native. The natural and true

line of life for him seems to me to be to help to uplift his own people.

(5) The position in America is made extraordinarily difficult by the man of mixed ancestry being classed and treated as a Negro. We must face the consequences of our own actions and admit these in South Africa to our opportunities and responsibilities.

(6) It is clearly shown that the Negro is not fitted for city life. His home life should be in the country, and it is as peasant farmers that the majority will find the sphere for which they are best fitted. I think the same may be said of the Bantu people of South Africa.

(7) The races are so different that to reduce antagonism and give each its full opportunity for race development, a conscious and reasoned attempt at race separation should be made. On lines I have already indicated it is the hope of the Negro race in America.

(8) Such separate communities should be under white guidance, assisted by the more advanced of the black race. Thus separated from the whites to a degree not hitherto attempted, scientific study should be given to the educational requirements of the black man, and every facility given for race development. The value of this I have shown in my sketch of Hampton and Tuskegee.

(9) Religion and morals should be given a high place in any educational system. The emotional side of the native mind should not be suppressed but guided. The history of the Negro in America proves this to be true.

(10) The great sin of the white man against the black lay not in slavery, nor in economic exploitation, but in the debauchment of the race by illicit sexual intercourse. This is the saddest page in the history of the Negro in America. At all costs we must preserve racial purity.

To these categorical lessons I would add a few words as to what practical steps we should take in South Africa to ensure better race relations :—

(1) We want a frank recognition that the races are different and that different treatment is necessary.

(2) While recognizing that white ideals and white rule must prevail, we must feel the solemnity of the responsibility thus resting upon us. We must not rule the land solely in our own interests, but in the best interests of both races, and this demands a measure of generosity and self-sacrifice never hitherto attempted by us.

But this end will not be achieved by good intentions only. We have to examine our methods, and find out how far our present system of government will enable us to carry out our intentions, however good they may be. To me this lies at the root of the native problem in South Africa. At present we are like voyagers without chart or compass on an unknown sea. As questions affecting the native people arise we deal with them on the spur of the moment, governed by the exigencies of a system of representative party government which we have imported ready-made from oversea, and in which the huge native population is unrepresented. We follow no plan, we have no principles to guide us. We have adopted as final a system of government gradually evolved by homogeneous peoples of Western Europe to suit their needs, and fatuously hope this will meet the totally different conditions of South Africa, with its many problems of race and colour, and where the outstanding fact is that a minority of civilized whites form an oligarchy, and rule over five times the number of a weaker people hardly emerging from barbarism.

To continue in this course is to court disaster, and we have to realize that this system, conceived under such different conditions, must be so far modified as to suit the peculiar conditions of our country.

The urgent need of the times is to devise machinery, within and subject to the present parliamentary system, which shall provide for the steady, continuous study of the ever-changing relations of the races, and enable the results of that study to be brought before the notice of Government and Parliament with an emphasis that cannot be denied.

I have frequently in previous writings referred to this and suggested as a first step :—

The appointment of a permanent non-political Council established under Statute law to study continuously the question of race relations in all its bearings. And the election of a limited number of European representatives in Parliament to speak for the Council and to voice native opinion.

The present is full of menace. The United States fifty years ago tried the experiment of giving to Africans the full franchise, and the result has been disastrous. The same course is impossible in South Africa. But it is the first duty of South Africa to find a better way.

CHAPTER XXXII.

BIBLIOGRAPHY.

Dr. Booker T. Washington, " Up from Slavery," " The Story of the Negro," " Working with Hands," " The Negro in Business, " " Character Building," " The American Negro," " The Man Furthest Down ". These books are all so well known that little comment is needed. Generally they dwell on the achievements and prospects of the Negro, and do not emphasize his failures and disabilities.

Alfred Holt Stone, " Studies in the American Race Problem ". Written by a planter on the Yazoo delta of the Mississippi, who knows the Negro intimately. He is not hopeful as to the future of the race. He carried on practical experiments on his estate with Negroes and Italians as workers, and found the former distinctly inferior. This book reflects the attitude of a large number of the better class in the South. Mr. Stone sees no solution but separation or absorption.

Cleland Boyd MacAfree (coloured) writes a review of this book in the " Journal of the African Society of London," Vol. VIII, from the point of view of an educated coloured man.

Ray Stannard Baker, " Following the Colour Line ". A valuable book full of information actually gathered while travelling in the South. He seems to think that the industrial awakening of the South may give the Negro his opportunity. He makes no definite proposals, but hopes that time may bring amelioration and mutual toleration.

Professor Kelly Miller of Harvard University, "Race Adjustment". A book of essays written by a coloured educationist. He shows much discrimination and fairness. Among them is a lively open letter to Thomas Dixon, the author of the "Leopard's Spots". Professor Miller sees something of hope in the voluntary separation of the races, which he favours.

A. H. Shannon, M.A., B.D., "Racial Integrity". The author gives the darker side of the problem, and says in a general way that the hope of the Negro race lies in it being able to avoid conflict and competition with the white race. Distinctly pessimistic.

W. P. Pickett, "The Negro Problem". A temperate book; the author arrives at the conclusion that colonization is the only remedy.

Dr. Shufeldt, "The Negro". This book is hostile to the Negro. His only remedy is segregation.

H. E. Montgomery, "Vital American Problems". A book of generalities; the author thinks that literary and industrial education may solve the problem.

Dr. A. B. Hart, "The Southern South". A book that must be read; full of facts and shrewd conclusions. I cannot gather that he has any definite solution to offer, though he favours race separation.

John A. Price, "The Negro, Past, Present, and Future". Written from the point of view of the Southern planter; and though published in 1907 does not reflect the opinion of a majority. Full of class prejudice. Quotes from Scripture to prove Negroes are predestined to inferiority.

G. W. Cable, "The Freedman's Case in Equity," and "The Silent South". Written in the eighties of last century and very valuable as showing the position then. The spirit of the books is hopeful. It is a call to the better South, to which the response has hitherto been disappointing.

Edgar Gardner Murphy, "The Basis of Ascendancy," and "Problems of the Present South". Two books which must be read. Scholarly, eloquent, and convincing, they voice the feelings of the best new South by one who has lived in and loves the Southland. He raises the question to a high level, is sympathetic yet practical. He favours recognition of race differences, but desires every opportunity for the Negro race.

J. E. Cutler, " History of Lynching ".   The authority on lynching which should be read.

Dr. E. W. Blyden, "Christianity, Islam, and the Negro Race ".   Written by an educated American Negro long resident in West Africa.   It does not deal directly with our-subject, but gives the point of view of a Negro who desires to stimulate race solidarity and race consciousness in his people.

W. P. Calhoun, " The Caucasian and Negro in the United States ".   Written by a Southerner and bears evidence that the author knows his subject.   Probably reflects opinion between the extremes, though tending towards repression.   Honest but hopeless.   Favours separate state for Negroes.

Professor Josiah Royce of Harvard University, " Race Questions ".   The distinguished author is much impressed with the better way in British Colonies and quotes experience in the West Indies.   I do not think he fully realizes the different conditions.   Did he visit South Africa he would hardly be so optimistic as regards the future of British administration.

W. P. Livingstone, "The Race Conflict ".   A short book giving an epitome of the position.   Should be read along with the same author's " Black Jamaica ".   He advocates as the only solution in the United States the guardianship of the Negro by the Federal Government.

" Cyclopædia of Thought by One Hundred of America's Greatest Negroes."   Gives the Negro point of view but is not very illuminating.   Many of the essays are wordy.   One cannot gather much from them.   Photos are given of the writers and it is significant that the great majority are partly white, some apparently quite white.

W. Laird Clowes, " Black America ".   This book

was published in 1891 and valuable as a standard of comparison. He sees no remedy but colonization; the absolute removal of the black man from the United States.

T. Nelson Page, "The Southern Problem". Hostile to the Negro; gives the extreme view.

C. Carrol, "The Negro a Beast". This reaches the climax of hostility; the author argues that the Negro is actually non-human.

William Archer, "In Afro-America". A recent work by an English writer. Discusses four possible courses and favours a separate State for Negroes within the Union. Is deeply impressed with the seriousness of the problem.

W. B. Smith of Tulane University, "The Colour Line". Is unfavourable to the Negro. Sees signs of race discouragement and thinks the race may die out.

Atlanta University publications. Among these are many dealing with phases of the subject: "The Negro Artisan," "Social Condition of Negroes in Cities," "The Negro Church," and others which should be read.

P. A. Bruce, "The Plantation Negro as Freedman" is a local study of the condition of rural Negroes in South Virginia.

P. A. Bruce, "Rise of the New South". Sees a time of trial for the Negro in the new industrial conditions, and doubts whether he can meet them.

Miss Mary Ovington, "Half a Man". A valuable monograph on the New York Negro. Full of sympathy and yet discriminating.

Wm. A. Sinclair, "The Aftermath of Slavery". Written by a Negro who gives many cases of hardship and discrimination.

W. W. Elwang, "The Negroes of Columbia, Missouri". An exhaustive monograph on the Negroes living in a small town in Missouri. Agrees with W. P. Livingstone in thinking that Negroes should be placed under protection of the Federal Government.

A. W. Tourgee, "An Appeal to Pharoah". Written from a Southern point of view and desponding.

Frederick Law Olmsted, "Journey in the Cotton Kingdom," "Journey in the Seaboard Slave States," "The Texas Journey," "The Back Country". I have already in the text given my opinion of these most valuable and interesting works which give living pictures of the country and society in the later slave times by one who was specially qualified.

W. H. Fleming, "Slavery". A thoughtful contribution to the subject.

J. P. Hoffmann, "Race Traits and Tendencies of the American Negro". Written by a professional statistician in much detail. He finds cause for thinking that the Negro has deteriorated since Emancipation. It seems to me that his case is built upon the city Negro, and he does not fully investigate the position of those living under rural conditions.

Dr. W. E. B. Du Bois, "The Philadelphia Negro". A valuable monograph, sympathetic to the Negro but fair.

Dr. W. E. B. Du Bois, "The Souls of Black Folk". An eloquent and touching appeal for justice.

Sir H. H. Johnston, "The Negro in the New World". A work dealing with both North and South America, and giving the history of the race on the Western continent. He travelled through the South and his conclusions are more optimistic than any of the other Englishmen who studied the question on the spot.

W. Hannibal Thomas, "The American Negro". Though a Negro himself this writer brings an indictment against his race so sweeping and scathing that it can only be equalled in this respect by the most extreme of white writers.

W. D. Weatherford, Ph.D., "Negro Life in the South". Gives the present position from the point of view of the best South. The author is himself a Southerner and one who has done work for the uplifting of the Negro.

Rt. Hon. James Bryce, "The Relation of the Advanced and the Backward Races of Mankind". A wide survey of the world position which should be read.

INDEX.